The Sound of Philade

The Sound of Philadelphia

Tony Cummings

A Methuen Paperback

Methuen paperback edition
First published by Eyre Methuen Ltd
11 New Fetter Lane, London EC4P 4EE

Copyright © 1975 by Tony Cummings

Printed in Great Britain by
Whitstable Litho, Straker Brothers Ltd.

ISBN 0 413 34080 5

Contents

Acknowledgements

It would require literally another volume to list everyone who has helped me. As, sadly, I have to be brief, I
must thank in particular: Denise Hall, who gave weeks
of her time to the awe-inspiring task of transcribing
over two-hundred hours of taped interviews; IPC
Specialist Press, which made available to me the files
of *Black Music* magazine and *Melody Maker*; and Joe
McEwan, a Philadelphia-raised disc jockey and writer
who came to see me to blow me out but ended up
giving me inestimable help and much needed encourage-
ment. Others who gave invaluable assistance are John
Anderson, Adam Finn, Rob Finnis, Charlie Gillett,
Vivien Goldman, Ian Levine, Alan Lewis, Tony
Philibert, Bill Millar, Clive Richardson, Roy Stanton
and Cliff White.

My special thanks go to Meg McLaurin and to my
wife Hilary for their incredible patience and endurance
in translating my unintelligible scrawl into a neat type-
script. Also, sincerest thanks must go to Weldon Arthur
McDougal III who never ceased in his efforts to help
my researches and became a good friend during my
month's stay in Philadelphia. And finally, an enormous
thank you to the hundreds of artists, producers, label
owners and disc jockeys who were so patient, cour-
teous and friendly to me during my interminable
search for information. It must be obvious that without their help this book could not have been written.

Note: the following books have been used for refe-
rence: *The Drifters* by Bill Millar; *The Encyclopedia
of Jazz* by Leonard Feather; *The Filmgoer's Com-
panion* by Leslie Halliwell; *The Gospel Sound* by Tony
Heilbut; *Pennsylvania: A Guide to the Keystone State*;
Rock On by Norm N. Nite; *The Sound of the City* by
Charlie Gillett; and *Those Fabulous Philadelphians* by
Hubert Kupferberg. In addition various issues of the
following magazines were consulted: *Billboard, Bim
Bam Boom, Black Music, Black Wax, Blues and Soul,
Blues Unlimited, Downbeat, Hot Buttered Soul, Let
It Rock, Melody Maker, New Musical Express, Rolling
Stone, Shout* (formerly *Soul Music*), *Stormy Weather*
and *Who Put The Bomp*.

Photographic Acknowledgements

The author and publisher are especially grateful to Weldon McDougal and Frank Virtue for supplying and giving permission to reproduce a number of previously unpublished photographs. McDougal's photos include the Philadelphia street shots, Sigma Sound Studios, the Uptown Theater, WDAS radio, and portraits of Luther Randolph with Johnny Styles, Jimmy Bishop, Georgie Woods, Carolyn Crawford, the Soul Survivors, Kenny Gamble, Leon Huff, Thom Bell, Bobby Martin, Norman Harris with Ronnie Baker, Bobby Eli and Earl Young, Bunny Sigler with Gerri Grainger, Tony Bell and Joe Tarsia. Virtue's photos include portraits of Howard Tate, Clara Ward with Russ Faith, Fantastic Johnny C with Jesse James and Bobby Martin with session men. He also courteously volunteered several photos from his private collection: the Virtues, Gabriel and the Angels, the old days at Virtue Studios and Prince Johnny Robinson.

The author and publisher would also like to thank the following record companies, agencies, journals and individuals for supplying and granting permission to reproduce photographs: Atlantic, Avco, Beacon, Bell, Buddah, Cameo, Chelsea, Chess/Janus, Columbia, Decca, Dot, Duke/Peacock, Gamble, Grand, King, Mercury, National General, Philadelphia International, Philly Groove, RCA, Relic, Roulette, Spring, Swan, Warner Bros. and Verve; Keystone Photographic Agency, London Features International, Matthews News and Photographic Agency and SKR Photos International; *Gospel News Journal* and *Record Exchanger*; Arthur Howes, Dennis Morris and J. Paul Simeone.

INTRODUCING: THE CITY OF BROTHERLY LOVE

"Money, money, money, money . . . money!!"
Three voices chant. As the first syllable of the last
"money" shoots into a shrill falsetto, a torrid dance
riff shudders from the gut of a synthesizer while a
phased drum snaps a back beat. The record begins to
fade while Eddie Levert snarls improvised asides. A
smooth brown voice announces from the taxi's radio
— "That was the O'Jays, and that was the sound of
Philadelphia."

The lyric of "For The Love Of Money" attacks
avarice yet, paradoxically, the song was recorded for
the label and the production team which have seen
more cash than any other music enterprise of the
seventies. For the sound of Philadelphia is much more
than the sound of soul — more than the vigorous
passion of the O'Jays, the falsetto lilt of the Stylistics,
the tortuous exhortations of the Blue Notes, the
simpering sexuality of the Three Degrees, the jazzy
cool of Billy Paul or the warm eccentricity of the
Intruders. The sound of Philadelphia is also the sound
of cashiers rubber-stamping money drafts and of bank
managers smilingly welcoming sharp-suited record
producers whose companies deal in tens of thousands. But Philadelphia is a major banking centre of
the East Coast and is well equipped to handle the
massive cash flow of Philadelphia International
Records or the Sigma Sound Studios.

Music has brought the money. But what brought
the music? Why is it that America's fourth largest city
(behind New York, Los Angeles and Chicago) has
been the place where soul music has again emerged
with all the power, energy and dollar capacity of
Detroit in the sixties? Sociologists will, no doubt, present theories to explain the phenomenon. The evidence,
however, seems to suggest that the Philly sound was
made possible because of a startling web of coinci-
dences. The right people in the right place at the right
time.

"The time is three thirty and this is station WDAS"
comes the voice again from the radio. "WDAS — the
tops for soul from the City of Brotherly Love." As
the cab cruises around the city, the driver begins to
point out the standard sights pointed out to a hundred-
thousand tourists in a hundred-thousand taxis. There
is Independence Hall. There, the Mercantile Library.
And over there, sprawling in an enormous seven-storey,

Where the hits are made . . .

four-and-a-half acre structure of white granite and marble, is City Hall.

"Yeah, there's a helluva lot of history in Philly", shouts the cab driver over the blare of the radio. "Helluva lot."

It was in settlement of a debt of £16,000 owed to his father by Charles II that an English Quaker, William Penn, was given a grant for almost all that is now the state of Pennsylvania. When Penn published "some account of the province" in 1681, offering easy terms for purchasing land, there was so much interest that he appointed four commissioners to locate "a Great Town". One withdrew, but the others, arriving on the Delaware in the spring of 1682, selected a site and, carefully choosing a name from the New Testament, called it Philadelphia (Greek for "brotherly love").

During the first year Penn and his followers erected eighty houses. By the beginning of the twentieth century Philadelphia had a population of 1,250,000. Streams of immigrants poured in steadily from Europe and after the emancipation of the slaves, a black population began to arrive from the South. By 1940, Philadelphia had a distinctly dual character. On the one hand, it was a sophisticated city famed for its social services and for its cultural facilities — art galleries, museums, historic sites and, above all, a world-renowned symphony orchestra. On the other, it had a population of almost two million, many of whom lived beyond the fringe of the city's beneficence in mile after mile of festering, crumbling slums.

In 1975 — despite local newspaper reports of "massive social reform" and the claim of a tourist-orientated guide-book that "today Philadelphia is well on its way to becoming a model of urban planning and revitalization" — the slums are still there. Like so many large American cities, Philadelphia seems firmly caught in a now classic urban pattern. In the centre lie its fine arts and big business. Circling this are decaying, densely occupied ghettoes. And on the outer perimeters are the immaculate suburbs where affluent businessmen live in middle-class comfort when not commuting to the nucleus.

As I glance from the cab I spot just such a businessman — a stereotype in grey suit, grey overcoat and grey expression — clutching his obligatory briefcase and the day's edition of the *Philadelphia Daily News* as he scurries into an office next to the Academy of Music on the corner of Broad and Locust Streets. Philadelphia has many music schools — and many formally trained musicians. History has seen to that.

The first public music concert in Philadelphia was given as long ago as January 25th, 1757 by John

Palina at the Assembly Room, Lodge Alley. Two years later English opera was presented for the first time at the Southward Theatre by the American Company, and in 1794 the Uranian Academy of Philadelphia was formed for "the instruction and practice of church music". By 1900 there was enough of an audience for classical music to make possible the founding of the Philadelphia Orchestra. Under the brilliant leadership of such highly acclaimed conductors as Fritz Scheel, Leopold Stokowski and Eugene Ormandy, the Orchestra has developed and maintained a reputation as one of America's best.

But, of course, Bach, Brahms or Beethoven in a live, exquisitely formal setting is not, and never was, the music of the ordinary worker in Philadelphia's textile factories or on the docks of the Delaware River. By the twentieth century the city had lost much of its Quaker character under a wave of European immigrants. Along with their families, the newcomers brought their music: the German march, the Polish polka, the English folk ballad. And, of course, the Italian opera. Throughout the nineteenth century the strains of Paganini and Verdi were heard not only in the concert halls erected by Philadelphia's merchants and bankers to indulge their cultural fancies, but in the homes of the poorer Italians of south Philadelphia as well. By the turn of the century they were able to herald their great hero, Enrico Caruso. Born in poverty in Naples, Caruso rose to become the world's greatest operatic tenor. In 1903 he journeyed to the U.S.A. and made his first recordings for the new-fangled phonograph which the Victor Talking Machine Company assured him would widen his appeal far beyond the world's concert halls. They were right and Caruso's cylinders and discs — particularly his glorious "Vesti La Guibba" — made him the first international recording star and gave the tens of thousands of Italian Americans a real musical link with home.

Caruso died, mourned by millions, in 1921. The same year in New York was born one Alfred Arnold Cocozza, claimed by the fanciful to be Caruso's musical spirit reborn. As Mario Lanza, Cocozza was to become Philadelphia's first superstar. As a child he'd moved with his family to south Philadelphia where he grew up listening to his father's treasured collection of Caruso records. He became determined to follow a career in opera and, at 21, studied under Irene Williams and then under Giacomo Spadoni, the 84-year-old former tutor of Caruso and Gigli. After two years in the Air Force, Lanza began giving concerts. Then in 1949 the barrel-chested, wavy-haired opera singer got an unbelievable break. He was picked by M.G.M.'s Hollywood movie moguls to star in a film,

Philadelphia's first superstar: Mario Lanza

The Midnight Kiss. That was just the beginning. Two years later he was given the title role in the film biography of his idol, *The Great Caruso.* It was a massive success, though the critics didn't like it. In *The Filmgoer's Companion,* Leslie Halliwell wrote that Lanza "proved to a surprised Hollywood that opera can be big business if given the right sugar coating".

It was a thick coating. Lanza, much to the displeasure of those who considered opera a "serious" art form, souped it up with theatrics and no small degree of chest-beating melodrama. And Lanza's material was by no means limited to the operas of Paganini. He melted the female hearts of the nation when he warbled the sentimental pop song "Be My Love" to Kathryn Grayson in *Toast Of New Orleans.* For several years Lanza played multifarious roles: serious performer of operas and religious music, singer of cloying pop ballads ("Because You're Mine" was Mario's third million-seller for RCA Victor in 1952) and eye-flashing movie heart-throb. Although his film roles continued well into the fifties — *Serenade* in 1956 and *Seven Hills Of Rome* in 1958 — Lanza's barrel chest turned to bulging paunch and his singing

style became increasingly anachronistic. Mario Lanza died in 1959 at the age of 58.

"Yeah, I liked Mario. He was a *singer* — you know what I mean? — a real singer. My ol' lady liked him too. Better than all that rock'n'roll stuff". Joe's head nods towards the radio which he's turned off while he engages me, his fourth fare of the day, in conversation. Joe has been driving taxis around Philadelphia for twenty-six years and has seen a lot of changes. "Yeah, I can remember when they'd be lining up outside Convention Hall for three hours to hear Mario. 1951 that would be. The only other singer I saw lines like that for was Eddie Fisher . . . he used to play the Latin Casino and they'd go wild."

Eddie Fisher was (and still is) a pop singer pure and simple with no pretensions about singing opera. And he's Jewish not Italian. But Fisher rose to popularity at the same time as Lanza and still dampens the eyes of nostalgic middle-aged Philadelphians when they recall the "golden age" before "the kids took over with their goddamn rock'n'roll." Yet crooner Fisher was as artificial and insubstantial as the older Philadelphians claim "all that rock'n'roll stuff" to be. Eddie Fisher was a product of New York's Tin Pan Alley, the establishment which for half the twentieth century successfully controlled the mass music intake of Philadelphia and most of the Western world. In his book *The Sound of the City* Charlie Gillett explained: "In the early years of the century the most (commercially) important source of new live music was vaudeville and music halls, and many publishers had their offices close to the 27th Street vaudeville theaters in Manhattan, an area that became known as 'Tin Pan Alley'. When stage musicals began replacing vaudeville in its role of introducing new songs, publishers began moving uptown. By the end of the nineteen thirties 'Tin Pan Alley' was the area in the forties and lower fifties close to Broadway."

For nearly fifty years Tin Pan Alley ruled with sousaphone-burping dance bands, oob-boop-be-doo Roaring Twenties whimsey, moon-in-June ballads and regular doses of melodrama, nonsense and sentiment. Change was painfully slow and anything that replaced a redundant style was equally facile. Then, in the fifties, a much needed and radical challenger emerged: rock'n'roll. In *The Sound of the City* Gillett shows in great detail the complex evolution of that "new sound". He also painstakingly traces the history of how the white mass audience gradually came into contact with the music of the black population.

"Yeah, man I can remember when a few brave white kids used to sneak on down to catch Lynn Hope and his Band rockin' it up in a club . . . or they'd

The streets of the ghetto

sneak over to the Uptown and catch the Orioles when they hit town.'

The day after Joe's taxi tour, Weldon Arthur McDougal III — one-time singer with the Larks and the Castelles, co-founder of the innovative Harthon Productions, former promotion man for Motown, and, today, head of artists' public relations at Philadelphia International Records, record producer (Love Commit- tee) and photographer — offered another one. Leaning gangster-style behind the wheel of his Mercedes, he cruised down Leigh High Avenue in the heart of the ghetto. There are no white marble edifices here. Just a converging jumble of images flashing past the window: wig shops, supermarkets, pimps, Afro stores, graffiti, dope merchants, tenements, children, record shops, hustlers. As Weldon slips a Cleveland Eaton cartridge into his car stereo, he begins to rap again over the blare of an electric piano.

"Those white kids listening to R&B . . . that was happening all over. It was only a matter of time before somebody like Bill Haley would come along . . . He was from near here". Haley's home-town was in fact Chester, only fifteen miles from Philadelphia while two of the composers of his legendary "Rock Around The Clock," Max Freedman and Jimmy DeKnight,

were Philadelphians. "Then of course Elvis Presley came and pretty soon 'rock'n'roll' was as much a white thing as black. . . A few black guys from the South, dudes like Fats Domino, Little Richard made out okay, but it was like when the kids discovered the beat they wanted to do it for themselves. Now they couldn't get the same sound but that's how they wanted it. . . The blacks kept with R&B but it changed from the old blues things. Doowops were big in the fifties and then the church, the gospel kinda sound started coming — that was like the beginning of soul."

For a few distressing years in the late fifties it looked as though the white teenager had absorbed black styles and evolved a new form of popular music only to have Tin Pan Alley recover from the shock of losing control of the record buyer and fight back with a new form of contrived ephemera. Philadelphia tele- vision launched a programme — American Bandstand — which had extraordinary effect and control on the "rock'n'roll" audience. New performers emerged with good looks and no talent, but with music-biz know- how behind them. Fabian, Frankie Avalon etc. rose to become major record sellers and by the late fifties pop music's quality had slumped once again. But that didn't worry the ghetto.

Philly street brothers

"Some R&B acts got on *Bandstand*. Dick Clark quite dug R&B, but black acts went their own way most of the time. Funny thing though, it was the white guys in New York, the record producers, who really got the soul thing movin'..."

McDougal suddenly stops his explanation of soul music's birth to point out the street where he and Kenny Gamble used to play. It's drab and desolate, and the walls are covered with a fresh layer of aerosol-can grafitti. Then he continues: "Yeah, those New York guys like Jerry Leiber, Mike Stoller, Phil Spector — Leon Huff used to do sessions with all those guys; Jerry Ragovoy — he's from Philly — Bert Berns. They were like the pioneers. They put strings and heavy rhythm and stuff with R&B singers and what came out they called soul . . . no, they called it 'Uptown R&B' first. They, and Motown in Detroit, they were doin' similar kinda things, they did a lot of the ground-work."

When the black artists on labels like Atlantic and Motown began making Dick Clark's *Bandstand*, the days of Bobby Rydell were numbered. And they ran out forever when the British beat invasion brought welcomed new pop acts, if no great new musical concepts, to the popular music mainstream.

"When the Beatles hit the scene, everything changed for the American pop singers. Only the black artists could *live* with the British groups. Like soul music was their inspiration. If any of those groups played Philly they'd wanna go down and check out the R&B acts." A few days later a record executive proudly recounted meeting John Lennon who was clutching the Atlantic *Saturday Night At The Uptown* album. "When the soul labels started forming in Philly it was only a matter of time before it got real big. . . there was so much talent around here. It was a gradual thing, like some of the big soul stars who now sell a whole heap 'a records used to really scuffle. But once Kenny and Leon broke pop for the first time it couldn't be stopped. People are always tryin' to figure out why Philly soul is bought by whites as much as by blacks. Some critic wrote somethin' about it bein' 'cause all the real soul feelin' had been taken out of the music an' that the O'Jays or MFSB or the Spinners aren't really where the black thing's comin' from. Now that's real dumb, like the Philly sound is the

The gold disc wall of the Sigma Sound Studio

biggest thing in the whole R&B scene. That dude just hadn't checked out a black club. If he had . . ." Weldon again stops in mid-sentence, this time to nod in the direction of a drab, crumbling brick building. Despite its disrepair, three posters on its face displaying a crude drawing of Jesus make it obvious that it's a church . . .

"So, you're gonna do a book on the Philly sound are you man?" Weldon smiles. "You'd better start there . . ."

One: The gospel truth; the Blue Gates of Harmony to Stars of Faith

On a cold Sunday afternoon in November 1974 Louise Williams rushed home from the WDAS radio building where she'd just completed hosting a four-hour gospel programme. An hour later she was walking up the aisle of the Christ Memorial Baptist Church on West Leigh High Avenue. The grandiose name veiled little more than a barn-like brick box — no polished mahogany or gleaming silver; stained plaster instead of stained glass. A threadbare red carpet covered the floor. The disc jockey celebrity was greeted excitedly by church officials. The congregation didn't often welcome such exalted guests, but this evening was something special. Louise was to be mistress of ceremonies for an "Appreciation Service" for the Rev. Mother Carrie G. Thomas ("we want to give her her flowers while she's with us"). For forty years Carrie had worked for the good of the depressed community of West Leigh High and now the crumbling little church had put together a little gospel programme for their beloved lady. There was no big name act like the Davis Sisters and certainly no star quartet like the Dixie Hummingbirds, just a small-time presentation with a handful of local acts.

Louise was ushered to the right-hand side of the hall, a literal hot seat between the radiator and the organist, and instantly — with a smash of tambourines — the William Gospel Chorus, ten women and girls in pink robes and five men in sombre suits, swelled into song. The young lead singer, a tall teenage girl, sang in a husky, blisteringly powerful contralto and as she swerved and dipped across the singers' chant of "the

Lord will find a way", a great sighing rose from the congregation. As the hymn spiralled to a climax, voices from the seated throng shrieked in a wall of ecstatically soulful sound.

In the overall order of things the William Gospel Chorus, or for that matter those with whom they shared the West Leigh High bill — the Barbour Gospel Singers, the Blue Gates of Harmony, Tina and Danny Odom and the Gospel Seven — are as far removed from the entertainment bright lights as it's possible to be. The women in the group are maids and housewives, the men clerks and labourers, and the only reward for their music is the sight of a congregation "upset" by their fervour and "happy" with their natural musical passion. Yet, unbeknown to any apart from the local audiences in ten-thousand store-front churches which butt against the sidewalks of frustration and squalor that are America's ghettos, groups like the William Gospel Chorus regularly display the very heart of American popular music. For the sound of gospel music is something, consciously or unconsciously, every one of us knows and recognizes. In one form or another gospel music has, with the coming of rock'n'roll, the ascendancy of "soul" and the proliferation of thousands of singers, black and white, who ape gospel's originality, totally reformed our listening expectations. The metamorphosis of an entire folk art, nurtured in an insular unworldly culture, into a "billion-dollar opiate of the music-grooving masses", promoted by super-sophisticated media and accepted and bought by countless millions, has meant that the seeringly soulful vibratto,

MON. EVE., JUNE 19, 1968
THE MET
Broad & Poplar Sts., Phila.

THE SOCIETY BOYS present

THE GOSPEL EXPRESS OF 1968!
FEATURING 5 TOP GOSPEL RECORDING GROUPS:

SWAN SILVERTONES
of Pittsburgh, Pa.

SWANEE QUINTET
of Augusta, Ga.

DAVIS SISTERS
of Philadelphia, Pa.

SOUL STIRRERS
of Chicago, Ill.

5 BLIND BOYS
of Alabama

LANE RELATION SINGERS
of Philadelphia, Pa..

THE MISSION SINGERS of Phila.   AND OTHERS
(The Swan Silvertones Will Have Their New Lead Singer - CARL DAVIS)

BONNIE DEE - M.C.

ADVANCE TICKETS $3.00 — AT THE DOOR $3.50

Tickets on Sale at: Paramount Records Shop, 18th & Ridge Ave.; Oak Lane Shop,
Limekiln Pike & Ogontz Ave.; Treegoob's, 41st & Lancaster Ave.

the haunting melisma, the sweet falsetto harmony, the almost subliminally anticipated climax and the very tensions and textures of the rock'n'roll big beat, are often considered the product of music-biz know-how – in spite of the token platitude "it all stems from the blacks".

Today, gospel music has almost come to terms with the merciless pillaging to which the entertainment world has subjected it for half a century. It has learned to tolerate singers who've screamed and hollered gospel anguish over a twelve-bar blues structure and called it rock'n'roll, "writers" who've "borrowed" beloved hymns and spirituals and called them original compositions; singers who've taken the churches' blue notes and soaring glissandos and called them soul; and countless Caucasion musicians who've never experienced pure gospel yet use the techniques, chord progressions and "feel" of the black church. Bitterness still occasionally shows through in some gospel singers, and a comment like "rock'n'roll is devil's music" expresses a cynical awareness of the enormity of the injustice of rock music's rampage as much as it speaks for any firmly held conviction of the inherent evil of secular lyrics. For the most part, though, the black church today quietly accepts what history and commerce have done to its music forms, neither fighting nor protesting against the massive music machine, and simply gets down, as it has always done, to its main role of communicating to its people . . . and its God.

Nowhere in America does the gospel sound reach the people, and permeate the very air, as it does in the heaving complex of Philadelphia. For though the significant gospel styles, songs and singers were born and originally flourished in America's South, Philly has become the Mecca of black religious music. Great gospel performers pour to the East Coast in a never-ending stream, several of gospel music's greatest figures live in the city, and each Sunday tens of thousands of black Philadelphians attend services and "programmes" where music becomes the ultimate means of bringing them closer to a heaven and a God they so passionately and eloquently believe in. And for those who do not pull on their mail-order hats and sombre serge suits to hurry off to the Pilgrim Rest Church of God in Christ or the Zion Apostolic Temple, there's always the radio where, every Sunday, gospel music brings the word of the Lord into thousands of ghetto dwellings.

Louise Williams, a beautiful black woman with a Harvard-graduate accent, sat in front of the mike in the cramped little WDAS studio used for her mammoth

A typical Philly gospel programme

gospel programme, surrounded by racks of cassettes labelled with such names as "Tasty Baking" and "United Artists – War". The James Cleveland record began to fade out and from the loose-leaf catalogue spread in front of her she started to read a "Len Robes" commercial: "They start at twelve ninety-five and with each robe you get a free item of Rodgers silverware". As she finished she slotted in a cassette and a commercial for a forthcoming performance of *Die Fliedermaus* ("The opera's in English so you can understand it") boomed out as Louise expertly cued up the third track on side two of a Swan Silvertones' album. At the exact second the commercial ended, she flicked the start switch and another slice of vibrant black religious music poured out. For the next four hours she sat in the cramped little room, leaving only to get some maple pancakes for breakfast. At this point her assistant, Melvin Hill, took over. Hill, who sings with the Savettes gospel group when he isn't playing disc jockey, flicked through an enormous stack of gospel albums piled in a metal cupboard which had buckled out of shape under the huge weight, occasionally selecting an item and passing armfuls of discs to Louise to make the final choice as to which Mighty Clouds of Joy or Isaac Douglas item will be spun. Each record is normally followed by two or three commercials, some glaringly incongruous in their crass exhortations to buy. Between Louise's constant announcements that "the Jacksonaires are in town soon" are dedications to the living – "to all those who cannot go to HIS house today" – to the crippled – "to Ellis Johnson of the great group the Harmonizing Four who as you know has lost his legs, but not his faith" – and to the passed-over – "this record is dedicated to the memory of the late Clara Ward" – the latter preceding Clara's "A City Called Heaven".

Clara Ward lived, and died, in the city of Philadelphia. She was the brightest of all Philly's gospel stars, an artist who rose in her mother's group from abject poverty to the kind of mink-and-cadillacs-stardom which seems incongruous compared with the careers of the Sensational Porter Singers or the Imperial Gospel Singers, whose brilliant evocative music has brought only richness of soul. But Clara's memory is cherished, partly because she showed that maybe, just maybe, a singer like the Imperials' Louise Smoke Brown stands a chance of getting fame and fortune out of the talent she so abundantly possesses without the harrowing and sometimes quite impossible process of "crossing over" to "rock'n'roll" (i.e. soul music). Then, too, the gospel audience is long of memory, remembering when the Ward Singers were staggeringly innovative and richly creative. As Melvin

Hill so rightly observed, "Without Clara Ward you'd never have gotten an Aretha Franklin". And without Gertrude "Ma" Ward there wouldn't have been Clara.

Gertrude Ward was raised in South Carolina. She grew up poor, but in body not spirit, and was raised on the old Dr. Watts hymns like "The Day Is Past And Gone", "A Charge To Keep I Have" and "Must Jesus Bear the Cross Alone" — blunt metaphors of physical trouble and spiritual transcendence. Gertrude sang as a mezzo-soprano soloist in the local choir before she moved with her husband in the mid-twenties to Philadelphia. There she bore two children, Willa and Clara. Times were savagely hard for the family. During the Depression Gertrude would stand on street corners waiting for white people to pick her up for day work. Then, in 1931, Ma claims she had a vision, a vision to go out and sing. She rushed home excitedly and formed a family gospel group. The music the Ward Singers brought to the churches of Philadelphia was something excitingly new and fresh: the new words of the Lord, not just the archaic spirituals of the old Presbyterian order but the vibrant, fresh compositions of such as Thomas Dorsey and Sallie Martin. Throughout the thirties the Ward Singers tore up the Philadelphia Baptist churches. With Clara hammering out rocking piano accompaniments, Gertrude would wail in her big, cracked voice which could leap octaves from word to word, a voice that could shout out a booming baritone and soar to a gravelly falsetto on numbers like "On The Jericho Road There's Room For Just Two" or "I'm Gonna Work Until The Day Is Done".

In 1943 the Ward Singers took the National Baptist Convention by storm and were acknowledged as America's greatest gospel group. By the late forties Mrs. Ward had added new members to the group: Henrietta Waddy, a middle-aged Philadelphian whose gutteral voice recalled the old blues singer Ma Rainey, and a teenager from Miami, Marion Williams. Louise Williams is rich in her praise: "Marion is one of the greatest singers of them all. She could make *any* congregation happy. When she sang the whole church would go wild".

They went wild over an extraordinary voice which ranged from a growling bottom to the airiest, most floatingly high soprano the gospel world had heard. It made the group. Over the next years they featured other great soloists: a powerful St. Louis contralto, Martha Bass; a rumbling near bass from Baltimore, Frances Steadman; and a shrieking soprano shouter from Trenton, New Jersey, Kitty Parham. But Marion

Clara Ward, queen of gospel music

Gospel artist Clara Ward at Virtue's with arranger Russ Faith

was the all-purpose singer, unbeatable on lead and the solid base of the group's background harmonics. Only when Clara herself sang in her exceptionally beautiful alto, with its penetrating nasality and rich vibrancy getting her named "the queen of the moaners", did the congregation react similarly. Clara's compelling phrasing on hymns like Dorsey's "Precious Lord" and "The Day Is Past And Gone" had the surging power and unquestionable conviction to fill churches . . . and sell records.

By 1948 small independent record labels like Apollo of New York, Savoy of New Jersey, Chess of Chicago and Specialty of Los Angeles were recording the "race" music ignored by the white-owned, white-orientated major labels. The phenomenal upsurge in popularity that Thomas Dorsey and his fellow composers brought to black religious music in the thirties ensured that the small-time entrepreneurs made as many recordings of gospel music as they did of the evolving rhythm and blues, and were rewarded with some massive-selling gospel hits. Among the earliest smashes were the Angelic Gospel Singers' "Touch Me Lord Jesus" and the Ward Singers' "How I Got Over", both for Gotham Records of Philadelphia. Apart from its unquestioned stars, the Ward Singers, Gotham recorded such successful acts as the Harmonizing Four, the Davis Sisters and the Dixie Hummingbirds — though when Gotham lost the Wards to Savoy Records in nearby Newark, New Jersey, they quickly declined and by 1954 were out of business. Savoy went on to become the dominant power among America's gospel labels and, in addition to the Ward Singers, had under contract the most successful gospel artist of all time, the Rev. James Cleveland. The Ward Singers sold well on Savoy. As Louise Williams explains, "Philadelphia really began to build up a reputation for being something special in gospel music in the fifties. The Ward Singers did programmes when thousands of folk would turn up. Soon all the big acts were coming into town to play the Met. Philadelphia had become Gospel City U.S.A.".

The Ward Singers' greatest records combined brilliant soloists, Clara's consistently inventive arrangements and exceptional material from the pen of the Reverend W. H. Brewster. Brewster, based in Memphis, was by the forties an acknowledged great with such shattering compositions as "Move On Up" (a million-seller for Mahalia Jackson), "Surely", "How Far Am I From Canaan" and "Weeping May Endure For A Night". His songs were structurally more complex than those of gospel's other all-time great composer, Thomas Dorsey. Brewster was the first to compose songs which began "slow and mournful" with melismatic cadenzas reminiscent of Dr. Watts hymns which picked up tempo and built shuddering, rhythmic climaxes. And "Surely" even introduced a new waltz rhythm into gospel.

The Ward Singers were also the first female group to feature the switch-lead tactics of the shouting quartets; and even in dress they set new precedents, forsaking staid church robes in favour of exotic, sometimes bizarre costumes and increasingly ornate wigs. In the early fifties the Ward Singers began touring with a thrilling preacher from Detroit, the Reverend C. L. Franklin — and touring with immense success. Clara Ward became the constant companion of the Reverend's daughter and in 1956 a fourteen-year-old Aretha Franklin paid tribute to her idol by recording a series of hymns which were not only taken from Clara's repertoire but were in every phrase and cadence the style of her mentor. When, more than a decade later, Aretha found superstardom with "soul", she was wholehearted in her praise of Clara, who was so instrumental in the formation of her vocal style. For the Ward Singers, tours, a continual stream of successful Savoy recordings and even a trip to the Holy Land followed. Their acclaim and success seemed beyond question. But in 1958, Marion

Williams, the most thrilling of all the thrilling Ward voices, announced that she and the rest of the Singers were quitting. Disgusted that the main bulk of the group's substantial fees found their way only to Gertrude and Clara, Marion decided to take her chances and form a new group. Mrs. Ward brought in new Singers, but without the captivating sound of old, the Wards' popularity began to wane — until 1961, that is. Then the Ward Singers came back big, but in a manner far away from that of the grassroots storefront churches which had brought them initial fame and fortune. First Clara, then the rest of the family, broke into the Las Vegas nightclub circuit. While the black gospel audience looked on in bemusement, the Ward Singers, who by then had moved home from Philadelphia to Los Angeles, began to caricature their musical roots for white middle-class America, and soon adulatory audiences all over the world. Clara and her hand-clapping, tambourine-bashing accompanists became a frequent sight and sound on Broadway, Vegas and television, and if the plump, middle-aged women boldly whooping up "When The Saints Go Marching In" on *The Johnny Carson Show* embarrassed the new militant black American, it did keep the group in the diamonds and minks to which they were accustomed. Clara continued to record steadily though without much restraint. But despite some excruciating pop-cum-soul-cum-gospel albums for Verve Records, Clara never quite lost her Philadelphia roots. In 1970 she returned to Philly for the funeral of the Davis Sisters' giant talent Ruth Davis, and, led on by an extraordinary emotional evocation by her mother, proceeded to upset the church when she hollered Ruth's immortal "Twelve Gates". In January 1973 Clara Ward finally joined Ruth and her maker whose praises she had wailed so passionately. Her spirit lives on. Happily, Marion Williams, the singer who rose to popularity as a result of her Ward Singers exposure, is still alive and still capable of producing soul-saving music.

Marion was born in Miami. She quit school to support her diabetic mother, working as a maid and in a laundry, but every weekend she sang in church and street-corner revivals. By her teens Marion was the recognized queen of the Miami soloists, her beautiful high soprano able to drop into the raw "sanctified twine", upsetting every congregation in Florida. She had offers to sing everything from blues to opera but gospel was Marion's only considered path. She joined the Ward Singers and quickly rose to become the group's star soloist. Her performance on the group's "Surely God Is Able" with a blistering climax of "Well surely, surely, surely, surely, He's able to carry you through" was one of the most terrifyingly intense moments in fifties religious music, while two of her other discs with the Ward Singers — "I Know It Was The Lord" and "Take Your Burdens To The Lord" — were unique marriages of the "gospel" and "quartet" styles. In 1957 Marion cut her second biggest hit, "Packin' Up", full of high notes, low growls and sanctified spirit. It was one of her last great performances with the Wards.

Marion's formation of the Stars of Faith in 1958 didn't, at first, bring the expected success. None of the singers had Gertrude Ward's managerial expertise and although Marion composed a few good songs based on old sanctified shouts like "We Shall Be Changed" and "Holy Ghost Don't Leave Me", her compositions lacked the compulsive fire of the Reverend Brewster, while her arrangements, although beautifully exploring the possibilities of female harmony, didn't attempt to show her startling vocal versatility which had so upset the congregations during her Ward days. Kitty and Frances sang the deeper numbers but it just didn't work. As Melvin Hill comments: "The old fire wasn't there. Like in the old days people would be crawling up the walls. But with the Stars of Faith the whole thing had gotten a bit subdued".

Then in 1961 musical producer Gary Kramer, inspired by Marion's Christmas album, commissioned a gospel musical scripted by the famed black poet Langston Hughes. *Black Nativity* was an immense success. Marion, the Stars of Faith and veteran Alex Bradford sang harder and with more fire than they had for years. Although the show, a simple adaptation of the story of the Nativity through the songs of the black church, was predictably showbizzy, with Christmas carols and spirituals souped up into tambourine-bashing extravaganzas, the Stars of Faith's commitment could not be doubted. The show broke off-Broadway records and then began a triumphant tour across Europe where it gave the people their first taste of something approaching authentic gospel. Although the staid white audiences were slightly bemused by the bluesy passion of "No Room At The Hotel", they reacted to "When Was Jesus Born" with genuine excitement.

The Stars of Faith and *Black Nativity* became inseparably connected. The group toured, appeared on television and were wooed as thrilling ambassadors of black religious music wherever they went. "Occasionally they'd come back home and do a show here", says Hill. "Some people thought we ought to be critical of them for taking gospel music out of the churches . . . but we were proud of what they achieved".

In 1965 Marion and the Stars of Faith parted company. Led by Frances Steadman the group all but forsook the storefront church gospel roots of their music. Today most of the time the group are in Europe, where, especially in Germany, the Stars of Faith still excite white audiences who feel that a rousing version of "Didn't It Rain" and "When The Saints Go Marching In" are the epitome of the black religious experience.

Marion too left for Europe, where she flopped in a new play, but on returning to America she began upsetting equally diverse audiences — Yale students, jazz fans and occasionally a roots gospel one. Today Marion Williams records for Atlantic Records of New York City. Despite some occasional rock accompaniments and songs (including Dylan and McCartney) Marion still wails with frightening passion and plays a fine piano on numbers like "Live The Life I Sing About" (Thomas Dorsey's greatest gospel blues) and the famed "I Have A Friend".

Not all of Philadelphia's gospel all-time greats have been as lucky as Marion. The Davis Sisters were never to attain the same kind of success seen by Clara Ward and Marion Williams. Yet, at their peak, their jazz-imbued harmonies and sanctified spirit made them artistically the equal of their cadillac-driving rivals. Louise Williams has enthused that "Nobody in the city is loved quite like the Davis Sisters . . . it's difficult to know why they didn't become bigger than they did. They were famous but broke".

Ruth "Baby Sis" Davis had the hardest, toughest, blues shouting voice in gospel. With sisters Thelma, Audrey and Alfreda and a superb jazz-inspired pianist, Curtis Dublin, the group upset every church on the East Coast in the fifties. They recorded successfully for Gotham Records ("Get Right With God") before transferring to Savoy Records where they made a stream of excellent recordings. Misfortune, however, stalked the group and four of them — Dublin, Ruth Davis, Thelma Davis and Leila Royster — died in starkly tragic circumstances. Although Audrey and Alfreda carried on the group, second lead Jackie finally decided on a solo "soul" singing career (where her brilliant recordings meant nothing to a mass audience). Today, the Davis Sisters still play the occasional gospel programme, satisfied at least in the knowledge of their own exceptional contribution to gospel music history.

Philly's most famous male "quartet" have wider horizons for, after nearly four decades, the "Birds" are at last becoming known outside the "Met" audiences who've adored them for so long. It was way back in 1940 that the Dixie Hummingbirds decided to

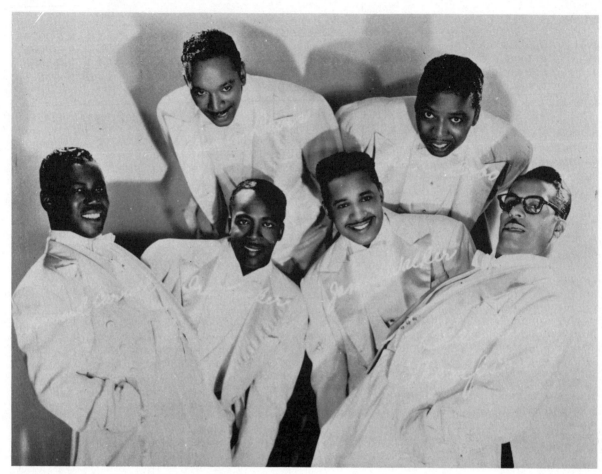

Zoot-suited gospel wailers, the Dixie Hummingbirds

join the relentless exodus of blacks from the rural South to the industrial North and settled in Philadelphia. By that time the group were well on the way to becoming the most influential performers of the "quartet" sound which, with its blue notes, slurs and controlled shrieks, was giving a new sense of dynamics and intense excitement to the black religious music experience. The Birds began, in fact, in Greenville as a barbershop harmony "jubilee" quartet led by baritone James L. Davis. But in 1939, after travelling up to New York to record for Decca, they won a "quartet song battle" against the Heavenly Gospel Singers at that group's hometown of Spartanburg, South Carolina, and in addition to winning the prize, gained two new members, William Bobo, the bass singer with the Heavenly Gospel Singers, and Ira Tucker, a fourteen-year-old who'd sung briefly with the Gospel Carriers and whose intense, tortured vocal style took him to the front of the group and reshaped their style.

When the Dixie Hummingbirds settled in Philly

they added a second lead voice, Paul Owens from South Carolina. By then the group's music revolved around frantic exhibitionism. Ira's seemingly spontaneous expressions of religious faith were not limited to the frenzied growls and glissandos of his vocal style — he would whip up the congregations with unashamed knee-dropping, hand-wringing, aisle-dashing showmanship.

Having cemented their reputation as gospel's most exciting live act, the 'Birds' started broadcasting on WCAC in Philly. In 1945 they began recording for Apollo Records of New York, and in 1949 for Gotham Records. But it was in 1952, when Paul Owens left the group for the Sensational Nightingales (and later the Swan Silvertones) to be replaced by baritone James Walker (previously with the Smith Jubilee Singers), and Howard Carroll (from the Nightingales) joined, that the group's most famous line-up was settled. With Ira Tucker (lead), James Walker (second lead), James L. Davis (baritone),

Beechie Thompson (tenor), William Bobo (bass) and
Howard Carroll (guitar), the group signed to Don
Robey's Peacock Records in Houston, an association
which has lasted twenty years.

"In The Morning", "Prayer For Peace", "Every
Day And Every Hour" — for two decades, a torrent
of searing, raw, anguished discs were released by
Peacock. Throughout the sixties the Dixie Hummingbirds remained at the top, often being voted Gospel
Group of the Year by the National Association of
Radio and TV Announcers. Then, in the seventies, the
"production revolution" finally got to gospel music as
well as to R&B. And when the Birds' guitar accompaniments were suddenly augmented by drums, bass and
even brass, Robey began to see the group's full commercial potential. In 1973 Duke/Peacock was purchased by the ABC monolith and a big push was made
to extend the classic group's appeal outside the insular
world of gospel. With extraordinary irony the Birds'
scored their greatest record triumph performing the
vocal back-up to pop singer Paul Simon, who'd just
"discovered" gospel music. Simon's "Loves Me Like
A Rock" gave the group a million-seller. Within months
the Birds had recorded their own version of the song,
which made the lower reaches of the soul chart, and
followed up their move towards a new audience by
playing the Whiskey A Go Go with soul-blues
singer Bobby Bland. Rock star Stevie Wonder has even
written a song for the group, "Jesus Children Of
America" . . . a fitting tribute.

Of course, Ward, Williams and the Dixie Hummingbirds are the jewels in Philly's gospel crown. There has
been no rock-star recognition for groups like the Harmonizing Four of Richmond, Virginia, whose smooth
eloquent harmonies, featuring three lead singers —
Tommy "Goat" Johnson, "Gospel Joe" Williams, and
Lonnie Sherman (and the famed bass voice of Jimmy
Jones) — were heard for over thirty years on Philadelphia's "programmes". Their rich, mellow sound,
the obvious root of the street-corner groups who
sprang into the secular limelight in the early fifties,
has been largely superceded by the wilder, more
frenetic sounds of gospel music, not just in the Whiskey
A Go Go or the Latin Casino (recently played by the
Mighty Clouds of Joy) but in the poor storefront
churches where gospel doesn't need slick choreo-
graphy or a sophisticated audience to move the spirit.

TWO: DOOWOP: THE STREETCORNER HARMONISERS

In 1949 five black children sat on the steps of a forty-year-old west Philadelphia tenement and began to argue. Should they go throw rocks at the housing project, steal a hub cap or two or do what their leader, George Grant, suggested and try copying the harmonies of the record they kept hearing on the radio? They decided to give singing a shot and soon the ragged little group could be heard practising every day. They'd sing on the tenement steps, in the subway or, best of all, in the corridors of the Sulzberger Junior High.

George Grant decided to call his group the Castelles — "it had a nice 'ringing' sound" — even though it was a pretty fancy name for a bunch of rough kids like Grant, Octavius Anthony, William Taylor, Frank Vance and Ronald Everett. But the kids had grit. They kept with music and by the time they hit high school they were playing the occasional school dance and the 43rd Street Y.M.C.A. What they were singing, although none of them, of course, realized it at the time, was the doowop sound, a sound which had eased onto the street-corner concrete from the storefront church.

By undertaking extensive tours, the innovating gospel quartets of the thirties had ensured that their music reached a massive ghetto audience. But not only did their unique harmonies move the soul and the spirits of religious congregations; consciously and unconsciously the gospel sound and style were absorbed into the black popular music mainstream. In the beginning the process was a gradual one. The slick barbershop harmonies of black Tin Pan Alley groups like the Mills Brothers owed hardly anything to church music. But by the late thirties the Ink Spots, through the falsetto lead voice of Bill Kenny, were making at least a nod in the direction of the religious style. By the late forties the essence of one of gospel music's styles, the intricate, precise har-

The Castelles

monies of the Harmonizing Four, had evolved completely into a secular alternative. In 1949 the Ravens of New York City were selling large numbers of records and it was only a matter of time before Philadelphia, the self-proclaimed "Gospel City U.S.A." spawned the first secular "R&B" groups.

With the Castelles' lugubrious line in harmonies set off by Grant's high, unbroken lead, the group continued to sing the hits of the era (the Ravens, the Crows *et. al.*) for four years. One such hit was a simpering ditty, popularized by Edna McGriff, called "Heavenly Father". One of the ironies of the lyric content of fifties black popular music was that songs tended either to be broad and outspoken in their sexuality ("Work With Me Annie") or conceived in the worst excesses of Tin Pan Alley sentimentality. Miss McGriff's song was definitely one of the latter: a sonorous saga about a girl whose boyfriend was overseas (particularly relevant due to America's bloody Korean involvement). Castelle Frank Vance was so taken with the song that he wrote a similarly inspired sentimental eulogy, but this time of a young man's love:

> The flowers are blooming, the birds are in the trees,
> The sun is still shining, and it casts a gleam on me,
> I am happy just because, my girl awaits me.

Frank's fellow group members loved his song so much that they trouped down to a city centre penny arcade and recorded it on a record-your-voice disc for twenty-five cents. Then, clutching their primitive recording, the teenagers scampered over to Treegoob's — a ghetto-based record shop on Lancaster Avenue run by Herb Slotkin. The kids asked to hear their unplayed record and Jerry Ragovoy, a young musician who worked in the shop, liked what he heard. He persuaded Herb Slotkin to become the group's manager and even more significant, Slotkin decided to form a label to record the group.

The fifties had seen the rise of literally dozens of independent record companies across America as astute businessmen noted the major labels' lack of recording activity in the newly developing "R&B" market. Philadelphia, in spite of its large black population and its vibrant music scene, wasn't particularly quick off the mark in the formation of R&B labels. The only important, black-orientated company which had been formed in Philadelphia was Gotham Records. But, in the main, the black harmony groups springing up all over the city had to look towards New York — only eighty miles away — for a recording contract (an example being Chris Powell and the Five Blue Flames who recorded for Columbia Records in 1951). That

situation wasn't to alter radically from the initial development of Philadelphia-based harmony groups to their contribution to the "golden group" era of rock'n'roll and through to their demise in the sixties. Herb Slotkin, with his little Grand Records, offered a local-based company, if not an alternative to New York sessions. Slotkin and Ragovoy took the youngsters (the average age of the Castelles was still only fifteen) up to New York. A couple of takes and "My Girl Awaits Me" was in the can. Its release met with considerable success, with the big Philadelphia deejays Jocko Henderson and Ramon Bruce spinning the disc constantly. In addition to selling well in Philadelphia, New York and Washington, it was — appropriate to its idyllic love lyric — a big hit among soldiers stationed in Korea. Possibly, if Slotkin had fully realized the potential of a black group which featured the high unbroken voice of a teenage lead, the Castelles could have broken through to the white popular market (a feat to be achieved three years later by another youthful group, but from New York — Frankie Lymon and the Teenagers, under the guidance of Philadelphian Richard Barrett). But despite having a national R&B hit, the Castelles' horizons were pretty limited. They played the Imperial Skating Rink at 60th Street and occasionally did a big R&B extravaganza at the Uptown Theater. But the group, still tied down to high school attendance, did no big-time touring. The dirge-like quality of "My Girl Awaits Me", with its minimal instrumental accompaniment and almost total reliance on sombrous wailing harmonies, was the group's archetypal recording. Their second one, "This Silver Ring", was written by Jerry Ragovoy.

Like his boss, Ragovoy was a white man, but unlike Slotkin he eventually achieved musical immortality in the annals of rock'n'roll history through a series of classic New York "Hit Factory" productions in the sixties. Ragovoy was a south Philadelphian of the apparently obligatory Italian origin who had learned piano and written his first song at the age of eight ("a direct steal from the Nutcracker Suite"). Ragovoy's discovery of the Castelles led to a regular job with Grand, though he still had to supplement his income teaching classical piano, recordings of which he listened to avidly. His familiarity with and fondness for the orchestrations of "serious" music were to contribute significantly to the revolution in recording technique which overtook New York City in the early sixties. This revolution was the direct predecessor of the classically influenced sophisti-soul of the late sixties and seventies Philadelphia sound. But back in 1954 it was a one-note-piano job that was required. The idea of "production" and all the complex orchestrations and technical wizardry that the name implied were a long way off when the first tin-whistle falsettos, wurbling basses and sweet harmonizing tenors were pulled from street corner to recording studio.

"This Silver Ring" didn't do nearly as well as the Castelles debut record, although their third, "Do You Remember", with its extraordinary flipside — a gurgling version of the Tin Pan Alley standard "If You Were The Only Girl" — generated big sales in Philly. Three more discs came out on Grand Records throughout the latter part of 1954 and into 1955 — "Over A Cup Of Coffee" — Grant's personal favourite; "Marcella"; and the song which had been the group's original inspiration, "Heavenly Father". George Grant also made a solo record, "It's Christmas Time", under the name George Castelle around the same time that another group of west Philadelphia youngsters, the Dreams, were taking their first faltering steps into the recording business. The Dreams, taken under the brotherly wing of the "big-time" Castelles, recorded for Savoy Records of Newark ("Darlene" and "Letter To My Girl") and the group's lead singer, George Tindley, made an arrangement with George Grant whereby either would step in for the other as a temporary Castelle or Dream.

But the Castelles weren't able to duplicate the sales of their first disc. And although Grand recorded other vocal teams who performed in a similar style, neither the Marquees nor the Dreamers had much sales impact. By 1956 Grand Records were in difficulties. Then the Castelles, having finally graduated from high school, got what might have been a much-needed big break. It wasn't. Record exec Pat Pignato entered into discussions with Herb Slotkin about the group recording for Atlantic Records, a label which by the mid-fifties had evolved into New York's biggest independent rhythm and blues label. In 1955 they formed a new subsidiary label, Atco, on which the Coasters were becoming another star attraction. Perhaps president Herb Abramson saw the Castelles in a similar light to the Leiber/Stoller team. The Castelles released one Atco disc, "Happy And Gay". It featured a revamped personnel of George Grant, Octavius Anthony, Billy Taylor and Clarence Scott, with Scott handling lead. The record had some of the Coasters' raunchy, drawling humour, but failed to achieve the same success. The Castelles fell apart, though another group, a white Californian one, used the name in the late fifties. George Grant, bitterly disappointed that stardom was not his, quit singing for a few years before briefly reappearing on the recording scene with the Modern Red Caps in 1961. He still lives in Philadelphia, still possesses a beautiful tenor voice and still

dreams of a show-biz return. Billy Taylor did some work with the Dominoes and the Spaniels; he eventually got back to recording with a revamped Orioles group and, like Grant, the Modern Red Caps.

The group Grant once so proudly led weren't, in fact, the first Philadelphia doowop team to reach a national audience. That honour was claimed in 1950 by the Capris (not to be confused with the white group of "There's A Moon Out Tonight" fame). In the late forties a gospel and R&B independent label had been formed in Philly by Irv Ballen called Gotham Records. The Capris' hit with Gotham was the eerily beautiful "God Only Knows". In the early years of secular harmony teams the Capris were almost unique in their usage of a girl lead singer. And a girl — not a woman — she most certainly was: sounding about thirteen she drifted and glided through a wistful prayer of teenage love while her fellow Capris warbled an appropriately respectful back-up capturing a mood of breathtaking innocence. The disc, mainly through extensive plugs by rock'n'roll's greatest disc jockey, Alan Freed of Cleveland, was a big R&B hit. But sadly, although the song over the next two decades acquired the status of a doowop classic, the Capris quickly returned to street-corner oblivion.

Weldon McDougal, one-time bass singer with the Castelles, theorizes about the short life of most doowop groups: "Groups like the Capris and the Castelles weren't hip enough to see that the record industry was what was important in show business and that revolved around New York. Labels like Gotham ('46), Grand ('52), Red Top ('57) were springing up in Philly, but to really get anywhere an act or an artist had to get to New York and hang in there and hustle . . . that's why Richard Barrett made it."

Richard "Ritchie" Barrett, a significant figure in New York City's doowop era, and originally a Philadelphian, tells an intriguing tale. "I was raised in Philly and I went to New York City in '54. Before that I was in the service. When I got out I got into the music business. I taught myself the piano . . . through loneliness and because I liked music — I was my folks' only kid. I had a very comfortable childhood. I learned about poverty when I got to New York, like it was a brand new thing to me. When I was in the forces I had written a song 'cause I thought I was in love. I put it in my pocket and I must have carried that song around for about five years. Eventually that number put me in the music business. You see when I got on the streets of New York, I started checkin' out poverty and stuff, and I found it wasn't too good . . . not eating that is. So I remembered my

song and went to the Brill Building on Broadway and
49th Street. That was where all the music companies
were. Now I didn't know whose door I should be
knockin' on, so I listened to all the guys — the songwriters — who were talkin' outside on the sidewalk.
And the publisher's name I heard most was Morris
Levy. So I went up and knocked on his door. He
bought the song. For years nobody did anything with
it. Then eventually it was given to Frankie Lymon.
That was 'Creation of Love'; it sold quite a bit.

"Pretty soon though I was back in Philly. I had a
vocal group called the Angels. One of the guys in the
group, Junior Booker, had a younger sister named
Kathleen. I used to tease her that I was going to write
a song about her. One day I arrived at her home with
a beat-up guitar and started to sing a song I'd written
for her called 'Tonight Kathleen'. She cracked up.
Buzzy Willis, he was a buddy of mine and a big name
with the Solitaires, called me and said there was a
group of guys who didn't have a lead singer and they
had no songs, they just harmonized. They were Mick
Francis, Raymond Briggs — we called him 'Pop' —
Eddie Edgehill and Ronnie Bright." (Ronnie subsequently went on to the Cadillacs and the Deep River
Boys, sang bass on Johnny Cymbal's "Mr. Bass Man"
and Barry Mann's "Who Put The Bomp" and is now
with the Coasters.) "So I joined the guys as lead singer
and songwriter. We called ourselves the Valentines. We
recorded 'Tonight Kathleen' with Old Town Records
with the Solitaires band backing us up".

It was in 1955 that Barrett joined up with Rama
Records run by George Goldner and started a working
relationship with him which was to be crucial in the
establishment of New York as the centre of doowop
group record activity. The Valentines recorded the
song "Lily Maebelle" for Rama and it was a smash hit.
Overnight Barrett and his fellow group members were
New York's favourite sons and Barrett went to live in
the Naked City. None of the Valentines' other recordings had quite the same level of success as the rocking,
finger-snapper "Maebelle". But by 1947 Richard was
moving in new directions as producer, songwriter and
talent scout. In partnership with George Goldner,
Barrett auditioned hundreds of black harmony groups
scuffling in New York City. Among them Barrett
found the Chantels, Little Anthony and the Imperials
and the Isley Brothers. But perhaps his greatest discovery was Frankie Lymon and the Teenagers. The
Teenagers were originally an all-Puerto Rican group
who, through a series of accidents, ended up recording
the song "Why Do Fools Fall In Love", written and
sung by black thirteen-year-old Frankie Lymon. The
record (for Goldner's Gee label) became an inter-

national success and for two years the group rode high
on the crest of a rock'n'roll wave. Tragically however,
Lymon died a drug addict in 1968.

After the Valentines split up, Barrett continued to
record as a solo. His smooth Nat Cole-styled tenor
could handle supper-club standards and in 1957 he
recorded "Smoke Gets In Your Eyes" for MGM
Records ("The Platters borrowed my arrangement and

Key-pin in New York's golden group era: Richard Barrett

they got most of the sales"). While building up
Goldner's rock'n'roll empire Barrett made discs for
Metro Records (1957), Gone Records (1959, a sentimental dirge called "Summer's Love" which, with the
Chantels shoodop, shooby dooby-ing a back-up,
closely resembled the Five Satins' classic "In The Still
Of The Night"), Twentieth Century Fox Records
(1960) and Atlantic Records (1962). Barrett's Atlantic
disc, "Some Other Guy", a frantic, gospel-styled Ray
Charles imitation produced by Leiber and Stoller,
subsequently became a minor "pop classic". It was the
influence of Leiber and Stoller and other New York
producers responsible for the "production revolution"
of the sixties which the Philadelphia veteran was to
take back with him when he returned to settle in the

City of Brotherly Love in 1963. By then, of course, the doowop era was well and truly over.

If New York was kind to the multi-talented and very flexible Barrett, it was less so to Philadelphia groups who relied on New York companies to release their discs. Groups like the Silhouettes — and the Turbans.

In 1955 Herman Gillespie — a businessman with an itch to get into show business — came across four Philadelphian teenagers, Al Banks, Matthew Platt, Charlie Williams and Andrew "Chet" Jones, who were performing a gig or two around town. Gillespie became their manager and came up with a name for the team, the Turbans, the ghetto's fixation with Eastern headwear having already produced Chuck Willis, the proclaimed Sheik of the Blues. With a set of natty turbans, a slick line in white suits and individualistic lead singer Al Banks, the Turbans were ready for the big time. Gillespie took the group to Al Silver in New York City and in July 1958 Silver released the Turbans on his Herald label performing a catchy rhumba, written by bass singer Chet Jones, called "When You Dance". With Al Banks' vibrant tenor warbling an opening line of "when you dance, be sure to hold her, hold her tight" and at the end of the verse swooping into a reedy falsetto — "such a thrill, aaah, when she's close to you" — its catchiness made it an instant hit record, even though its Latin American rhythms were far removed from the norm of drooling, street-corner harmony or the raunchy rock'n'roll big beat. With the chart success of "When You Dance" the Turbans toured up and down the eastern seaboard.

But the group were never to get another big chart record. Although an up-tempo finger-snapper, "Sister Sookey", moved out of the Philly-Baltimore-D.C. airplay circuit it didn't quite go, while their subsequent releases all failed to make the best sellers. These included "B-I-N-G-O", an attempt to turn a national pastime into a jaunty rock'n'roller; a "When You Dance" soundalike, "It Was A Nite Like This"; and a simpering ballad with tinkling celeste and lovely harmonies, "Valley Of Love". Al Silver began to lose interest in the group. Although "The Wadda-Do"/ "Congratulations", released in the Christmas of 1957, was played in the South and some Northern cities, the group's reliance on old style rhythms began to appear increasingly anachronistic. The Turbans underwent extensive personnel changes with only the flexible, fluid voice of Al Banks remaining a constant factor. But discs on Red Top, Imperial, Cameo and Roulette didn't do anything. Today, Al Banks, no doubt comforted by the "acknowledged classic" status of "When You Dance", still lives in Philadelphia and recently

did some gigs with the Charlie Thomas-led group working the clubs under the Drifters' name. Not an auspicious end to a music-biz career. But lamp assembler Richard Lewis, contractor Raymond Edwards and clothes presser Earl Beal haven't even got that link with the bright lights which once shone on them as members of Philadelphia's first chart topping group.

The Silhouettes had formed in 1955 as a gospel group, the Gospel Tornados. Consisting of Billy Horton (lead), Richard Lewis (tenor), Earl Beal (baritone) and Raymond Edwards (bass), the group "crossed over" and, as the Thunderbirds, were singing "blues" around the local clubs. In 1957 the group met Philadelphia disc jockey Kae Williams of WDAS. Kae liked the group but not their name so Earl Beal came up with the Silhouettes. Williams became their manager. Newest group member Richard Lewis presented the young group with a song he'd written while in the Army called "Get A Job". Compared with the standard simpering sentimentality performed by black vocal groups its lyric was revolutionary, a detailed description of the frustration of continual unemployment. Perhaps it was its unmistakable social implications (it *was* only 1957) that led arranger Howard Biggs to disguise the song's revolutionary tone behind a welter of vocal gimmicks when the Silhouettes took it to the recording studio. Paradoxically, the nonsense scat chant intro Biggs devised ("sha na na na, sha na na na na na" and "yip yip yip yip yip yip yip yip, boom boom boom boom boom") was, in its very ludicrousness, both the record's chief selling point and part of its continual place in retrospective rock romances (eulogized by authors Charlie Gillett and Nik Cohn and "rock revival" group Sha Na Na). When the jaunty finger snapper with its compulsive droning chant was released on Kae Williams' Junior Records, it became an instant local hit. Mr. Williams took the tape to Al Silver in New York whose Herald/Ember label was firmly established in the big-time rock'n'roll league. Its subsequent release in late 1957 led to an immense national hit (hitting Number 1 on 11 January 1958). "Get A Job" seemed the anthem of the age. Even an answer, "Got A Job", by a new Detroit group, the Miracles, sold quite well. The Silhouettes were overnight "stars", but it was a peculiarly false kind of stardom. In between appearances at a number of big East Coast theatres the group recorded a follow-up with a similar lyrical bent. "Heading For The Poorhouse" seemed a sure-fire formula for success, but the mass audience (black and white) who'd reacted so strongly to the infectiously bizarre rhythms of "Get A Job" obviously felt it was the song, not the singers, they were buying. "Heading For The Poorhouse" became ironically prophetic, flopping badly. Rock'n' roll's "one-hit-wonder" tag never seemed more appropriate. The group struggled on for a while with more releases on Ember ("Bing Bong/"Voodoo Eyes", selling a few locally and then on Johnny Vincent's Ace label where they recorded the standard "I Sold My Heart To The Junkman" — a song later to figure significantly in Philly's musical history when it was recorded by the Bluebells in 1962. But another hit wouldn't come up for the Silhouettes, not with wur-baburping novelties, not with sweet doowop harmonies — and not with the soul music they tried in 1967.

The same year that the Silhouettes were recording their classic hit for Kae Williams, another small independent R&B company was starting in Philadelphia. In 1957 Doc Bagby, a successful organist and band leader well known on the East Coast formed Red Top Records with Irv Nahan and Marvin Schwartz. Bagby took a teenage group, the Students (not the Checker Records' hit group of the same name) into the studio and the resulting disc, "My Heart Is An Open Door", sold 25,000 in Philadelphia. It was a fair start. By the spring of 1958 Red Top were causing national interest when their recording of "Oo We Baby" by the Ivy Tones was picked up for coast-to-coast distribution by the major label, Liberty Records. The original Ivy Tones consisted of John Ivy (lead), William Brown, James Green, James "Peewee" Thomas and for a short while Little Joe Cook. "Oo We Baby" was never quite the national smash hit it could have been but the lugubrious doowop sound did show that John Ivy (who, with his son Michael, has now organized a contemporary group, the Naked Truth) was a sadly underestimated talent.

It was a group from York, Pennsylvania, who were to give Red Top its only national R&B hit. The Quintones featured the warbling lead voice of Roberta Haymon and with Ronnie Scott, Phyllis Carr, Caroline Holmes, Kenneth Sexton and Eunice Cristi performing a slow harmonic back-up, the group's "Down The Aisle Of Love" proved such a big Philadelphia record that Red Top turned it over to Dick Clark's Hunt label for national distribution. Sadly, as with so many of the fifties doowop teams, the Quintones, despite making a Number 6 in *Billboard's* R&B chart in September 1958, were quickly forgotten. For three years Red Top Battled on, recording a girl group (the Sharmeers), an Italian doowop team (Tony and the Twilighters who, as Anthony and the Sophomores, were to gain some success in the early sixties oldies and goodies revival), and even an instrumental group (the Kingsmen, put together by Chicago soul man

Curtis Mayfield). But the latter record was in 1961 and by that time Schwartz, a veteran music man with a management career stretching back to the Dells and the Spaniels in 1954, was running Red Top/Jalynne Records with only Irv Nahan's help. Doc Bagby had departed to a new company. Bagby teamed up with Eddie Hart and Felix Valdera, owner of South Street's Paramount Record Shop, to form Val-Ue Records. And the group Bagby contacted to launch the label was the one who'd been hanging around the fringes of the Philly scene for four years, the Blue Notes.

It was in 1956 that Bernard Williams, Harold Melvin, Jesse Gillis Jr., Franklin Peaker and Roosevelt Brodie had trouped over to Josie Records in New York City. Josie were hitting big with the Cadillacs and the Blue Notes hustled a recording contract. They made their first record, the Tin Pan Alley standard "If You Love Me" ("if the sea should suddenly run dry . . ." etc.) and it sold locally. But the group were just one of dozens trying for a big hit disc. The Blue Notes played around the Philly clubs before recording another local hit in 1959, "I Don't Know What It Is", for Brooke Records. Then — in the fall of 1960 when Doc Bagby moved in — the Blue Notes really got a break.

Bagby produced the group performing an ancient standard — "My Hero". In addition to a high reedy lead and burbling back-up, Bagby — influenced no doubt by the developing New York production revolution — conceived a quasi-classical accompaniment with dramatic concert piano and all-enveloping strings. The fact that the strings were dubbed on with appalling amateurishness drowning parts of the group's histrionic vocal didn't seem to matter. The disc still captured a commercial mood of hand-wringing sentimality. "My Hero" made 78 in the Hot 100. The group played the Apollo and at last felt they were on their way. But it was difficult for Bagby to choose a coherent direction for the Blue Notes. The black market for old-style doowops had by 1960 disappeared and Philadelphia's use of the "beat concerto" production techniques was still in its emergent stage. The Blue Notes' follow-up, "Blue Star" "Devoted", didn't sell, despite or because of the bizarre gimmick of a bagpipes intro on "Devoted". As Val-Ue Records began to stumble into difficulties, the Blue Notes began to revamp its personnel and its musical direction. John Atkins and Lawrence Brown replaced Gillis and Peaker, and the group became on-stage performers of sophisticated cabaret material; and on record, the performers of something which was taking over from the old order of cool harmony — soul music.

It is the big-money-soul-of-the-seventies world that one Joseph Cook, occasional performer of unsuccessful soul discs, now longingly pursues. Yet the small-time Cook isn't without his fragment of fame. In a November 1974 interview with *Black Music* magazine, black rock superstar Stevie Wonder was asked what was the first song he sang as a child in the back streets of Detroit. "Peanuts uh oh, uh oh!" he ruefully replied. "Peanuts" was the fleeting claim to rock immortality for a popular bunch of Philadelphians, Little Joe and the Thrillers. The group consisted of Little Joe Cook, Harry Pascle, Farris Hill, Donald Burnett and Richard Frazier.

"We sang on street corners and things. Arnold Maxim heard about us and came around to my house. We did some acappella for him and he really liked what he heard. He set up a date for us in New York to record for the Okeh Record Company."

A Cook-penned dance novelty, "Let's Do The Slop", was the Thrillers' first release on the Columbia Records rhythm and blues subsidiary. But it was an even sillier number, warbled in a squeaky falsetto, which was to push the group into the Top 30 in the summer of 1957. "The falsetto on 'Peanuts' came from a girl who couldn't speak very well. She would say 'You come back here, uh oh, uh oh'. That was it. I wrote 'Peanuts' in five minutes in my house. We went on Dick Clark's *Bandstand*. It got heavy play in New York and Philadelphia, but the fellow who really broke 'Peanuts' was Dick Clark".

Sadly, the Thrillers' big success had all the banal ingredients of a one-off freaky hit. Signed to an ambitious five-year contract, Little Joe couldn't find another successful record. The follow-up, "The Echoes Keep Calling Me", didn't make it, and when the group disbanded and Joe struggled on as a solo his discs, despite his forsaking the gimmicky falsetto in favour of a gospel baritone, went nowhere, though Little Joe Cook was to re-surface briefly onto the national scene in 1962 with the Sherrys.

Considerably more secure financially than Cook is Philadelphia International Records' executive Weldon Arthur McDougal III. He has scuffled too, however. "I started off like all the other kids, trying to imitate Sonny Til and the Orioles. They were out of Baltimore but their records were played on the radio. They were a real influence, everybody was trying to sound like them. After I'd got my ass kicked out of the Castelles and the Dreams I thought, man, I ain't gonna have that happen again . . . I'll form my own group. That was the Larks. That was me – I sang bass – Bill Oxydine, Calvin Nicholls and Jadie Marshall, he was the lead. It was a real scuffle, we were trying to get a break into

show business and everybody had regular jobs. I used to work as a cab driver, another guy worked with the Naval base, stuff like that. I used to pick up all the guys in my cab, and tell them to get on the floor. Then I'd put the flag up and drive off to a gig. We kept together quite a while playing gigs around Philadelphia. In 1960 I wrote a tune called 'It's Unbelievable'. We cut that for Sheryl Records and it was quite a hit (69 in the March '61 Hot 100). Then we had a thing called 'Fabulous Cars And Diamond Rings' which went okay. But it was difficult to break out of the East Coast. Like the Hearts had three national hits and they never did that . . ."

Lee Andrews and the Hearts had emerged back in 1954, were at their height in 1957 and today, as a reformed group playing out-of-town nightclubs and the odd rock'n'roll revival show, remind the long-of-memory of a bygone age. It was at one such show that the specialist doowop magazine, *Stormy Weather* (issue 4), interviewed Lee Andrews in 1970. "We started because of poverty. We wanted to get out of a hard life. At that particular time music was one of the few means by which black people could lift themselves out of the ghetto. . . . We auditioned for a disc jockey and he liked us and took us over to Rainbow".

The group, consisting of Lee Andrews, Roy Calhoun (first tenor), Wendell Calhoun (bass), Ted Weems (baritone) and Butch Curry (second tenor), recorded for Rainbow Records in 1954, including a particularly dirge-like version of "White Cliffs Of Dover". "We left Rainbow because we didn't get paid. We went to the Gotham label with Irvin Ballin. We recorded a few things with Mr. Ballin ('Bluebird Of Happiness'). They were local hits. But he kept putting us off and saying 'I'll give you a session later'. After about a year of pleading and begging and him putting us off, Roy Calhoun and I decided we were gonna contact Jocko, who was a big disc jockey . . . to see if he would be interested in doing something. . . . He gave us an audition and he liked us. We then recorded 'Long Lonely Nights' ".

When the group's rendition of "Long Lonely Nights" appeared on Jocko Henderson's Mainline label it became a local hit. Andrews' voice with its pure, vaguely metallic tone was startlingly similar to that of another black vocalist who had emerged that year out of San Francisco, but who was to move in a completely different musical environment: Johnny Mathis. But although Andrews' beautiful modulated lead had the stamp of real "class", the group's sighing back-up made the Hearts a classic sound of the streets. The master of "Nights" was picked up nationally by Chess Records of Chicago, and the disc rose to 45 in the Hot Hundred. A follow-up, another wistful ballad of unrequited love called "Teardrops", was an even bigger hit for them. However, a situation which should have seen the group established in the big-time quickly soured. Andrews claims that most of the royalties never found their way to the team. "Jocko was sick of it and he couldn't get any satisfaction so he put us on United Artists and our next record was 'Try The Impossible' ".

United Artists actually picked up the master for "Try The Impossible" from the Casino/Gowen label. The item, with its lightweight, skipping tempo, proved to be the group's last chart record, though the Hearts continued to record steadily. "We did 'I Wonder' and the answer to 'Baby Come Back' and the answer to 'Teardrops' called 'Together Again'. But in those days or even now it was all exploitation . . . "

The group broke up in 1959. Lee Andrews and the Hearts had had three national pop hits, yet through constant subjection to the wheelers and dealers in which the fifties record industry abounded came out with next to nothing to show for the era when they'd topped the bill at the Apollo and been "real big record stars". But it wasn't just disgust with the brutal exploitation which had led to the disintegration of the Hearts. Weldon McDougal explains: "There was a time in the fifties when doowops were everything, like groups like the Castelles and Sonny Gordon and the Angels and Lee Andrews and the Hearts were local heroes and were a real big deal. But things changed. New music was coming along and all of a sudden nobody wanted that 'I love you, doo-dooby-doo' shit nomore. By '59 or so that old group thing was dead".

And dead it was to remain for the ghetto audience. The days when hundreds of black teenagers would surround the Uptown Theater jostling for a chance to see and hear a dozen groups stand on stage in baggy suits and processed hair and ooze cool, cool harmonies into a blinding spotlight were never to return. But, amazingly, doowops *were* to have a revival — a revival born in Philadelphia and a revival paradoxically brought about by white record buyers. Sid Payne, who today runs Jerry's Records, one of Philadelphia's most successful record retailers, explains the phenomenon. "Around '59 or '60 or so Dick Clark had Philly sown up. If *Bandstand* plugged a record once, it hit. But Clark was getting in with the guys who were plugging Avalon and Rydell and all those white kid things and some of us didn't dig that. Now the mass did, they went along with that pretty boy thing, but some of the record fans weren't happy.

Now there was a disc jockey called Jerry Blavat. Around '59 he began playing old rhythm and blues records on his radio programme. He played things like the Harptones and the Chantels and the Hearts . . . things that some of the kids hadn't heard when they originally came out and sold to black folk. Pretty soon Jerry Blavat was a real big-time personality. He'd play record hops and 2,000 people would come to hear all those doowop things. It just got bigger and bigger. Hundreds of crazy white kids from south Philadelphia were running around trying to find all these old doowop things, these oldies and goodies as they were called".

The oldies and goodies craze wasn't just restricted to Philadelphia. Irving "Slim" Rose owned a record shop in New York City's Times Square which quickly became the Mecca for the hard-core doowop "collector". The phenomenon didn't simply end with the hoard of fanatical Italian and Jewish record collectors obsessively searching out discs of a bygone black music era. Their presence eventually broke overground. The collectors formed a powerful lobby able to chide record companies into re-issuing some of the discs whose lugubrious tones were oozing from the East Coast airwaves as treasured oldies and goodies. And with the start of the re-issues, amazing come-back stories began to evolve. The Shells, the Five Satins, the Chanters, Johnnie and Joe all came back to the charts. Groups who'd never played to a white audience before and had disbanded with the bitter taste of ghetto apathy or exploitation, suddenly found the white kids in Philadelphia, New York and all over, raving for their "pure" sound of engaging naivety. As the craze continued new doowop groups emerged, like Slim Rose's Timetones or Little Caesar and the Romans who performed "Those Oldies But Goodies Remind Me Of You". Original Sound Records in Hollywood and Roulette Records in New York City bought up the rights of dozens of doowop classics and started massively successful *Oldies But Goodies* album series. All over America record labels dug into their vaults to release *Best Of The Golden Groups* compilation LPs and Jerry Blavat's plump face smiled from a dozen album sleeves as he offered his "personal choice" of goodies by the Harptones, the Hearts and others. So Lee Andrews' group suddenly found themselves once more in demand. The Hearts reformed and began recording again. Lost Nite Records on Philly's Chestnut Avenue was a record label offshoot of the Record Museum record shop which started out by re-issuing Andrews' oldies like "The Bells Of St. Mary's" (as well as others in demand such as the Bosstones'

A Relic Records doowop reissue album

"Mope-itty Mope" and the Capris' "God Only Knows") and by 1961 were recording new material on the Hearts. But it was of specialized interest.

One development of the oldies but goodies craze was the recording of groups who sang in the style of the fifties street-corner harmonizers, but without accompaniment. But as most of the acappella groups (as they were named) were white — and musically inept — their sometimes painfully flat notes were in fact the final death knell for the oldies but goodies craze. By 1964 the British beat group invasion swept doowops from the pop radio airwaves. The Hot Hundred doowop craze died.

Although the mass interest in the sound of the streets subsided as suddenly as it had begun, it left behind the hard-core fanatic. Today Philadelphia is noted as *the* city — with the possible exception of New York — which does most to remember the cool sounds of pure black harmony. Harvey Hill is a disc jockey on WDAS who every Sunday presents an oldies but goodies show which, although partially complying with the requests to hear old Motown hits, mainly pours forth a potent musical brew of fifties black harmony. "One of my most requested things is by the Cobras . . . then I still get asked for the Quintones, the Harptones, the Orioles. Man, I could go on and on. Philly is still very much into those old things . . . okay, not the black audience, but you've still got companies who re-issue piles of old group stuff. And the originals are still bought and sold in Philly. There are super-collectors like Val Shively".

Shively is a legend within the strange, insular world of doowop collectors. His personal collection of priceless "rare" records is one of the largest in the world. He writes for specialist collector magazines like *Bim Bam Boom* and *Record Exchanger* and runs a successful shop, R&B Records, specializing in discs from the fifties. It was in his shop on Lebanon Avenue that a customer, whose Italian accent displayed his south Philly origin, spoke with passion as he clutched a rare new purchase by the Buccanneers. "These group sounds are the pure R&B. You listen to the Stylistics or the Delfonics, they've simply taken the doowop sound and put in all that strings and shit. You don't need that. It's the harmonies I wanna hear, not a symphony orchestra. You take something like the Castelles, now that's really beautiful . . . what a sound . . . but a sound like that will never come back." As I started to agree he began to sing "My Girl Awaits Me".

Philadelphia: home of the doowop fanatic

Three: Jazz fragments: roots to freeform

"There's always been plenty of jazz musicians coming up in Philadelphia . . . but that's all they seem to do. They learn their trade here and then they leave and make it in New York". Organist Luther Randolph knows only too well Philadelphia's apathetic attitude towards the jazz musician. Some of the all-time jazz greats have been associated with the city, yet there is little sign within Philadelphia of much active support for jazz: no jazz recording, few paying customers and fewer gigs.

"I know jazz has declined everywhere, anyway; a historic club like the Birdland closed down in New York, and nobody seemed to care. But in Philly it's not a decline situation. There never *were* many jazz clubs. The Red Rooster, the Downbeat, but not many. Like, John Coltrane moved out of Philly soon as he could . . . he'd have *starved* here".

Coltrane wasn't the first giant to live in — or leave — the cold wastes of Philadelphia for the warmer climate of New York City. Cornet ace Rex Stewart, who found fame and acclaim during the thirties and forties as omnipresent Duke Ellington sideman, was born in Philly in 1907. The greatest female blues singer of all, Bessie Smith, lived in the city with her Philadelphia policeman husband. And Ethel Waters, the vaudeville-cum-jazz singer who swept to stardom as a silver screen actress, wowed local audiences way back in 1915 as Sweet Mama Stringbean.

But Coltrane is the greatest of all Philadelphia's many fine post-war musicians. John William Coltrane was actually born in Hamlet, North Carolina in 1926,

coming to Philadelphia to study music at the Granoff Studios and the Ornstein School of Music. He was a brilliant pupil who showed early promise of greatness, but on leaving Ornstein all the young tenorman found was a few cocktail lounge gigs and a lot of frustration. Then he was drafted. In the U.S. Navy, Trane played in the forces band, and on his discharge in 1946, took the first significant step in making a full time career out of music — though at first it was urban blues music. Coltrane joined the band of altoist and blues shouter Eddie "Cleanhead" Vinson touring the chittlin circuit with the singer throughout 1947 and 1948. Trane's gruelling blooding continued when the young tenor player joined Dizzie Gillespie's big band, with a role restricted to sax section ensemble work and with little chance to solo, and in 1952 John was back on the chittlin circuit with the Earl Bostic Combo. Bostic's band was a big act along the East Coast: the alto saxman was one of innumerable jazzmen dubbed "rhythm and blues" by an industry anxious to pigeonhole the results of the tremendous upheaval in Negro big band jazz styles throughout the War years. Raucously swinging bands like those of Lionel Hampton and Lucky Millinder had simplified and re-directed big band jazz into a more aggressively blues-orientated style which, although lacking the technical brilliance of a Duke Ellington, was more appealing to the mass black audience who sought bands which could deliver the required driving dance beat. Bostic, born in Tulsa, Oklahoma, had played with many New York bands before forming his own unit at the Mimo Club, Harlem in 1941. After two years with Lionel Hampton's Orchestra, Earl started on his own again and in 1945 cut a few sides for Majestic Records in New York. Yet it was with a smaller group playing raunchy twelve- and sixteen-bar blues that Bostic's combo first began to attract the R&B audience. The company for which Bostic recorded thirty-three sides between the summer of 1946 and the winter of 1948 was Gotham Records. But the popularity of Bostic's Gotham recordings was overshadowed by the immense success that was to follow. In early 1949 the bandleader signed to King Records of Cincinatti, which also bought up his Gotham Masters. Bostic's extrovert, vibrant music quickly captured the mass audience and black location juke boxes across the country became crammed with his band's smash hits like "Sleep", "Flamingo" (a purported million-seller) and "Moonglow". Coltrane stayed with Earl Bostic for a year, recording two sessions, one in Cincinatti (which spawned "Moonglow") and one in L.A.

When Trane left in late 1952 it was to join Johnny Hodges. Hodges, the companion of Duke Ellington from 1928 until 1951 had, sensing where the gigs were, formed a Bostic-style R&B combo, who hit nationally with "Castle Rock" for Mercury Records. But Coltrane's stay with the former Ellington altoist was as brief as that with Bostic. It wasn't until 1955 that the gnawing restlessness and boiling urgency manifest in the young Coltrane first came close to finding an appropriate outlet in music. For in 1955 Trane joined an emerging trumpet player called Miles Davis. Coltrane's work within Davis' newly formed quintet was exciting, vibrant and fearsomely original. It also brought barbs from the conservative jazz establishment. For example, critic John S. Wilson, as referred to in *The Encyclopedia of Jazz*, wrote: "He often plays his tenor sax as if he were determined to blow it apart, but his desperate attacks almost invariably lead nowhere". More astute observers recognized, however, that Coltrane's passionate music with its overtones of Sonny Rollins and Dexter Gordon plus the rooty swagger of R&B contained in its groping, snarled strangeness a whole new concept as to exactly what constituted "jazz". In 1957 Trane left Davis for a few months to work with composer/pianist Thelonius Monk and when he returned Trane's playing was more assertive. His new confidence made his subsequent albums with Prestige, Blue Note and Atlantic, with and without Miles Davis — with whom Coltrane played intermittently — stunning contributions to the changing improvisational vistas of post-Charlie Parker jazz. Trane had evolved an extraordinary style which came to be referred to as "sheets of sound". Critic Robert Palmer described

it in *Black Music* magazine in February 1975: ". . . A permutative approach to harmonic extensions which involved every note in every possible extension of every chord. By grouping these mercurial clusters of tones in series, and often in asymmetrical five- and seven-note groups, he achieved an excruciatingly thorough improvisational method, and extended the length of saxophone solos so far some traditionally-oriented listeners felt decidedly uncomfortable".

When, with his Atlantic recordings, Trane added soprano sax to his technical armoury, his playing also began to take on an additional spiritual exultancy, the logical extension of the mystical beliefs to which Trane had been introduced by experimental jazzman Sun Ra. Two crucial albums were made in 1959,

Giant of tenor sax, John Coltrane

Giant Steps, in which Trane applied his "sheets of sound" technique to one of the most demanding chord progressions in jazz history, and Miles Davis' *Kind of Blue*, in which chord changes were reduced to a bare minimum or discarded in favour of modal or scalar structures. *Blue* was staggeringly innovative. Although it was to be only a brief stop in Trane's stylistic search, many of today's jazz and soul musicians, such as Kool and the Gang, are still exploring *Blue's* implications.

In 1960 Coltrane formed his own quartet: bassist,

Jimmy Garrison, drummer, Elvin Jones and a young pianist who shared with Trane a Philadelphia background, McCoy Tyner. Tyner was born in Philadelphia in 1938. His mother played piano and encouraged her son to learn, and McCoy eventually enrolled at the West Philadelphia Music School followed by the Granoff Music School. While still a student Tyner played a gig or two.

"I played a little bit of R&B and a little bit of jazz back then", remembers Tyner. "I had my own seven-piece combo. When I was seventeen I did a gig with Calvin Massey's band at the Red Rooster and that's when I met John Coltrane. I thought he was a very down-to-earth person but he was definitely on a different plane as far as his mission was concerned. . ."

In 1959 McCoy joined the Jazztet, the group led by Benny Golson — the Philadelphia-born tenorman whose frenetic musical past had included spells with Tadd Dameron and Lionel Hampton in 1953, Johnny Hodges in 1954, Earl Bostic from 1954 to 1956, Dizzy Gillespie from 1956 to 1958 and Art Blakey from 1958 to 1959. In the fall of 1959 Benny, with trumpeter Art Farmer, formed the Jazztet. McCoy stayed with the group for six months mainly gigging on the East Coast. But in early 1960 Tyner got the opportunity to check out at close quarters John Coltrane's "different plane".

"I joined Coltrane's Quintet when it was only two weeks old. John felt that music was like the universe. That influenced me. You look up and see the stars but beyond them are many other stars. He was looking for the stars you can't see."

The search for invisible stars was almost an obsession. In the exact style of *Kind Of Blue*, Coltrane used the chords of the Rodgers and Hammerstein opus "My Favourite Things" as the basis for his own improvisations. With Elvin Bishop's polyrhythmic drumming laying down a hypnotic rhythm, the maestro's eerie soprano sax created an exotic Eastern mood of shattering force. *My Favourite Things* (Atlantic) brought considerable acclaim for Coltrane — and for his sidemen. Tyner's style had the critics in raptures. He re-emphasized the lower half of the keyboard with dark, thickly textured, fumbling passages perfectly complementing Coltrane's mystical flights. Coltrane, Tyner and co. became accepted leaders in the new jazz movement. Coltrane became even more engrossed in Indian improvisational techniques, and although some critics attacked his harsh, passionate, often excessively lengthy solos as "ugly anti-jazz", his innovative introduction of Indian and modal concepts helped sweep away more of the old conceptual barriers for the sixties' jazzmen. True to his roots,

however, Trane still found time to record a series of vibrant blues and also cut two albums devoted to ballads played with a combination of sensitivity and intensity.

In 1963 Tyner had left the Coltrane Quintet (to be replaced by Alice Coltrane) to begin working under his own name, and commenced an artistically successful association with Blue Note Records. Eighteen months after Tyner's departure, Rachied Ali joined Coltrane's group. Drummer Rashied was born in Philadelphia (and like Coltrane and Tyner was a student of the Granoff School). Ali had worked with saxophonist Len Bailey and various local R&B bands before being forced to take a regular job (cab driving) for two years. He resumed playing with Arnold Joyner before eventually leaving Philadelphia in 1963 to work in New York. There he played with many of the new wave of experimental jazzmen like Archie Shepp and Sun Ra. Ali joined Coltrane in November 1965 and, for a short while, worked alongside Elvin Jones as part of a two-drummer line-up of explosive percussive power. With his new line-up Coltrane's music became increasingly diverse and his recordings increasingly prolific. Recorded for ABC's Impulse label (where producer Bob Thiele gave full rein to the master's burning musical search), albums like *Ascension* (the definitive avant-garde big band jazz album featuring "guests" like Archie Shepp, Pharoah Saunders, Freddie Hubbard and many others), *Om* (a stunning Eastern mantra) and *Interstellar Space* (duets with Rashied Ali) became acknowledged classics of the avant-garde.

Trane burned with energy. He began to study the bass clarinet and flute. When not performing awesome solos which pushed his horn and its player further than any previous musician had dared to go, Trane was exploring Eastern philosophy. Then, on July 17th, 1967, John William Coltrane died suddenly of a heart attack and post-war jazz lost one of its most eloquent voices.

Coltrane's memory will, of course, live on. McCoy Tyner, the key associate of Trane, has now developed into an internationally acclaimed jazzman. Tyner's albums for Blue Note between 1965 and 1970 each gained him an expanding reputation as a fluidly inventive keyboard man. But Tyner's reputation really blossomed when in 1970 he changed musical direction and his playing became less linear in its development, with a new emphasis on shapes — note groups and blocks of sound. Tyner's albums for Milestone Records — *Sahara*, a spiritual evocation stemming from the musician's Islamic religion; *Song For My Lady*, wistfully inventive and considered by some his finest album; *Songs Of The New World*, with a massive brass ensemble and sweeping string section; *Echoes Of A Friend* where dense chords and stirringly articulated arpeggios flashed dramatically — all reflected Tyner's new creative impetus. They were followed by the commercial success of Tyner's *Sama Layuca* album, which featured the superb supporting band of Bobby Hutcherson on elegant vibes and Gary Bartz on soulful alto drawing strength from Tyner in the creation of exotic, Eastern-flavoured mood pieces.

"Philadelphis should give Tyner the keys of the city" laughs disc jockey Perry Johnson whose Philadelphia station programmes "jazz and progressive soul music". But then he sadly reaffirms Luther Randolph's criticism: "The contribution made by musicians like Tyner — or Philadelphia's other great modern jazzmen, Coltrane, Stan Getz, Philly Joe Jones, Gerry Mulligan, Lee Morgan, Bobby Timmons — hasn't been recognized in Philadelphia. They all had to leave the city to get work."

And the place Getz, Mulligan, Jones, Morgan and Timmons made for was New York. Tenor sax great Stan Getz who, with his post-bop "cool" sound, rose to prominence with Woody Herman before breaking through with his much copied small group and even, with guitarist Charlie Byrd, gained a massive pop success with the bossa nova "Desafinado"; Philly Joe Jones, the veteran drummer who found acclaim for his work with Miles Davis before blossoming into one of the sixties' most influential percussionists; Gerry Mulligan, the baritone saxman who worked with Gene Krupa and Miles Davis, then formed his own piano-less quartet which swept him to the top of the modern jazz tree; Lee Morgan, the fluid trumpeter now sadly deceased who toured with Dizzy Gillespie and Art Blakey and worked in Philly with Jimmy Heath before his bluesy recordings for Blue Note (particularly the classic "The Sidewinder") made him a national name; and Bobby Timmons, the soulful pianist who came to the fore through his churchy work with Art Blakey and Cannonball Adderley before forming his own trio — all made for the Big Apple frustrated by Philadelphia's reluctance to support them. Ironically, one band who was able to find support in the City of Brotherly Love was the unit led by Lynn Hope — ironically, because Hope was never to achieve the jazz establishment acclaim of a Getz or Mulligan.

Bobby Martin, now a behind-the-scenes soul star, played in the successful Lynn Hope Band. Martin, born in Cincinatti, had learned piano in high school and "got hooked" on music after seeing Lionel Hampton playing "Flying Home" in Kentucky. "I got a music scholarship but I only went for a year before joining

Lynn Hope. Lynn came from Cincinatti and his band used to play around town. One night he was playing in a place outside of town called the Smokey Mountain. It was amateur night so I got up and played 'Caldonia' and 'After Hours' on marimbas which my mom had bought me. Lynn dug me and I joined his band as pianist. At first it was the Lynn Hope Trio but later he got a sextet. Lynn played sax, a real raunchy, blues kinda sound, a bit like Earl Bostic but wilder. We got very popular and played cities like Cleveland, Louisville and St. Louis. We began recording and in 1950 came off with one of the biggest R&B hits of the year 'Tenderly' for Premium Records. We toured up and down. We got booked to do a job at the Showboat on Lombard Street in Philadelphia but we got there five hours late. When we arrived there was no one there. The man had fired us but Lynn asked him to give us a chance to play. We said we'd work through 'til two without a break. So we started playing, the place got filled up and that went on night after night. The man signed us up for five years. So that's how Lynn and I got to Philadelphia."

Lynn Hope's swaggering, honking, bluesy music was like Earl Bostic's, the very root of rock'n'roll. And among the vocalists who roared a boogie or shouted a blues with Lynn's raunchy combo were two later to find a rock'n'roll audience: Frankie Brunson, who today sings with the soul group Peoples Choice and, for a brief spell, one Jalacy Hawkins, a singer who was to show precisely how the black music mainstream was a totally fluid entity. Just as big band jazz styles had been coarsened and simplified to produce rhythm and blues, so that very modification was itself to undergo traumatic reshaping in the evolution of rock'n'roll. Hawkins was born in Cleveland, Ohio in 1929. He learned piano and listened to the big band singers. After a spell as a boxer he landed a job as pianist with the Tiny Grimes band. Guitarist Grimes had a substantial music background. He worked with Cats and a Fiddle, Art Tatum and Slam Stewart before forming his own group, the Rocking Highlanders, and toured the Midwest until he finally settled in Philadelphia in 1955. Grimes and band members backed Hawkins on his first recording, a blues ballad "Why Do You Waste My Time" for Gotham. The disc didn't sell but it did clearly show Jay's original influences . . . exuberant shouters like Bullmoose Jackson (like Hawkins, a singer from Cleveland who, after working with Lucky Millinder became a popular R&B name in the forties and early fifties before retiring to run a Philadelphia bar in 1959) and sophisticated jazz intonated balladeers like Ernie Andrews (a Philadelphia-born singer who moved to

L.A. and had popular recordings on G&G in 1945 and Aladdin in 1947).

Jay himself possessed a rich, resonant, baritone voice, which although somewhat pedestrian for slow, sentimental ballads, did lend itself fairly effectively to up-tempo boogie shouting. By 1954 Jay had begun to write his own decidedly eccentric material. In New York City he recorded songs of hard drinking — "Baptise Me In Wine" (Timely Records, 1954) — and flabber-mouthed women — "She Put The Whammee On Me" (Mercury Records, 1955). But they didn't sell. Then came Jay's metamorphosis. Disc jockey Alan Freed, anxious to pull more and more black rhythm and blues artists into the big-money world of rock'n'roll, advised Jay to exaggerate his raucous city blues style and to adopt outfits and performance to emphasize the macabre side of his humour. Screamin' Jay Hawkins emerged: a lunatic madman in polka dot tie, yellow suit and zebra stripe shoes, who leapt from a coffin in which he was carried onto stage, and whose bizarre antics terrified an audience into attention. Previously, in May 1955, Herb Slotkin had taken Jay to New York for a recording session and one of the songs cut for Slotkin's Grand Records was an under-stated, but somehow eerily threatening, blues ballad called "I Put A Spell On You". The Grand disc hadn't sold, but on September 12th, 1956 Screamin' Jay re-recorded the number and Hawkins had a disc which captured the demented atmosphere of his bizarre stage performances. The session which produced "I Put A Spell On You" and "Little Demon" for Columbia Records (for release on their Okeh sub-sidiary) was, if rock'n'roll history is to be believed, a riot of alcohol. But the man in the control booth was sober enough. Caught on tape was a performance of intense, devilish, power.

In *Black Music* for April 1974 critic Cliff White described it thus: "Over a thumping waltz tempo laid down by drum, bass, sax and a banjo looms Jay's resounding baritone — shouting, snorting, chuckling and demanding. It is an amazing sound. Nothing much to do with rock and roll or blues or any other normal form of music, just one helluva record."

The classic "I Put A Spell On You" was a smallish hit and soon Screamin' Jay was terrifying audiences all over America on big rock'n'roll extravaganzas. But he was never again to quite capture the blistering sound of "Spell". He recorded a series of bizarre, self-composed songs with imagery snatched from the dark side of the mind — songs of voodoo and black magic and even cannibalism — and also saw fit to perform excruciating ballads in an embarrassing pastiche of Billy Eckstine — but the records, for numerous New

York companies, didn't sell. In 1961, Screamin' Jay returned to Philadelphia for a final session for Chancellor Records, then split to Honululu, Hawaii to open a nightclub. By then, of course, Screamin' Jay Hawkins was an anachronism, an eye-rolling, skull-waving museum piece who, despite a "cult" following in England (where he subsequently toured), seemed destined to remain a grotesque curiosity or a reminder of the cruel fickleness of the teenage audience, no longer of interest to the pop record buyer and certainly of none to the jazz enthusiast.

The lack of "acceptance" by the jazz establishment was something encountered by artists considerably less bastardized than Jalacy Hawkins. The accusations of "gimmickry" or simplistic "playing to the stalls" fell on a whole area of jazz music. Luther Randolph explains: "There used to be this thing called the organ circuit. Philadelphia was the city that pioneered the organ as a jazz instrument. Most of the great jazz organists come from here or round about. But the critics were really down on the music . . . they said it wasn't jazz or that it was a gimmick. The audiences wanted to hear organs though. So as a Bill Doggett or a Doc Bagby couldn't get bookings at the established jazz venues this special club circuit opened up on the East Coast . . . it was like half R&B, half jazz, mainly black and really pretty wild. Until Jimmy Smith came along the organ wasn't 'respectable' as a jazz instrument".

The pioneer of the electronic organ was one William Strethen Davis from Glasgow, Missouri. In 1945 Davis had joined Louis Jordan's Tympany Five as pianist and arranger and four years later recorded a couple of organ-led tracks with the popular bandleader. Davis' subsequent recording of "Make No Mistake" for Mercer Records caused a furore in jazz circles. It combined all the elements of single line bop improvisation with full-blooded chord effects and a surging beat which made the artist credit of Wild Bill Davis particularly appropriate. Immediately, other jazz pianists began to look at the organ in a new light. Milt Buckner, for years the pianist with Lionel Hampton, began to get organ-ized while the successor in Louis Jordan's band, one William Ballard Doggett, enraptured by the pulsating sound achieved by Davis, got a Hammond too.

Bill Doggett was born in Philadelphia in 1916. He'd played piano with Jimmy Gorman and briefly led his own band in 1938 before working with the innovative jazz-cum-R&B orchestra of Lucky Millinder. Near the end of the Second World War, Bill worked as pianist with the Ink Spots vocal group, before joining singer/altoist Jordan whose raucous, good-humoured, good-times music was a key factor in the soon-to-develop rock'n'roll. It was 1951 when Bill Doggett took up the organ. He accompanied Ella Fitzgerald on some recordings and, encouraged, proceeded to form his own trio. Doggett signed with King Records and commenced recording. Discs like "Big Dog", "Moondust" and

Bill Doggett, the "Honky Tonk" million-seller

"Real Gone Mambo" showed the potential of the organ to swing loud and long and with Doggett's Davis-inspired heavy chorded passages, seemed the perfect instrument for simple, riffing blues. In the main, purist jazz fans threw up collective hands in horror, but the rhythm and blues audiences took Doggett's exciting, raunchy sound to their bosoms and clubs. Doggett, Wild Bill Davis and Jackie Davis (yet another ex-Louis Jordan sideman) began the endless trek around East Coast bars and grills. On record, the greatest triumph for the Bill Doggett Combo was to come on June 16th, 1956. On that day Doggett, along with saxman Clifford Scott, guitarist Billy Butler, bassist Carl Pruitt and drummer Shep

Sheppard, recorded an insidious blues jam which they dubbed "Honky Tonk". The disc became the instrumental smash of the year, selling a million copies. Paradoxically, the phenomenal R&B and rock'n'roll success of "Honky Tonk" was, in the long term, to play against Doggett. The organist was, not surprisingly, never again able to come up with such a massive success and his constant attempts to try — "Slow Walk" in 1956, "Ram-Bunk-Shush" in 1957, "Blip Blop" in 1958 and "Smokie" in 1960 — although fairly successful, restricted Doggett in the eyes and ears of the public as a mechanical purveyor of repetitive, lolloping, rather mindless dance riffs. The impression was reinforced in 1961 when Doggett, by then on Warner Bros. Records, hit the charts with "Let's Do The Hully Gully Twist". By the mix-sixties Doggett had finally moved away from the rooty, blues-based, shuffle beat and, after albums on Columbia, did a LP with Ella Fitzgerald and later one with Della Reese. But by the late sixties Doggett was again entrenched in the rhythm and blues field, now evolved as "soul", and recorded an album with the James Brown Band (*Honky Tonk Popcorn* no less). The seventies saw Doggett still occasionally recording a little R&B in New York. But by then of course the music world had well and truly passed by the performer of one of the fifties' classic instrumentals.

The Bill Doggett Combo's influence is unarguable, however. And among the dozens of pianists who turned to the Hammond organ as a result of the driving music which throbbed from the fifties organ circuit was a Norristown, Pennsylvania-born musician called James "Jimmy" Smith. Jimmy's parents were both pianists and even at the age of nine their son showed considerable talent, winning the Major Bowes Amateur Show and, as a result, playing on several Philadelphia radio programmes. In 1942 James Sr. and James Jr. formed a song-and-dance team, their first job being a spot at Norristown's Coconut Grove. Then Jimmy was drafted. After a brief spell in the Navy serving in the Pacific, the young musician gained his first formal musical training. He studied string bass at the Hamilton School of Musicians in 1948 and piano at the Ornstein School during 1949 to 1950. Then in 1952 Jimmy joined a Philly group, Don Gardner and his Sonotones.

Gardner, born and raised in Philadelphia, is today a reasonably successful soul singer. Back in 1952 there was no such classification. "I started off singing the blues. I'd hang around the clubs and when they played a song I knew I'd get up there and start singing. I did my first record with Gotham Records. That was

called 'Trees' and after that I did a spell with Jimmy
Shorter's Band. Anyway, in '53 I did a thing with
Bruce Records in New York who were hot with the
Harptones. My thing was called 'How Do You Speak
To An Angel' and was a small kinda hit so I was able
to get my own little band together. Jimmy played
piano for awhile around Philly. He was a fantastic
musician even then".

By a strange coincidence Don Gardner's singing
partner a decade later was to be greatly influenced by
Jimmy Smith, then established as the king of the jazz
organ. For, after a steady stream of New York recordings for labels like King and Jubilee, Don Gardner
teamed up with Dee Dee Ford. The duo's quasi-
gospel vocals were accompanied by Dee Dee's bluesy
organ work and the stream of sixties releases by Don
and Dee Dee clearly showed that, by then, Smith's
influence had extended even into early soul.

Jimmy Smith's first steps to becoming a major
musical influence were pretty tough ones. Playing
piano by night he wood-shedded by day and in a Philadelphia music studio laboriously taught himself the
use of the Hammond's multiple keyboards, multifarious stops and the co-ordination complexities of
foot pedals. Jimmy saved enough money for a down
payment for his own instrument and, storing it in a
rented room in a warehouse, spent hours of studious
concentration. Then, in the summer of 1955 Jimmy
Smith emerged from his warehouse and, booking himself into a club in Atlantic City, New Jersey, prepared
to shatter the jazz world. Smith's playing was startlingly original. By unique usages of stops and showing
real improvisational flair, Smith gave the instrument a
variety and colour, a percussive, rhythmic impact and
a range of dynamics and moods undreamed of by the
pedestrian Bill Doggett. One of Smith's most effective
devices was the technique of holding a note or chord
with one hand, while the other embarked on a wild
series of eights or a jagged row of rhythmic punctua-
tions resembling the urgency of a Morse code trans-
mission. The Jimmy Smith Trio hit New York in 1956
and immediately bathed in the limelight. Smith began
recording and the stream of albums for Blue Note
Records clearly showed that his appeal was broader
than any other organist — before or since.

DJ Perry Johnson tells the story: "He got a kind of
acceptance that a lot of the other organists didn't get.
Guys like Bill Doggett worked more or less in R&B gigs
and the guys who came up after Jimmy, in his shadow
so to speak, artists like Jack McDuff, Groove Holmes,
Johnny 'Hammond' Smith, Larry Young, Lou Bennett,
Jimmy McGriff and Shirley Scott . . ." — the latter

nearby Newark and Camden respectively — ". . . got
called 'jazz funk' and 'soul jazz' by the critics and
really just got to play the organ circuit. Not that the
critics really took to Smith 'til the sixties, but the
public grooved to him and he was kinda tolerated."

Smith, as the father of organ-led "soul jazz", was
lucky. He appeared at the Newport Jazz Festival, Birdland and drew forth such comments as "the eighth

Pioneer of the jazz organ, Jimmy Smith

wonder of the world" from Miles Davis. His Blue Note
albums such as *Sermon, Home Cookin'* and *Plays
Pretty Just For You* poured forth in a torrent of
rhythmic pungency. By the sixties Smith even became
a teenage cult figure. Bluesy tracks like "Midnight
Special" and "Back At The Chicken Shack" were
pulled from his Blue Note albums and made the Hot
100. And when Smith joined Verve Records in 1962
and combined with the big band of Lalo Schiffrin to
work out a blistering arrangement of Elmer Bernstein's
"Walk On The Wild Side", its massive sales success

seemed not only Smith's biggest personal triumph but the highlight of the jazz-for-the-masses movement championed by those anxious to see jazz music, in however modified a form, become "accessible" again to a mass audience. Acclaim and poll-winning trophies were scattered on the "Hammond genius". And with hit singles and albums like *Hobo Flats* and *The Cat* (the latter winning a Grammy in 1965), the claim by Smith's management that he was "the biggest selling post-war jazzman" was pretty convincing. But para-doxically in his gigantic acclaim lay Smith's fall from favour. Jazz critics, annoyed by his reliance on a certain stylistic formula and distressed with the welter of Smith-inspired combos that flooded the catalogues of every major jazz label, began to be even more virulent in their criticism of the "mindless funk purveyed by Smith and his ilk". Jimmy seemed to over-react. In 1966 Smith, possibly anxious to ridicule his critics by extending his mass Hot 100 audience even further, began to perform vocals: "Got My Mojo Working" and "I'm Your Hoochie Coochie Man" (both from the repertoire of bluesman Muddy Waters). No doubt reasoning that his lack of voice (he performed in a rasping, perfunctory grunt) would in no way sound amiss in the era of gritty soulmen, Smith made a major error of judgement. His vocal discs, although heavily promoted by Verve, didn't really take off with the teenage audience and their recording lost him a considerable chunk of his credibility with the jazz audience. Disappointed and upset by the violent criti-cism, Smith largely withdrew from serious recording and performing. Despite a few isolated releases on Verve, and recently an album on Pride, Smith — the brilliant technician whose fluid fusion of improvisa-tional flare and gritty blues/gospel funkiness — seems now to have been overtaken by other jazzmen who've followed his lead in finding a large audience but put-ting their improvisation in a funky framework. Don Gardner observes: "Jimmy made a whole lot of money out of his music so even though he's slipped from view he's done *fine*. And nobody can say he ain't been a major influence".

One of the musicians influenced was Jimmy McGriff. Born in Philadelphia in 1936, Jimmy played bass with various Philadelphia groups before his friendship with Jimmy Smith led to a switch to organ. He formed his own trio, playing the East Coast. After touring with artists like Don Gardner and Arthur Prysock, McGriff played the Vanity Club in Newark where he was spotted by Joe Lederman who recorded the trio (McGriff, organ, Morris Dow, guitar, and Jackie Mills, drums) on an old Ray Charles standard, "I Got A Woman", for his local Jell label. The disc's wickedly throbbing drive made it an instant local hit and the master was picked up by Sue Records, the New York company run by Juggy Murray. "I Got A Woman" became a smash R&B and pop hit (20 in the Hot 100 of October 1962) and although another hit of that enormity didn't emerge, McGriff did well in the R&B market with numbers like "All About My Girl" (in 1963) and "The Last Minute" (in 1964) before leaving Sue Records. Since then McGriff has toured exten-sively and recorded steadily for Solid State, Capitol and Groove Merchant (including an intriguing album with bluesman Jr. Parker).

Juggy Murray reminisces, "Jimmy was not what you'd call real jazz; he said it was old-time swing with a jazz effect but he's ripped up some audiences in his time. Now you take an artist like Shirley Scott, she's got more technique but she's never got as popular as Jimmy".

Shirley, one of jazz music's most respected female musicians, put in the seemingly obligatory attendance at the Ornstein School of Music. She first of all took up trumpet, winning a scholarship before switching to piano and playing in her father's private club in her brother's band. In 1955 she joined the trio of tenor saxman Eddie "Lockjaw" Davis. A swinging soloist, Shirley stayed with Davis (recording for Roulette and Prestige) until she left to form her own trio (albums on Prestige and Imperial) and married band-member Stanley Turrentine, the soulful tenor saxman who has made a name for himself in the seventies on Fantasy Records. Shirley has still to get Jimmy Smith's acclaim or a similar bank balance but she has at least made a significant mark on the jazz world. Such a mark has still to be made by a brilliant organist who today regularly plays at the Roundtable on Philly's 62nd and Walnut Streets. Yet that musician, Luther Ran-dolph, has made a massive contribution to the music in Philadelphia though in a manner which, parallel to his jazz obscurity, has brought him neither fame nor wealth. But Randolph isn't bitter. "I've contributed my part and I just hope the Philadelphia music scene continues to grow as a result of it . . . I wasn't actually born in the city, I was born in a place called Meida, which is about fifteen miles away. I played piano in church and I was in a gospel quartet called the Gems of Harmony who did some radio shows when I was about twelve. When I was fifteen I met Marcus Welgrave who was one of the leading jazz trumpeters in the area. So we started this little group, playing Charlie Parker things. Later I switched over to organ and worked with Hilary Hamilton's group. Then I went to art school and had a spell in the Army. When I came out I studied at the Granoff Music School and I got with a dixieland group and played Bermuda. Then, after a spell with Bunny Sigler who was just starting up, I worked a lot of jazz gigs like the Village Gate. Around '61 I did a session with Duke Ellington. But I never much cared for New York and when I met this guy called Johnny Styles who was tired of being out on the road I decided to team up with him in Philly and see where it took me".

Guitarist Johnny Styles had also been around quite a while. "In the beginning I had a group called the Medallions. We were singers but we started learning instruments and we re-named ourselves the Manhattans. We did a record or two in Philadelphia, a thing called 'Live It Up' for a little label here. It did well so we went up to New York and did something with Sy Oliver. The Manhattans started touring, there was me, Darrell Small, Bobby Gregory and Hollis Floyd. We did another record or two, we had a thing 'Ebb Tide, Parts 1 and 2' for Sid Nathan in Cincinatti (King Records). I played violin on that. But mainly we were out on the road. We backed Sonny Til for a year or two when he'd split from the Orioles, so we worked as the Orioles. But I got tired of the small club thing, I wanted to come home. The record business was what I wanted to break into . . . and I just felt Philadelphia would be the place to do it".

Four:
Bobbysox, Bandstand and Beatles

A group of teenage girls shivered by the entrance to WFIL-TV on 46th and Market Street one December afternoon in 1959, waiting for Bobby Rydell to come out. Inside the studio Bobby couldn't get his lip synch right. He never did, but it didn't really matter. His manager had told him that his even flashing teeth were his main asset, so Bobby always sang in an unwavering ear-to-ear grin. "Wild one, I'm gonna tame you down" — his voice warbled across the studio — "Wild one, I'll clip your wings". The tempo increased and Bobby made a few half-hearted leg and trunk movements to acknowledge the skipping dance beat, though nothing drastic enough to crease his shiny, lapel-less suit or to fool the cameraman. Around Bobby hoards of young permed and prettied girls and exuberant, perspiring youths twirled and bobbed in self-conscious stiffness or head-shaking abandon, constantly glancing up to see if "they" were on the programme monitors.

As the record faded, *American Bandstand's* other camera zoomed in on Dick Clark. He's older and plumper than Rydell, his suit a little more conservative, his hair a little shorter, and his manner considerably more confident. He tells the viewers that they've been listening to "Wild One" available on the Cameo label and continues, clutching a hand mike in a neat, manicured hand, with the information that they've got a great show lined up: "There's Connie Francis, Fats Domino and Frankie Avalon's going to look in to sing his new record 'Don't Throw Away All Those Teardrops'. . ."

American Bandstand, hosted by Clark, did much more than pull Philadelphia into the very centre of popular music activity, where hits were made, stars were born and dollars were amassed. Eventually, the programme's blatant manipulation of the vulnerabilities and buying habits of American youth came ironically close to smothering rock'n'roll, the music which brought so much wealth to Clark, WFIL-TV and the city of Philadelphia. But before then, before the rise — and fall — of Rydell, Fabian, Avalon and the other pre-packaged teen idols offered by *American Bandstand*, even before the first waves of rock'n'roll rose out of the Southern states, Philadelphia was helping Tin Pan Alley in its relentless pursuit of the American record buyers' dollars.

In the forties popular music, a strange commodity consisting of melodramatic ballads, sentimental swan songs and novelty ditties, changed very slowly, if it changed at all. By the end of the Second World War the emphasis had shifted away from dance bands and towards individual vocalists, though in fact many of the songbirds and crooners who jockeyed for post-war radio space were former dance-band singers. But, even though the styles remained rigidly stereotyped, there was always a need for new balladeers to give the appearance of variety to the endless schmalz of Kay Starr, Jo Stafford and Philadelphia-born Kitty Kallen.

The music moguls of New York looked to the East Coast nightclub circuit for crooners of Italian or Jewish extraction, and if the singers they found were seldom able, like New Jersey/Italian Frank Sinatra, to transcend the mawkish excesses of Tin Pan Alley, they noted something which was to serve them well a decade later: that a disc's musical content wasn't the only, or even the main reason the young female record buyer bought a particular record. Veteran music arranger Peter DeAngelis explains: "Every woman has an ideal of the handsome man she would want to fall in love with. In the same way every guy likes to fantasize about the beautiful blonde. The movies tapped that, they created stars, handsome leading men, beautiful heroines, which huge, big audiences related to. The music business did the same thing. After Sinatra, what the singer *looked* like became as important as what he sounded like. The girls bought the records and they wanted singers who were handsome. So singers like Frank Sinatra and Vic Damone were sold as much on their good looks as their talent for singing".

By 1949 Philadelphia, with its thriving Italian ghetto, had begun to spawn smiling, wavy-haired vocalizers with enough talent to croon in the flat unemotional manner which was the pop balladeering norm of the day. But in fact Philly's first post-war crooning star was Jewish, not Italian. Eddie Fisher was born in Philly in 1928 and had sung over local radio stations before going to New York as band vocalist and production singer at the Copa Cabana Night Club. In 1949 Fisher was spotted by Eddie Cantor, who signed him for a cross-country tour, and the following year began recording with RCA Victor Records under the uninspired direction of Hugo Winterhalter. By 1951 Eddie's bland, modulated voice was striking gold ("Anytime", "Tell Me Why", "Lady Of Spain", "I'm Walking Behind You" and others) while his TV show and highly publicized marriages to Debbie Reynolds and Elizabeth Taylor kept him firmly in the public eye. Then in 1957 Fisher's career and personal life suddenly took a downward turn. In a sense Fisher found the same thing with the swooning young ladies who rushed in their millions to buy "I Need You Now" that Fabian was to discover with the *Bandstand* ans six years later: a career based on a good profile and a Brylcreemed wave hiding the sterile anonymity of Tin Pan Alley music, could crumble fast.

More resilient and unquestionably more talented than Fisher was Armando "Buddy" Greco who today still trundles around the Vegas night spots. His "Ooh Look-a There Ain't She Pretty" was a purported million-seller for Musicraft Records in 1948. Buddy's vocal style had enough finger-snapping appeal to catch the middle-American audience of the fifties and sixties, though this success was, perhaps, a loss for the jazz world. Greco (a pianist and singer with Benny Goodman from 1949 to 1952) was an inventive keyboard-

man in the style of George Shearing, capable of more scope than the smooth, self-conscious swing vocals which were demanded of him. Also thrown up in the pre-rock'n'roll era was Al Martino. Born Alfred Cini in south Philadelphia in 1927, Al had gone to the same school as Mario Lanza but was at first considerably less successful than the quasi-opera star. Martino worked as a bricklayer and sang in a nightclub or two before eventually winning on an *Arthur Godfrey Talent*

Crooner Al Martino

Show. Shortly afterwards, in a Broadway restaurant, he met composer Bill Borelli who, with Pat Genaro and Lou Levinson, had written a sentimental ballad called "Here In My Heart". Martino and Borelli raised a couple of hundred dollars and recorded the song for the tiny independent BBS label. By the time Martino completed a drive across the States visiting disc jockeys to promote his disc, the record was shaping into a hit and the major label, Capitol Records, moved in to sign the balladeer. "Here In My Heart" was an international chart topper, certified gold in 1952. The singer cut a follow-up hit, "Take My Heart", and commenced a lucrative career as nightclub entertainer and slick-haired heart-throb. The immense success of his first record enabled "Mr. Heart" Martino to spend

most of the next six years in Europe and when he
returned America — thanks to Dick Clark — seemed
to have the alien sounds of rock'n'roll firmly under
control. Martino hits like "I Can't Get You Out Of My
Heart" (for 20th Century Records) carried on his
main theme and in 1962 the singer re-signed with
Capitol Records. He hit with "I Love You Because"
in 1963 and "Spanish Eyes", a 1965 recording which
made the British charts in 1973. With a new twist to
his career — Martino made an acclaimed acting debut
in *The Godfather* — the singer might now escape the
reactionary, ageing sentimentalists who make up the
music industry's current "middle of the road" market.
But, as a famed disc jockey once observed, "old
crooners don't change, they die of inertia".

The Four Aces died of rock'n'roll. The Aces were
a Philadelphia group featuring the rich, virile baritone
of lead singer Al Alberts. They first worked out their
stiff barbershop harmony at Ye Old Mill club, near
Philadelphia, until in 1951 they pooled their meagre
resources and recorded a melodramatic ballad called
"Sin (It's No Sin)", paying for the session themselves
and financing its release on the Victoria label. "Sin"
began to sell and a major record company, Decca,
moved in and signed the group to a long-term contract. The Four Aces' first with Decca, "Tell Me Why",
with a lyric written by Alberts, became a million-
seller. "Sin" also eventually passed the million mark
and for the next half decade gold records like "Stan-
ger In Paradise" in 1953, "Three Coins In The Foun-
tain" in 1954 and "Love Is A Many Splendored Thing"
in 1955 won them the industry's billing as "America's
top vocal group". Their quasi-operatic note holding
and self-consciously melodramatic harmonies also
became the model for dozens of similar Italian-origin
groups. Then, after nearly a decade, the Four Aces'
image began to appear as backward as their music. The
group struggled on without Al Alberts for a while and
made some sad attempts to update their image, record-
"Rock And Roll Rhapsody". But by the sixties the
Four Aces were chart has-beens. In 1952, however,
they ruled the airwaves. And as the Aces' "I'm Yours"
— Eddie Fisher also had a version out — jostled for
airtime with Martino's "Here In My Heart", nowhere
were they as heavily plugged as on WFIL radio.

WFIL pushed pedestrian musical fare on the Philadelphian population, except the blacks of course, who
had their *own* stations. And the deejay most adept at
finding slick intros for Patti Page or dedicating an
Eddie Fisher was one Bob Horn. At the beginning of
1952 Horn was joined on the WFIL roster by a fresh
young kid from Mount Vernon, New York, who'd
entered radio by broadcasting on the student station at
Syracuse University, bounced around Syracuse and
Utica as a deejay and newscaster, and moved to Philadelphia in late 1951 — Dick Clark. A radio announcer
who remembers Clark's entry into Philadelphia
broadcasting recalls: "He was hired onto WFIL radio
as a summer replacement. I think the manager and
Dick Clark's father co-owned a TV station — in Utica
or Syracuse. Anyway, he was the second of two guys
hired, and after the summer, they had to drop one of
them. Normally, the first one would have stayed, but
he used to do a network feed from the Epiphany
Church, and every time he did it, he'd mispronounce
it as Epi-fanny Church. So they fired him for that,
and Dick got to stay".

But Clark was small fry compared with Bob Horn.
It was no surprise when Horn was offered a chance to
expand his career into television. With a rotund veteran
television link man, Lee Stewart, Horn was given
an afternoon programme on WFIL-TV. Dick Clark
talked about what happened to Ben Fong-Torres of
Rolling Stone magazine (August 16, 1973): "They
were almost like a disc jockey comedy-oriented team
because they had nothing to fill in the afternoon on
the ABC station. I can remember those guys walking
around the music library, practically saying 'What the
hell are we going to do?' And they had old musical
films of people like George Shearing, Peggy Lee and
Nat Cole. They determined they would play some of
those. They would make like 'Dialling For Dollars'
calls to viewers at home. And interview guests that
came to the studio. They asked to have a studio
audience. The studio was at 46th and Market Street,
it was out of the way. The only people in the area
were the girls who went to West Catholic High School.
So the only people that came by that first Monday or
Tuesday were little girls in their Catholic school uni-
forms who sat in the studio bored to tears. And the
music came up and they said, 'Could we dance?' So
the two girls would dance together. A bright-eyed
cameraman turned the camera on the girls and the
director said, 'that's interesting' and punched it up.
Couple of peopled called in and said 'that's fun, let's
watch the kids dance while the films or the records
play'. By the end of the week the response was overwhelming. And then they remembered that in the
movies, people never really sang, they did a lip syn-
chronization. So they brought artists in and they
would mime their records. And the format never
changed in twenty years."

The format didn't, but the deejay — and the music
— did. "Bob Horn and I", continued Clark, "did a
radio DJ show in the afternoon the same time the TV
show was on. He would come on and do the first 15

or 20 minutes with me. He was the shill — the well-known disc jockey the station used to put his name up on so that they could sell it, and hopefully draw an audience, then he'd split and do a TV show. And I did the rest of the show and he would occasionally come in and do a 15-minute thing at the end. It was a bad setup. He was being used. He didn't like it. He didn't like me. He made it abundantly apparent that he hated every minute of it and I can see why, in retrospect."

Horn hadn't liked Lee Stewart much either and quickly rid himself of his *Bandstand* partner. He was that kind of man, powerful and rich. In his book *The Deejays*, Tom Donahue, who worked at Philly's WIBG radio, remembered Horn as "the closest thing to a Roman Emperor I've ever known". Donahue, who knew a lot about payola, also remarked that "Horn was making a *lot* of money". Then, in 1956, disaster struck for *Bandstand's* all-powerful presenter. As Donahue explained, "Horn got busted for drunken driving. He could not stop, getting busted driving a hundred miles an hour. Also, young girls . . ."

Bob Horn, now dead, was accused of the statutory rape of a fourteen-year-old girl, herself alleged to be part of a teenage vice ring in Philly. He was acquitted of the rape charge but the payola — the first disc jockey to be tried and convicted — and the drunken driving finished him. As the owners of WFIL also owned the *Philadelphia Inquirer* newspaper, which was conducting an anti-drunk-driving campaign, Horn had to go. And so it was that in July 1956, clean-cut good guy Dick Clark moved on to *Bandstand*. Clark in fact wasn't *that* wholesome ("I smoked and drank and swore and all of that in private life"). But he *looked* the innocent, all-American boy and the television audience took to him immediately. But that audience, and the music *Bandstand* played, was changing.

Clark was perfect for the part of rock'n'roll master of ceremonies when the big beat hit the East Coast. He was younger and hipper than Bob Horn, but he wasn't so young or so hip that the TV audience felt he was on a par with the rhythm and rhyming, bebop-talking disc jockeys springing up in radio land. Clark was young enough to profess an empathy with the teenage record buyers who were suddenly being seen by the record industry as the only market worth worrying about — but bland enough not to offend the establishment. When Chuck Berry or Jerry Lee Lewis or Fats Domino hit Philadelphia, WFIL always jumped on them to ensure their appearance on *Bandstand*. Amiable Dick Clark would introduce the artist, remind everyone when they could buy the disc they'd just heard, and often conduct a short inoffensive, little

interview. There was still mainstream Tin Pan Alley, of course: Gogi Grant — born in Philadelphia, raised in Los Angeles, recorded in New York — struck gold in 1956 with "The Wayward Wind". But it was the rockin' big beat that Philadelphia's teenagers lapped up — and soon, so did the kids all over America.

Combining his still-paltry WFIL salary with the rich takings of personal appearance "record hops", and making "at least $50,000" in his first *Bandstand* year, Clark was pretty appalled to learn that WFIL-TV was about to be taken over by the American Broadcasting Corporation. This, in effect, might well have meant the end of *Bandstand* if ABC decided to replace the localized WFIL outpourings with networked coast-to-coast TV fodder. Clark, with supreme acumen, made his move. Ben Fong-Torres described it like this: "Clark scurried up to New York, to pitch ABC on his dance party. After much hounding, the heads of ABC began to seriously consider the show. Clark, naive as he may claim to have been, snuck a friend, a record plugger, pretending to be a sponsor, into the meeting. Clark got back the word: They thought he had droopy eyes and a lousy set, but network-quality lighting and staging could make it work. They agreed to send it out, to 67 ABC stations."

Dick Clark was confident that the show, now renamed *American Bandstand*, was going to make it. "In order to show them that we had people watching in the first three or four days we were on we ran a contest on 'Why I'd like a Date with Sal Mineo' (the movie actor who cut records). It drew 40,000 pieces of mail. The next month we ran the annual dance contest that had been going on since '52 and drew 700,000 pieces of mail."

American Bandstand became every American teenager's essential piece of television. Ben Fong-Torres wrote: "They caught the beat, and they could dance to it. They gave it a hundred, and Chuck Berry gave it top billing in his 'Sweet Little Sixteen'. Suddenly, along with *Dig* magazine, sock hops, soda shop juke boxes, and drive-ins, they had their own TV show, this combination big-name record hop and teen-love soap opera."

The love soap opera was supplied by "the regulars", Kenny Rossi and Arlene Sullivan, Bob Clayton and Justine Corelli and the blondes like Franny Giordane, Pat Molitierri and Carol Ann Scaldeferri. They were part of the *American Bandstand* "scene", dancing and hanging loose before the endless stream of pop stars who flew in to Philly to lip-synch their hit or their newie, two a day, ten a week. But in a sense the *Bandstand* dancers were the stars. As Clark said, "Within a year they were drawing 15,000 pieces of mail a week, addressed to Kenny and Arlene and Pat. People would look in and fantasize about what was happening. Just the images and you'd say, 'Oooh, look at the look she gave him.' 'They're not holding hands today,' or whatever, and they'd do this whole mind trip. It became a . . . national phenomenon.''

But above all else *American Bandstand* was about music, the relentless big beat. And, with a kind of shuddering predictability, Philadelphia began to supply more and more of it. Around Christmas 1956 Philly saw the birth of a new company, Cameo Records, formed by two composers, Bernie Lowe and Kal Mann. By the mid-fifties it was clear to the entire music world that the smouldering, heavy-lidded rockabilly star Elvis Presley was the king of rock'n'roll. So Mann and Lowe wrote a song firmly in the vein of The Pelvis' hits and proceeded with the rather unlikely task of finding in bustling Pennsylvania a singer able to generate the fire and duplicate the music of the Memphis star of stars. Amazingly, they found a singer who could almost do it. He was called Charlie Gracie.

Born in Philadelphia in 1936, Charlie was taught guitar by his father and made his television debut at the age of sixteen when he appeared on *Paul Whiteman's Talent Show*. After graduating from university, Charlie began gigging around Philly and Pittsburgh. He made a few unsuccessful recordings but did manage to land a thirteen-week television series on Pittsburgh TV before Lowe and Mann "discovered" the twenty-year-old singer/guitarist. The song on which they modelled Gracie's first Cameo disc was Presley's "Don't Be Cruel". "Butterfly" had the same panting Presley quality and the same chanting back-up group, and Gracie's producers made sure their protégé's fiery guitar was kept well in the background. When Charlie appeared on *American Bandstand* to mime the disc, the kids went wild ("Philly's very own Elvis") and it shot into the charts. By February 1957 "Butterfly" had been certified gold even though a cover version by an establishment pop crooner, Andy Williams, was an even bigger hit. Within a couple of months both Gracie and Lowe/Mann had cemented the success of "Butterfly" by penning hits for others: Gracie wrote Tab Hunter's "Ninety-Nine Ways" and, ironically, the Cameo bosses composed "Teddy Bear" for the artist whose style had given them original inspiration and success. Gracie, the spirited Elvis-style rock'n'roller didn't last too long. After another smash hit, "Fabulous", and another small one, "I Love You So Much It Hurts", he was on the slide and two British tours didn't really help. But Cameo had considerably more than one string to their rock bow.

The Rays for instance. The Rays were black, and

The rockin' Charlie Gracie

from New York. Hal Miller and Davey Jones had worked with the New York doowop team the Four Fellows, whose "Soldier Boy" was a fairish hit in 1955. Then Miller and Jones formed a new group which, on the suggestion of their arranger Jimmy Duggan, they called the Rays. The group recorded for Chess Records where they met songwriters Bob Crewe and Frank Slay Jr. who signed them to their XYZ label. Rock'n'roll legend has it that while Crewe was riding a train through Pennsylvania, it stopped at a town and the composer spied a couple silhouetted in the window of a house and came up with an idea for a song. He took his idea to Frank Slay, the duo wrote a ballad called "Silhouettes" and went in the studio with the Rays to record it. "Silhouettes" with its unashamedly sentimental content would have been wretched schmalz in a pop crooner's hands, but Hal Miller's warm, rich lead and the group's doowahing back-up were able to give the record a rock-a-ballad edge. Bob gave a dub of the disc to Hy Lit, a popular WFIL disc jockey, who took it home to listen to with a dozen others. Legend goes the deejay fell asleep while the records were being spun on his automatic record player and "Silhouettes" got half a dozen spins before Hy Lit woke up to shut off the machine. He was so taken with the song that he took it with him to play on his show the next day. The master was quickly picked up by Cameo and by September 1957 "Silhouettes", together with the popular flip, the Walter Ford-led rocker "Daddy Cool", was in the charts. By 1960 Crewe and Slay had transferred the New York group back to their XYZ label, for whom they had two chart records, but the million sales of "Silhouettes" kept Cameo's bank account healthy until their real ascendancy.

"Silhouettes" was the first of a series of songs that, with *American Bandstand* exposure, became hits for the composing team of Crewe and Slay. Stanley Robert Crewe was born in Newark and grew up in Belleville, New Jersey. In the mid-fifties he worked in New York as a male model, moved to Detroit and tried a career as a pop balladeer, recording "Penny, Nickel, Dime, Quarter" for Spotlight Records before moving to Philadelphia. There, at a party, he met piano player Frank C. Slay Jr., a Texan who'd worked for the British Information Service in New York. The two got on well together and joined up as a composing team.

Towards the end of 1957, around the time XYZ were leasing the Rays to Cameo, Philadelphian Bernie Bennick was forming a new independent record label, Swan Records. Like Cameo, Swan was immediately successful, though with Dick Clark holding a 33 1/3% interest in the company, it was hardly surprising. Swan were ensured of favourable *American Bandstand* exposure, but their first smash must have seemed an unlikely bet. For "La Dee Dah", a Crewe/Slay composition which hit the Top 10 in December 1957, was by a veteran black bandleader and, given that it was a coy Latin American cha-cha, it was far

removed from the *Bandstand* big beat. Yet Billy and Lillie made it.

Billy Ford was born in Bloomfield, New Jersey in 1925. He learned the trumpet as a child and played for a time with jazzman Cootie William before leaving to form his own unit, the Thunderbirds. The band appeared in the Hollywood Brown Derby and New York's Paramount and their riffin' boogie-based jump music was firmly in the swaggering, gutsy mould of Lucky Millinder and Louis Jordan. After a series of recordings in the early fifties, backing such artists as blues shouter Google Eyes August, in 1957 the Thunderbirds took on a female vocalist from Newburg, New York, Lillie Bryant. The previous year in New York City, Mickey Baker and Sylvia Vanderpool (now Sylvia Robinson) had broken through with a million-selling duet, "Love Is Strange". Billy and Lillie's emergence was obviously influenced by the manner in which a rhythm and blues act had been able to reach a mass audience by performing vapid harmonies in a duet. But where Mickey Baker's blues guitar had been able partially to offset Sylvia's cloyingly twee voice, there was no such compensation in the Swan duo's work. If anything, Lillie's voice was even closer to the sound of the Tin Pan Alley warblers than Vanderpool's, while there was no attempt whatsoever on the part of Swan, Crewe/Slay or Billy and Lillie themselves to work within a R&B framework. Billy and Lillie's discs were straight pop and quite extraordinary for their total lack of Negroid characteristics. After the Latin American rhythm and foolish lyrics of "La Dee Dah" had sold a million, the duo stuck with the Slay/Crewe team for such trivia as "Happiness" and "Lucky Ladybug", the latter with an even more nonsensical lyric, a Top 20 hit in 1958. Of course Billy and Lillie's novelty couldn't last, and it didn't. But Swan Records were away and hitting.

If "La Dee Dah" and "Lucky Ladybug" were silly, Swan's other early hitmakers were positively absurd. Dicky Doo and the Don'ts press-release story is almost as unlikely as their name — two Philadelphians, Gerry Granaham and Jerry Grant, write a song called "Click-Clack" one night while riding on a train . . . they take it to Dick Clark . . . Clark takes it to Bernie Bennick . . . around the end of 1957 a group is formed with Grant (lead), Granaham (tenor), Harvey Davis (baritone), Al Ways (bass) and Ray Gangi (tenor) . . . Bandstand plugs them and by February 1958 Dicky Doo and the Don'ts and Swan Records have a Top 30 hit. They had more — who could ever forget the immortal "Nee Nee Na Na Na Na Nu Nu" — while their "Leave Me Alone" was a 1958 hit and the rock-a-

ballad flip, "Teardrops Will Fall", a 1959 success
(though the million sales claimed are surely an exag-
geration.) But Dicky Doo didn't last too long despite
having a rocking "No Chemise Please" chart disc for
Sunbeam in 1958 by plain old Gerry Granaham.

In November 1957, at the same time that the
Don'ts were in the initial throes of creativity, another
group of Philadelphian street punks were finding themselves at the very top of the American charts. Danny
and the Juniors' "At The Hop" smash didn't come
without a struggle. In 1955 Danny Rapp got together
with some buddies, Dave White, Frank Maffei and Joe
Terranova, and formed a vocal group called the Juvenairs. The kids were south Philadelphians but their
sound was quite removed from the Four Aces and
the other Italian-origin barbershop harmony teams of
the pre-rock'n'roll days. For parallel with the development of the black harmony teams who doowahed
their way from the ghetto to the recording studio, the
high density "little Italy's" of the East Coast also
threw up hundreds of teenage harmony groups.
Although the young Italian groups that flourished
from 1955 to 1963, particularly in the Bronx, borrowed most of their initial inspiration from the black
harmony groups — with "Italian doowops" often
sounding fairly close to the original form — some of
them utilized additional elements of the frantic
rock'n'roll bigbeat to produce an intriguingly original
style. The Juvenairs harmonized in the subway until
somebody told them where record producer John
Madara lived. They soon scurried around to his house
to sing at his window and "be discovered". While all
they got initially was a "shut up — you're waking the
kids", eventually Madara listened to the Juvenairs,
liked them and took them to disc jockey Larry Brown
and Larry's partner Artie Singer, who ran the small
label, Singular Records. The group sang their three
original compositions for Singer, "I Feel So Lonely",
"Sometimes" and "Do The Bop". Larry and Artie
liked the last one, but their buddy Dick Clark suggested the title be changed to "At The Hop". The
group were signed, changed their name to Danny and
the Juniors and soon their Singular recording of "At
The Hop" was in the shops. But very few. Despite an
electric atmosphere generated by a frantic rock'n'roll
piano which drove along behind wurbling chants and
excited shouts, the disc didn't sell well. Then Danny
and the Juniors got their break.

One 1957 summer day, Dick Clark called Artie
Singer to say that a group scheduled to appear on
American Bandstand hadn't showed up and he needed
an immediate replacement. Artie sent over the

Danny and the Juniors

unknown Danny and the Juniors, nervously clutching
a copy of "At The Hop". When the group mimed it
in front of the swirling hoop skirts and greasy DA's,
the effect was sensational. WFIL's switchboard was
jammed with calls wanting to know about the record
and the major label, ABC Paramount, rushed in to
pick up the master and the Danny and the Juniors
contract. "At The Hop" was a huge national hit with
sales of over two million and for the next year the
group toured steadily across America, basking in the
star limelight, but always returning to Philly for their
Bandstand plugs. But though "Rock And Roll Is Here
To Stay" and "Dottie" were sizable chart records for
the Juniors in 1958, their next four ABC discs failed.

However tough it was for a rock'n'roll act to main-
tain success once they'd found it, at least Danny and
the Juniors had *some* chance of reasserting themselves
with the fickle teenage mass because they were more
or less in the musical mainstream. Such a situation was
never possible for one John Zacherle, the most
unlikely, and undoubtedly the most bizarre, product
of the whole Philadelphia rock'n'roll era.

Zacherle was an actor, not a singer. One of the
most popular television programmes on the East Coast
in the mid-fifties was a series of horror movies called
"Shock Theater". Zacherle was the presenter of the
show and, as the character Roland, was forever emerging from coffins, drinking blood and holding up
brains in bottles. "Roland's" WCAU-TV audience
took in a pretty large chunk of Philadelphia's youth —
including the children of Cameo president Bernie
Lowe, who raved about the skin-crawling Zacherle to
their father. Lowe assembled a band of the best
session men Cameo could find — mainly top line jazz
musicians — and invited the TV star into the studio.

Lowe had come up with the concept of "crossing" horror and rock'n'roll. The resulting disc, "Dinner With Drac", was a masterpiece, partly because the eerie clanging guitar riff and Buddy Savett's honkingly soulful saxophone made the accompaniment one of the most excitingly convincing rock sounds to emerge outside of the South; and partly because the song's startlingly nasty lyrics, written by Sheldon and Land and recited in a conventional Boris Karloff monotone by Zacherle, were among the most attention-grabbing popular music ever produced. Together with hilarious asides like "Igor, did you water the brains today" and "Come in . . . whatever you are", "Drac" spoke verses like:

> There once was a mummy called Irene
> Whose hair was a bright shade of green,
> When asked if she dyed it
> She simply replied it's
> Dyed with the juice from my spleen.

Released on Cameo and played first on Philadelphia radio, "Dinner With Drac" not surprisingly captured immediate interest. But what was amazing was that clean-cut Dick Clark was soon presenting the two-part disc on *American Bandstand*. It rocketed to become a national Top 10 hit and although the record brought forth a virulent stream of criticism from the media, the establishment and the church — its lyric seeming to support the contention that rock'n'roll and the lowest forms of depravity were inseparably linked — the protests, if anything, stimulated sales. Overseas, the record was less successful, though no less controversial. Britain's *Daily Mirror* launched a major campaign against "this loathsome filth", while radio stations banned it completely.

In retrospect, what is really surprising about "Dinner With Drac" is that a record with such a savage rock'n'roll beat and so flagrantly distasteful in its lyrical content, should have been recorded by Cameo, the company soon to project a cleaner than clean image. And that it should have been plugged by Dick Clark, the epitome of wholesomeness, and have emanated from Philadelphia which by 1958 was becoming more and more cynical in its treatment of the original rock'n'roll form. The first label to kick rock'n'roll in the guts — or kick the guts out of rock'n'roll — was Chancellor Records.

Formed at the end of 1957 by Bob Marcucci and Peter DeAngelis, Chancellor was a pretty Tin Pan Alley-orientated set-up. The duo were "composers" in the pre-rock sense of the world. South Philadelphian DeAngelis who'd studied music formally, played with a "semi-jazz" group, the Four J's, and was "pretty unique" because he could write arrangements, met and teamed up with lyricist Bob Marcucci in the mid-fifties. "We went to New York a lot, you had to go there then. I was one of the first people to bring a completed master to New York companies rather than just a demo. But we really started off trying to sell our songs. We were heavily into publishing. The first thing was 'Calypso Paraqueet' — that sold about 100,000. Then we had 'I Love My Girl'. The third thing that really got us off the ground was 'With All My Heart'. . ."

Jodie Sands' "With All My Heart" hit in May 1957. But the artist who really got Chancellor Records off the ground was a south Philadelphian former child protégé called Frankie Avalon. Born Franklin Avallone, he had won his first talent show at the age of six singing "Give Me Five Minutes More" and winning a scooter. He was playing trumpet in a band, Rocco and the Saints, at the Steele Pier in Atlantic City at twelve, and was blowing the standards on the Jackie Gleason, Paul Whiteman and Ray Anthony TV shows before he'd moved to long trousers. Then his father Nick Avallone opened a nightclub where the horn-toting whiz kid rubbed shoulders with visiting big-timers like Steve Lawrence and Tony Bennett. But in 1956 the club burned down, Avalon Sr. was hospitalized and Frankie and his sister Theresa had to work after school to help pay the medical bills. Then the composing/publishing team stumbled across Frankie.

"We found this young kid who lived near us that played trumpet and sang a little bit", recollects Peter DeAngelis. "He was a good-looking kid so we said let's sign him: that was Frankie Avalon. We got him to dump the trumpet and get with what the kids wanted. Now I listened to rock'n'roll and I said, 'I can write that' — I was used to a lot more complicated music. At the time Philly only had one good studio — that was called Reco-Art; that's Sigma Sound now. We did a few sessions with Frankie there. But mostly we went to New York until we got our own studios. We got our first hit off Frankie in '58."

In terms of musical aesthetics, Frankie should have stuck to trumpet. He sang in a pinched, brittle voice totally devoid of emotion or a feeling for the gutsy spirit of rock. Frankie's Chancellor discs of "Teacher's Pet" and "Cupid" both failed, even though the first received a big plug in the 1957 movie *Disc Jockey Jamboree*. Then, the myth goes, at the end of 1957 Avalon was in the studio recording another DeAngelis/Marcucci dittie of mind-numbing mediocrity called "Dede Dinah". For a joke the singer pinched his nose while singing the song, the producer decided to retain the gimmick and, with some massive

Just another pretty face . . . Frankie Avalon

plugs from *American Bandstand*, American females took the pretty, seventeen-year-old, rock-a-ballad singer to their collective bosoms and purse strings. The disc was in the Top 10 by January and throughout 1958 such dire Avalon hits as "You Excite Me", "Ginger Bread" and "I'll Wait For You" were a depressing foretaste of the anaemic music which was to follow soon after when the other Philly companies "found their own Avalon".

While Cameo and Swan were beginning their search, another Philadelphian independent label was breaking through to the national charts, though not with Philadelphia recordings. Jamie Records were formed at the end of 1957. One day their president, Harry Finfer, received a package postmarked Phoenix, Arizona from a disc jockey-cum-record producer, Lee Hazlewood. In it was a dub of an instrumental by a new young hopeful named Duane Eddy. Contracts were exchanged and by February 1958 Duane Eddy's "Moovin' And Groovin' " was edging into the charts. Producer Hazlewood conceived an original instrumental

sound for Duane, a growling low-down guitar, with extensive use of tremelo in front of claps, shouts and honking saxophone which all exhorted the guitarist to "twang" (a word coined by Hazlewood's partner Lester Sill) simple, rocking melodies. Duane Eddy and the Rebels quickly became America's most successful instrumental act coming through with smash hits like "Rebel Rouser" in 1958, "Forty Miles Of Bad Road" in 1959 and "Because They're Young" in 1960. The Eddy and Hazlewood sound was excruciatingly formula-ridden and boringly simple but it did keep Jamie Records in the big time without the bother of having to record the music themselves. It goes without saying that in 1958 Duane Eddy was heavily plugged on *American Bandstand*, along with the contrived Philadelphian regulars and infinitely more interesting rock'n'roll stylists such as Chuck Berry, the Everly Brothers and even a San Francisco blues singer turned performer of teenage novelties, Jimmy McCracklin, whose "The Walk" became a *Bandstand* dance monster and a Top 10 hit. Extensive plugs also gave the *Bandstand* heroes some pretty strange chart companions who nobody today has the inclination to ask "whatever happened to?" The 1958 chart-makers included: the Honeycones, a New York studio group who picked up on the Bandstand hip expression "Op" and made a record of the same name on Ember; the Playboys, a Cameo Records studio group who cut "Over The Weekend"; the Quaker City Boys, who had the instrumental "Teasin' " on Swan; and the NU Tornados who presented that unforgettable Carlton recording "Philadelphia U.S.A.".

In mid-1958 Dick Clark moved into the big big-time and began commuting to New York where he'd present the *Dick Clark Show* each Saturday night from the Little Theater. A seated, non-dancing audience would roar to the delights of the Royal Teens, Duane Eddy and Robin Luke, while six million TV viewers echoed their enthusiasm at home. Saturday night was to last two years . . .

Around the time Clark began his New York show, an arranger/ producer who was to play a key part in Cameo Records' Philadelphia ascendancy was tasting his first success. Dave Appell was born in Philly in 1922. By the early fifties he was leading a vapid instrumental/vocal group, the Dave Appell Four, and recording for the major label, Decca Records. Decca's Paul Cohen suggested the group change their name to the Applejacks but despite an attempt to update their sound with a little "rock'n'roll" — they appeared in one of Alan Freed's early rock movies — the group didn't appeal to the teenage audience. Then Appell landed a job as leader of the studio band for Ernie

Kovak's show on Philly TV. From there he joined Cameo as a staff producer. In the summer of 1958 Appell got an idea from the Philadelphia String Band of a "marching type song with a dance beat". "The Mexican Hat Rock" emerged and when recorded by the studio band and given a big *Bandstand* push it became the Applejacks' first chart record. The Applejacks went on to hit with "Rocka-Conga" and "Bunny Hop". However, within a year or two, Dave Appell's career, aided by Cameo's other music-biz veterans Bernie Lowe and Kal Mann, was to take a new twist.

Three months after the Applejacks' initial hit slipped from the charts, another instrumental combo emerged into the Hot 100 led by a man who became very important to the Philly music scene in the sixties. In March 1959 Frank Virtuoso — now Frank Virtue of Virtue Studios — saw his group the Virtues climb to Number 5 with "Guitar Boogie Shuffle". Although Frank's rockin' guitar boogie captured the 1959 teenagers, he wasn't one of them himself. "I started right back in the forties. I learned violin, then bass guitar and then guitar. When I came out of the forces I started my own combo. We were known as the Virtuoso Trio and we did a lot of society functions. We

The Virtues

were pretty big and we worked with Sinatra, Nat Cole and did quite a bit of radio and TV."

Then rock'n'roll emerged. "The whole music situation changed and so eventually it became obvious that I'd have to get with the new music that the kids wanted." So the Virtues emerged. The line-up was Virtue on lead guitar; Jimmy Bruno, guitar; Ralph Frederico, piano; Sonny Ferns, sax; and Barry Smith or Joe Gillespie on drums. "An old Navy buddy of mind, Arthur Smith, had written this number called 'Guitar Boogie'. In '58 we decided to record it. We actually cut it in my basement. I had electronics as a hobby and I just built a little studio . . . we even recorded the Ted Williams Orchestra down there . . . anyway, we changed 'Guitar Boogie' around quite a bit and it became 'Guitar Boogie Shuffle'. We took it to Dick Clark and he put it out on Hunt Records which was a label he'd started. . . . We appeared on *Bandstand* many times; we were standby. When somebody didn't turn up, they used to call us."

The Virtues did quite a lot of touring as well on the strength of their mechanically twanging hit. The group couldn't get another big American success, though "Vaya Con Dios" was a hit in Germany and a 1962 disc, "Guitar Boogie Shuffle Twist", crawled into the charts. But the Virtues' gold record was a good enough launching pad for Frank to open his "first real professional studio" in 1962 and reserve his guitar playing simply for accompanying some of the scores of acts who began to troop to him for a stardom break.

Back in 1958 Robert Louis Ridarelli was looking for just such a break. He found it as Bobby Rydell. Born in Philly in 1942, Bobby had worked in Philadelphia night clubs by the age of seven, appeared on Paul Whiteman's amateur show which was broadcast from Philly at the age of nine and was playing drums with Rocco and the Saints at sixteen. One of the Saints, Frankie Avalon, had been whisked away to *American Bandstand* and stardom by 1958, but Rydell had to wait a year for his turn. His manager Frankie Day took Bobby to Cameo Records soon after Avalon's "Dede Dinah" had made it painfully apparent that good looks counted far more than note holding in the charm-bracelet and ring world of the nation's Bandstanders. Rydell's first Cameo disc went nowhere, but in the summer of 1959 the label's extensive "personal grooming" of their young would-be Avalon began to pay off. He recorded a sickly little ditty called "Kissin' Time" which, with a big *Bandstand* effort, made Number 11 in the pop charts. The next disc, a Lowe/Mann composition called "We Got Love", went even higher, earning a gold disc. Rydell, who sang in a

Bobby Rydell (left) with the man who made him, Dick Clark

near-crooning style with an occasional burst of finger-snapping "swing", was away.

By that time Chancellor Records, the label which had clicked with Avalon, had another contender to feed into the *Bandstand* machine. Because he was prettier, more languid and patently less talented than any other teenage star of the era, he has subsequently been acclaimed in various histories of popular music as "the worst pop star the world has known". He was born Fabiano Forte in 1943 — but in 1959 the world learned of him as Fabian. Chancellor's Peter DeAngelis tells the story: "We were talking to Frankie (Avalon) one day and he said he knew this fifteen-year-old kid at Southern High who looked like a cross between Elvis and Ricky Nelson. So Bob (Marcucci) went over to take a look at the kid. He was so pretty we just knew he had to be a commercial proposition so we

signed him up. We taught him a few things vocally but he never really did go much on singing. . . . Anyway, in '58 we did a thing on him called 'Lillie Lou' which sold a few around Philadelphia. We were spending quite a lot of money on publicity getting him known you know. His next thing was 'I'm A Man' and when he did that on *Bandstand* the girls went wild. Then came 'Turn Me Loose' and 'Tiger' — that sold a million — and we had a monster . . . "

A monster in more ways than one. Fabian couldn't sing and however much Marcucci and DeAngelis tried to hide the fact behind chirruping girls and dancing violins, the fact was abundantly clear to all save the squealing girls who clamoured for their idol. Chancellor used strings on almost all of their recordings. "I'd been schooled in serious music", explains DeAngelis. "I just saw strings as a way of making rock'n'roll more

Pretty boy Fabian

Massachusetts, and had picked up guitar as a kid. He, in fact, made his record debut way back in 1956 when at fifteen he played guitar behind the multi-racial doo-wop team the G-Clefs and watched excitedly when their "Ka-Ding-Dong" became a hit. The following year he started singing in Lynn, Massachusetts, and eventually formed his own group. While working as a truck driver Freddy recorded a song that his mother had written called "Tallahassee Lassie" and sent the tape to Swan Records. In Philadelphia Frank Slay and Bob Crewe took the tape and "added some things to it", came up with the name Freddy Cannon and the resulting disc, after exposure on station WMEX in Boston, started to break. Freddy quit his truck, got up to Philly, and *American Bandstand* did the rest. In retrospect Freddy wasn't of exactly the same pre-fabricated ilk as Fabian and Rydell. His hits, like a souped up, rocked-up version of the standard "Way Down Yonder In New Orleans" in 1959, "Buzz Buzz A-Diddle-It" in 1961 and "Pallisades Park" in 1962 had a frenetic, everyone-dance-and-shout atmosphere and were considerably less wooden than the Philly-

appealing to more people. Like Frankie Avalon. When I went to record 'Venus' with him everybody said I was crazy. They said 'that thing will never work with him', but I said 'it'll be a Number 1'. And it was." In Feburary 1959. "Okay, looking back perhaps some of those records weren't the greatest music in the world, but they were what the kids wanted."

Or what *Bandstand* ensured they wanted. Chancellor's Avalon and Fabian and Cameo's Rydell were promoted restlessly and they were quickly joined by two new handsome hunks.

James Ercolani became James Darren when he was spotted while attending Southern High by Joyce Selznick of Screen Gems. She signed James to a contract with Columbia Pictures and in 1958 he appeared in the movie *Gidget.* On celluloid he was pushed as a soppier James Dean and on record — making his debut with the theme from *Gidget* for Columbia's Colpix record subsidiary — he came on as a cross between Avalon and Rydell. "Gidget" was only a small hit, however, and in fact it wasn't until 1961 with two out-pourings of obnoxious, blaring melodrama — "Good-bye Cruel World" and "Her Royal Majesty" — that Darren finally began to repay the money poured into his career by the Columbia Pictures publicity machine.

More talented than Darren and more immediate in his success after *Bandstand* exposure was one Frederick Picariello. Freddy was born in Revere,

The explosive Freddie Cannon

born pretty boys. But they were also woefully con-trived and often laughably silly — "if you were a rock and roll record, you would be a hit I know". Anyway, for four years Freddy recorded a stream of moderate sellers for Swan, occasionally hitting big and regularly inspiring the dancers on *Bandstand* with calls to do the latest dance.

But when it came to getting people on their feet, Cameo Records were about to play their master stroke, though it took a couple of years for the music indus-try and the fans to realize fully its impact. Cameo were doing well in 1959 and decided to expand, form-ing a subsidiary label called Parkway. Soon after its formation, Henry Colt, the owner of a Philadelphia poultry store, went in to see Cameo's Kal Mann to enthuse about his chief chicken plucker, Ernest Evans, who among the flying feathers entertained the custo-mers with his singing and impersonations. Mann checked him out, felt he had something and signed him. The pseudonym devised for Evans on his first Parkway single — an impersonation novelty called "The Class" — was based on the famed New Orleans big beat boss, Fats Domino. Evans was transformed into Chubby Checker. One fan who saw Chubby's first *American Bandstand* appearance recalls: "He was black but nobody really thought of him in that way. He always looked sorta cute, so happy'n smilin'. And although he was kind of plump he really used to dance real good."

Before Chubby had a chance to show *how* good, a bomb-shell hit Dick Clark, *Bandstand*, and the whole American music industry. The *Daily Mail* newspaper of November 24, 1959 reported to startled British readers what was happening in America this way: "The deeper the TV investigators dig the more malodorous the mess. Today, one disc jockey after another skipped forward and said he had accepted payola, which means a bribe in cash or kind for plugging a record to boost its popularity on American radio and television networks. . . The most famous of all the disc jockeys and the acknowledged king of the airwaves is the all-American boy Dick Clark, the young man with the clean-cut face and the choirboy manner. Dick insists his record and his records are clean, although the payola probers say 'Dick could be on both sides of the record'. Clark who is worshipped by the teenagers and embraced by the Church for his true-blooded 100 per cent Americanism is getting rid of his extensive interests outside radio and television, including a one-third interest in Swan Records . . . The American pub-lic is so aroused that the politicians now promise a full-scale top-to-bottom investigation of the TV industry."

The subsequent "top-to-bottom investigation"

predictably had its scapegoats. Among them, tragically, was the pioneer of all rock'n'roll deejays, Alan Freed, who was thrown off ABC radio and, the following year, convicted and imprisoned for payola. Yet Dick Clark, the champion of the Philadelphia record indus-try, the man who'd owned labels in whole (Hunt) or in part (Swan) and who was by 1958 immensely, fabu-lously rich, came through it all. In between *American Bandstand*'s Clark — vigorously protesting his inno-cence — was called before the House Subcommittee. Years later, in the August 1973 interview with *Rolling Stone*, he was still doing it.

"They (the Government) went to one of the biggest broadcasting chains in the world that was riddled with payola. Rotten fucking, lousy, stinking mess. They arrived on a Thursday night, said, "We'll be back tomorrow to examine the logs.' Somehow or other when they went back on Friday there weren't any logs. They had disappeared. One of the biggest spokes-men in the broadcasting business, who was looked upon as sitting at the right hand of God, said, 'I'm aghast at this,' on and on. And it all went, zappo, to Dick Clark, 27-year-old cat in Philadelphia. 'You want the records? Here they are! Look at them!' I could've burned those mother-fuckers in two minutes. I had them examined; the examiner said 'You're right, you're straight.' They thought — dummies — I mean, 'How could a kid in Philadelphia make that much money?' They thought people came in with carloads and bagloads of cash and put it in my office. I found a better way to do it; to be in the music business. It was offensive to me, they thought I was that ignorant." The fact that one of Clark's labels admitted paying people to play records "blew their minds, but that's not what they were after. They wanted to prove I was the taker of bribes."

They never did, so Clark dumped some of his cor-porations and got back to the serious business of "breaking" hits for Rydell, Avalon, and even the Joiner, Arkansas, Junior High School Band. But rock history was to immortalize 1960 for another Dick Clark contribution. Joe Tarsia, once chief engineer with Cameo/Parkway and today the owner and chief engineer of the Sigma Sound Studios, recalls those days clearly: "I remember Dick Clark saying the kids were really dancing to this new thing called 'The Twist'. The record was by Hank Ballard and the kids loved the record. Hank Ballard was supposed to be coming to the show. I don't know what happened, but he didn't show . . . Clark recommended that someone cut a twist record, so Cameo went in and cut 'The Twist'. Bernie believed in it so little that it was the 'B' side, and Chubby Checker wasn't even supposed to do it.

The track was cut by a group of staff musicians who were in the house. Dick Clark wanted Danny and the Juniors to cut it, but Chubby's manager Henry Colt took Chubby into the studios and put Chubby's voice on it instead. I was the engineer. The rest is history."

Bernie Lowe's lack of confidence in a song that consisted of little more than a few lines like "come on baby, let's do the twist, come on baby, it goes like this" is perhaps understandable. Hank Ballard, the fiery black vocalist with the molasses-in-the-mouth enunciation whose early fifties Cincinatti recordings with the Midnighters like "Work With Me Annie" and "Sexy Ways" had made him a rhythm and blues superstar, wrote "The Twist" in 1959. Or so Hank says. Little Joe Cook told *Bim Bam Boom* magazine a different story in December 1973: "I had this group, a gospel group from Philly called the Davis Sisters. They were my group — I taught them. I took them to Atlanta in '58 to meet another gospel group who called themselves the Nightingales. Anyhow, we were getting together one time and Jo Jo, Bill and Jeff handed me this song called 'Let's Do The Twist'. I took it back to New York for my manager Arnold Maxim to look at. He said 'no way, man, that's too suggestive.' "

Then, Cook claims, the Nightingales gave the song to Hank Ballard who "changed the tune a bit" and called it "The Twist". If the story is true, it is even more confusing that Ballard's "new" melody ended up sounding so very similar to the Drifters' "Whatcha Gonna Do".

Whatever the origin of the song, the Midnighters recorded it as the flip of Ballard's "Teardrops On Your Letter" and both sides made the R&B chart in March 1959 without Clark's help. It's interesting, if academic, to surmise what might have happened to Hank Ballard and the Midnighters' career if they had decided to plug their version to the white teenagers. Chubby Checker's "The Twist" entered the charts in May 1960. Chubby sang the inane lyrics in a high nasal whine behind a rigid band, sounding like the R&B dance riffs of a hundred black hits being played by a group of robots.

Although Chubby can't claim the song's invention, he does make such claim to the dance. "Cameo asked me to put some new dance steps to it. I got together with my two younger brothers, Tracey and Spencer, and worked out the actual dance steps, the actual movements."

As the "movements" consisted of little more than jerking the legs and trunk furiously from side to side and holding the arms bent chicken fashion, it was not

Twistin' Chubby Checker

too surprising that after massive TV exposure brought Chubby a Number 1 hit, he didn't follow up with another "twist" record. Instead he chose a new dance — or, to be correct, an ancient one, as he simply revived the old Paul Williams' R&B hit, "The Hucklebuck". After that had made the Top 20, there came *another* new dance, "Pony Time". The proliferation

Chubby (*ca* 1973), from the movie, *Let The Good Times Roll*

of dances wasn't simply limited to Chubby Checker. Author Charlie Gillett described the phenomenon in his book *The Sound Of The City*: "A result of the audience dance format (of *American Bandstand*) was that the previous patterns of locally differentiated dancing styles was replaced by a nationally homogenous set of styles derived from the programmes. Whereas previously a dance style might have taken up to year to move across the country, becoming obsolete in one area as it was picked up in another, the turnover now became much faster. And the increase in turnover of styles modified the meaning of the word 'change'. Whereas previously the word had meant the substitution of one style for another, or at least a decisive alternative, it now came to mean a relatively minor modification. Since the change itself no longer was as clear cut, the emphasis put on it was increased."

The formula had been established for quite a while before Chubby broke through. Back in May 1959 Dick Clark told New York columnist Den Grevatt: "If a record isn't danceable it has a tough time. The new dances are tied in closely with hit records. We've started the chalypso (*sic*), the circle dance and the walk on our show. The kids love dancing."

They particularly loved Chubby Checker's "Pony Time". The song was written by Don Covay and John Berry who'd previously sung together in the Washington doowop team, the Rainbows. When the group disbanded, Covay and Berry began writing together while Covay pursued his career as an artist at the same time. None of Don's New York records really sold until he cut "Pony Time" at the end of 1960 for the tiny Arnold label. "The pony" wasn't much different from any of the other of the dozens of teen dances, but Covay's disc began to pick up sales. Then Chubby Checker moved in and his cover version, with the *American Bandstand* backing, swept all before it and hit Number 1 by January 1961 (Covay's version barely made the bottom of the charts). Ironically, two years later, Don Covay was signed as an artist by the company who'd done him out of a smash.

Chubby Checker was happy to continue to climb the charts with production-line dance hits and in the spring of 1961 he was exhorting Bandstanders to "Dance The Mess Around" (a little too explicit?). Then it was back to the twist. "Kal Mann and Dave Appell wrote this song called 'Let's Twist Again'. I recorded it and it hit the Top 10 in June. Then as winter started to come in, all the established and expensive clubs in New York started featuring the twist. All of a sudden the twist seemed to have caught everyone's imagination. In November of that year Zsa Zsa Gabor was photographed doing the twist at the

Peppermint Lounce. And Joey Dee was discovered. The whole world started going twist crazy. By that time I had a new hit, 'The Fly', but while that record was moving up the charts 'The Twist' was selling all over again. It went all the way to Number 1 — that's the only record that's ever done that twice . . . then 'Let's Twist Again' was a hit all over again! I was the biggest recording artist in the world!"

But at what a price. Chubby's music was mechanical and stupifyingly inane. And as New Yorkers Joey Dee and the Starlighters and soon dozens more jumped on the twist bandwagon, Tin Pan Alley predictably treated the boom as if the minor modification of the rock'n'roll beat was a major new form of music. But as thousands of clubs changed to a "twist policy" and everybody from film stars to congressmen was photographed and filmed doing the new gyration, Cameo, the label which had stumbled across the new fad, established themselves indisputably as *the* Philadelphia record label.

One of the acts that in 1961 helped them to do just that was the Dovells, a group which made the big time at the second attempt. Formed in 1957, the Dovells consisted of Leonard Borisoff, Jerry Summers, Mike Denis, Arnie Satin and Danny Brooks. In an interview in 1965 Borisoff, by then a solo star known as Len Barry, remembered: "We had a kinda reputation for being a bunch of rich kids that just sang for kicks. Well, we sure weren't rich but we did sing for fun. We did a record called 'No No No' which sold around Philly but we didn't get too far and we just kinda disbanded. But singing was in our blood I guess 'cause in '60 we reformed again. We auditioned for Dave Appell who was the A&R director at Cameo/Parkway in '61 and he dug us and we were signed up. Dave Appell and Kal Mann wrote a tune for us called 'The Bristol Stomp'. We cut it and it became a big hit for us."

"Bristol Stomp" with its basic thumping beat, bass-voice chant and Len's high wavery lead was gimmicky but had a certain primitive charm. With the Dovells in their mohair suits, Slim Jim ties and jar-of-Brylcreem hairstyles appearing regularly on *Bandstand*, the disc made Number 2 in the charts, easily selling a million. The group went on to hit with more, pretty gross ditties like "Do The New Continental", "Bristol Twistin' Annie" and "Hully Gully Baby" but even on the worst material, Len's voice had an attack which few other Philly artists possessed. The group *looked* pretty tough as well.

"We had a gangster-type image once. We used to pretend we were tough. Like the first time we met Brian Hyland was around the time of 'Sealed With A

Kiss' (June 1962). I went up and grabbed his lapels and warned him in this James Cagney voice I put on: 'Boy, you get a haircut before the show tonight, or else . . .' Brian ran around for three hours looking frantically for a barbershop.''

Totally different in image were Cameo/Parkway's other big new acts, the Orlons and Dee Dee Sharp. Both were black but not very noticeably. Like Chubby Checker's, their music was carefully censored for any offensive rhythm and blues content which would alienate the *Bandstand* kids who danced in front of the crisp, smart, hair-straightened stars. The Orlons evolved from a group formed in junior high school and consisted of Shirley and Andrea Brinkley, Marlena Davis, Rosetta Hightower and Andreena Frazer. When the group broke up, lead singer Shirley Brinkley teamed up with Steve Caldwell and deciding to form a new group, bringing in Marlena and Rosetta. They played some gigs around town, often with a local group the Cashmeres, later to find fame as the Dovells. Eventually in 1960 the Dovells' Len Barry arranged a record company audition for the Orlons and in 1960 they debuted on Cameo with a dirge-like Marlena Davis-led rock-a-ballad, "I'll Be True", which in overall style closely resembled the etherial sound of the Chantels. It didn't make the charts, however, and their 1961 release of "Happy Birthday Twenty One" fared even worse. Then, in 1962 with the nation reeling under a welter of *Bandstand* dance fads, Mann and Apell penned yet another one called the "Wah-Watusi". Certainly, compared with the stiff-as-a-board sound of Cameo's other dance discs, "Wah-Watusi" was positively lilting with the girls singing in tight, shrill, unison harmony over a skipping beat. The watusi dance, which had nothing but its name in common with the African subculture, became yet another gyration spotlighted on TV and the single rose to Number 2 in the charts. The Orlons, however, nearly destroyed themselves with the follow-up, a dance called "The Conservative", which appeared just a little too much like mockery of the *Bandstand* style. But the flip-side, a catchy novelty about a girl telephoning her boyfriend called "Don't Hang Up", burst through instead. Steve Caldwell, who throughout his tenure with the Orlons was kept totally in the background, delivered in a frog-in-the-throat bass the words "oh no" after each chanted hookline. Caldwell was never again called on to contribute as much.

The Orlons' potential to sing with any real fire was smothered by twee material, mainly from the pens of Mann and Appell, and by their almost unvarying use of regulation, Andrews Sisters harmony over the contrived twist beat.

Marginally more interesting in vocal style, if not in material, was Dee Dee Sharp. Born Dione LaRue in Philly in 1945, Dee Dee sang in her grandfather's church choir and learned to play the piano. Then in 1961 she saw a Cameo Records advertisement in a Philadelphia newspaper calling for someone who could read music, play piano and sing. She fitted the part, went along, got the job and was soon being used as background singer on a number of Cameo sessions. It was at one of them that she got her break. In early 1962 — with the whole world twist crazy and with Mann and Appell busily scribbling such gems as "La Paloma Twist" — Dee Dee did a session backing Chubby Checker on "Slow Twistin' ". The song was a transgression for Chubby. Although the lyric was still dully perfunctory ("there'll be no no twistin', but a slow, slow twistin' tonight"), the slow tempo at least gave his high tenor a chance to sing with something resembling feeling. But the "star" of the record was Dee Dee. Uncredited on the label, it was Dee Dee's bluesy harmonizing and asides like "now take it easy baby" which made the disc mildly erotic and infinitely more black than anything Chubby had done previously (or was to do for the half decade). Had Cameo but known it, the duo's singing with its distinct churchy overtones was almost an example of the emergent

Dee Dee Sharp, the "Mashed Potatoes" girl

"soul" music. But both Chubby and Cameo failed to grasp the musical implications of the arrangement on the song — despite its success (it made Number 3) — and Chubby quickly returned to wind-me-up dance ditties. But Dee Dee's vocal caused a considerable stir of interest and Cameo immediately began recording the lady by herself. Dee Dee was still at Overbrook High School when she cut a song penned by Kal Mann and Bernie Lowe which was even sillier than some of their other dance inventions. But "Mashed Potato Time" was a massive million-selling hit and with *Bandstand* featuring the pretty little girl in the full skirt and bouffant hairstyle showing everyone how to mash potatoes with their feet, its very ludicrousness seemed to work in its favour. The disc was in due course followed with — what else? — "Gravy" and Dee Dee had a third Top 10 hit in 1962 with "Ride!" Her vocals were shrill and a little lacking in range, but her bite and enthusiasm made her infinitely preferable to the posturing puppets with whom she so often shared the *Bandstand* rostrum. Only the songs let her down. And later, when Cameo began to see her potential as a "soul" singer, some of the mashed potato had stuck.

In the early sixties, though, there seemed to be no end in sight for Dee Dee, Rydell (who'd come through with smashes like "Volare" in 1960, "That Old Black Magic" in 1961 and "The Cha-Cha-Cha" in 1962) and and the boss of them all, Chubby Checker. With the twist being picked up by every kind of vocalist from crooners to blues singers, the Cameo bosses felt confident enough to extend further the dance empire of the undisputed "king of the twist". So Chubby told everyone about the "Dancin' Party" in June 1962, grabbed a bamboo pole and a calypso rhythm and got down to the "Limbo Rock" in September, and for good measure had a flip-side of "Popeye The Hitchhiker" (two dances in one). Cameo even thought of the Christmas market and in 1961 and 1962 "Jingle Bell Rock" — a Bobby Rydell/Chubby Checker duet — hit the charts. Dee Dee Sharp had launched a successful career as a result of her association with Chubby. Another Checker spinoff were the Dreamlovers.

The Dreamlovers had formed way back in 1956 and were very much a product of the ghetto streets. They'd doowahed on the sidewalks and for four years scuffled for gigs. Then in 1960 they got a kind of break when they were given a session doing a vocal back-up impersonation of the Midnighters on Chubby's "The Twist". The session led to plenty of work, both on stage and on future records, but the constant role of background nonentity interminably chanting "boogly boogly shoo" became pretty dispiriting. When Philadelphia record producer Jerry Ross formed Heri-

tage Records with Murray Wecht and asked the group to sign, they jumped at the chance. For their Heritage debut the Dreamlovers (Tommy Ricks, lead; Cleveland Hammock, second tenor; Cliff Dunn, baritone; Morris Gardner, baritone; and Ray Dunn, bass) recorded a ballad written by a former member, Donny Hogan. Surprisingly the record, "When We Get Married", although recorded in 1961 was, with its powerful beat, falsetto fill-ins and wurbling bass voice, pure doowop. Even more surprisingly, the disc became a big pop hit, making Number 10 in the Hot 100. The Dreamlovers never had such a big hit again. Despite "If I Should Lose You", which made the charts for them the following year on End Records, subsequent Dreamlovers discs on labels like Swan emerged when the public were beginning to expect soul from a black vocal group and they faded from national attention.

By 1962 the Italian pretty boys were beginning to fade too. Although Bobby Rydell continued to make the charts with Cameo until mid-1964 when he joined Capitol Records, he increasingly pursued the role of middle-of-the-road, "adult audience" entertainer with less and less *Bandstand* appeal. Frankie Avalon and Fabian moved into movies where Avalon showed a little talent for acting and Fabian none whatsoever. In view of the decline of their teen idols, the major Philadelphia record labels predictably looked more and more for inspiration to the rich and by then all powerful Cameo Records, and began signing black acts.

In 1962 Chancellor's president Bob Marcucci (DeAngelis had left the label the year before) signed a pretty young black girl from Macon, Georgia called Claudine Clark. Claudine had lived most of her life in Philadelphia, had studied musical composition at Coombs College and had recorded a little for Gotham and Herald Records. When signed to Chancellor, Claudine went in the studio and recorded a slow ballad called "Disappointed", written by Bob Marcucci and Russ Faith. The arrangement was skilfully conceived by Jerry Ragovoy to bring out the full drama of Claudine's emotive, vibrato-filled, broken delivery. It was a stunning disc from the company who'd given the world the insipid Fabian, and with its strong gospel overtones, was a fine example of the emergent "soul" music. Ironically however, it was too heavy for the only audience Chancellor understood — the white teenager — and only when flipped over did it grab attention. The reverse was a blaring Clark composition "Party Lights", arranged by Russ Faith. With Claudine hiccoughing a boyfriend-at-the-party lyric straight out of the pages of *Dig* magazine, the number developed into a major hit making the Top 10 in June 1962. But it was the kind of smash that wasn't really to help

Claudine. At future sessions conducted by Russ Faith, she was asked to fight a constantly losing battle with a squealing girl group and discs like the strangely titled "Walkin' Through A Cemetery" failed miserably. Jerry Ragovoy, disappointed by "Disappointed", learned that, as with Checker, the Orlons et al, black styles still sometimes needed considerable modification to be sure of making it with a mass white audience.

In the summer of 1962 such a modification brought Ragovoy his first Top 30 hit. "I began writing with Ed Marshall — who'd hit big with 'Venus' for Frankie Avalon", recalls Ragovoy. "We came up with this song called 'A Wonderful Dream'. It was a complete and total contrivance on my part. I said to myself at the time after listening to the radio: 'What's missing in the marketplace? A high falsetto voice.' I had an understanding with Bill Fox who managed this group called the Majors (Rick Cordo, Frank Trout, Ronald Gathers, Eugene Glass and Idella Morris) and so I made this lead singer (Cordo) perform in a falsetto. It was a piece of crap and I devised 'A Wonderful Dream' as such . . ."

A commercial "piece of crap". When the master was sent to Lew Chudd for release on his West Coast Imperial Records, the effect of the shrill, squeaky voice warbling a catchy inane lyric took the charts by storm. In a sense Rick Cordo's bizarre falsetto was the model for later black (Donnie Elbert) and white (the Newbeats) squeaky voiced acts. "Because there was a girl in the group a lot of people thought she was the lead . . . The follow-up was a thing called 'A Little Bit Now' which I wrote with Van McCoy". He later produced the Stylistics. "That started to break but some jocks were playing the other side, 'She's A Trouble-maker', and so both sides made the charts but low down . . . People forgot about the Majors pretty quickly."

They forgot about the Sherrys with equal speed. Little Joe Cook, who had a taste for the big-time after his 1957 smash with the Thrillers, formed a girl quartet based wholeheartedly on Cameo's Orlons. Consisting of two of Cook's daughters and two of their girlfriends, the Sherrys possessed minimal vocal talent but Cook nursed and rehearsed them until they could just about manage a turgid little harmony. After looking around to see what dance was big on *Bandstand*, Cook wrote a song called "Pop Pop Pop-Eye". In fact the Popeye originated in New Orleans and was one of the few dances Philly hadn't spawned. But even though the record Cook recorded with the girls had none of the rolling New Orleans Popeye beat, Cook was able to sell the tape to Harold Lipsius, president of Jamie Records. Jamie released the Sherrys on their Guyden subsidiary

and, with appropriate Bandstand promotion, it made 35 in the charts. A follow-up based on a dance that barely made it — "Slop Time" — only just made the 100. Another disc or two and then it was back to high school for Cook's protégées.

One hit black group missed by all Philadelphia's major labels were the Sensations, a team who had to be patient in their wait for national success. They had formed way back in 1954 as the Cavaliers and utilizing a girl lead voice, Yvonne Baker, trangressed a little from the normal black street-corner harmony teams. Atlantic Records of New York began recording the team as the Sensations and in 1956 the group made a version of "Yes Sir That's My Baby" which trans-formed the happy finger-snapping standard into a doo-wop chant. When released on Atco Records it became a minor R&B hit. But the group couldn't gain another success; Yvonne eventually left to marry and raise a family and the Sensations disbanded. Then in March 1961, encouraged by the amazing come-back stories that the "oldies and goodies" boom was creating and convinced that Yvonne Baker's warm, rather coy, voice had pop music potential, the Sensations' bass singer Alphonso Howell persuaded Yvonne to return to show business. Philadelphia disc jockey Kae Williams began recording a re-formed Sensations con-sisting of Yvonne Baker, Richard Curtain, Sam Arm-strong and Alphonso Howell. Williams concentrated on fast, skipping songs with much emphasis on a relentless, snapping drum beat, and the resulting disc, "Music Music Music" — not be confused with the Tin Pan Alley standard — was quickly leased to Chicago's Chess Records for national release on their Argo label. "Music" was an airy, catchy song which fell into an intriguing middle ground between an authentic R&B style and the computorized whimsey of *American Bandstand*. It became a sizable pop hit but at the end of the year, "Let Me In", despite its almost identi-cal skipping rhythm pattern, was a much bigger hit, becoming a million-seller. Yvonne and the Sensations embarked on a national tour and Argo Records got another fairish hit with "That's My Desire". But that was the Sensations' last big success and within two years the group had disbanded. Yvonne was to spend the next decade recording unsuccessful solos and try-ing to come to terms with the soul music which was now resounding from cities like Detroit in increasingly powerful waves.

Back in 1962, however, Motown's threat to Phila-delphia's ascendancy seemed pretty distant. *American Bandstand* continued to push trivial music onto the waiting teenager and if the Miracles or Marvin Gaye now rubbed shoulders with Brian Hyland or Duane

Eddy there was always Cameo to distract the kids with a new dance. One Philadelphia independent label which gained a taste of national success with a non-dance record was Arlen Records, founded by former Jamie executive Harry Finfer in 1962. Like Jamie, their biggest hit came with a disc recorded outside the city. Releases by the Nomads, Little Floyd and the Companions didn't go. But in August 1962 Bill Lowery of Lowery Music of Atlanta, Georgia, brought Finfer a tape of an Atlanta group, the Tams, singing a song called "Untie Me". The Tams were black and sported a lead whose harsh voice was distinctive over a catchy pop arrangement of dancing strings. The record was a fairish hit, but follow-ups flopped and the Tams moved on to the major, ABC Records. Arlen just disappeared from view.

One of the strangest pop and R&B hit stories emanated from Philadelphia. In *Let It Rock* magazine of July 1973, Roy Buchanan, guitar hero of the seventies, reminisced about bumping into a white drummer called Bobby Gregg who was getting some jazz musicians together for a session at the Sound Plus Studios. Roy went along, wrote down some chord changes and he and the renegade jazzers cut a raunchy, repetitive instrumental, "The Jam". The disc was released on a new Philadelphia independent label, Cotton Records, and credited to Bobby Gregg and his Friends. "Actually, we weren't friends at all. The people responsible for puttin' that record out promised me I was gonna get things released. I do stuff and they'd call me back in the office and say 'we don't know how to tell you this but we can't put your name on the label.' Gregg had a show when 'The Jam' was popular. No one else could play guitar on that tune so I figured I'd get even. They were about to go and I decided I wouldn't do it — waited 'til the last minute to tell 'em. The kids were screamin' and boin' them. Heh! . . ."

"The Jam" was a Top 30 hit and Bobby Gregg and his Friends saw a few sales with a follow-up, "Potato Peeler". But neither they, nor Cotton Records lasted out 1962. The year also saw the rise and fall of other diverse, one-hit-wonders. There were Gabriel and the Angels, whose Puerto Rican personnel created a bluesy, semi-doowop sound and hit with "That's Life (That's Tough)", now regarded as a minor punk-rock classic; Mark Valentino who, under the guidance of Bob Marcucci, changed his name from Anthony Busillo and in October exhorted everyone to do "The Push and Kick"; the Rockin' Rebels whose "Wild Weekend" was a throwback to the rock'n'roll instrumentals of the fifties; and Little Joey (Hall) and the Flips who released the unforgettable "Bongo Stomp". With the exception of Little Joey, all were on Swan Records and all only hit once.

"That's Life That's Tough" hitmakers, Gabriel and the Angels

1963 arrived and Chubby Checker still ruled supreme. He didn't make Number 1 anymore, but four double-sided hits in one year was an impresive achievement and his hectic social and romantic life ensured that his "cute" face beamed constantly from the world's newspapers. Despite the hits, Chubby's 1963 recordings (except "Twist It Up") kept away from the twist, even though he had told Britain's *Melody Maker* the year before that the twist was "gonna last forever" and "will take its place with all the other dances that have ever been invented." In fact the twist *was* beginning to wane. And as Cameo explored the possibilities of new bandwagons onto which Chubby could jump, such as the quasi-folk "hotennanny" craze ("Black Cloud") and surfin' music ("Surf Party") to be met with only moderate success, it might have begun to dawn on them that if the adult audience followed the kids' lead and dumped the twist, Chubby, its "creator", would be in trouble.

They had few other worries, however. Dee Dee Sharp was now flapping her arms and telling Bandstanders to "Do The Bird" while the Orlons went from strength to strength with trilling hits like "South Street" and "Not Me", the latter from the repertoire of Gary (U.S.) Bonds, the black singer from Norfolk, Virginia who'd mixed wild rock with calypso to become an early sixties *Bandstand* favourite.

In the spring of 1963 Cameo came through with yet another money-spinning act — and a pretty unlikely one it was. The Tymes — whose "So Much

In Love" hit Number 1 in June 1963 — were a black vocal group who used none of 1963's "commercial" styles. They sang neither frenetic, empty teenbeat nor fiery soul music. Neither, for that matter, were they another Dreamlovers, coming on with a nostalgic wave of doowop. Their sound, so polished and so precise in its modulated smoothness, was a throwback to the barbershop harmonizers of the thirties and forties. What stopped "So Much In Love" from being unbearable schmalz was its gentle, wistful air accented by clicking fingers and a beautiful drifting summery melody. The Tymes had had to wait a long time for their breakthrough. They had formed in 1956 when Norman Burnett and George Hilliard met at summer camp. A few months later they teamed up with Donald Banks and Albert "Caesar" Berry and, as the Latineers, worked local supper clubs until in 1960 lead singer George Williams joined the group and the team, now a quintet, changed its name to the Tymes. In April 1963 they appeared on a WDAS radio talent show, were heard by a Cameo/Parkway executive and signed to the company.

Producer Billy Jackson was assigned to the group. Jackson, who today produces the team's successful "soul" recordings, remembers: "George Williams had this idea for a song. He originally called it 'The Stroll' and had the basic melody and the first verse. I loved the song right away and me and the arranger Roy Straigis changed it around a little and it became 'So Much In Love'. It was my idea to put the seashore sounds and the birds and things because I felt it would make it more romantic."

George Williams' pure lead voice sounded at times startlingly similar to Johnny Mathis and after the massive success of "So Much In Love" the resemblance was quickly worked on. Mathis' "Wonderful Wonderful" was revived and brought into the Top 10. For the next two years the Tymes' under Billy Jackson's tight control veered further and further into the world of show tunes, "quality" songs and Tin Pan Alley standards. But by 1965 it became apparent that the nightclub world didn't really want *black* purveyors of bland "good" music and the Tymes changed direction — towards soul music.

By 1964 black acts were taking up more and more of *Bandstand's* hard-sell effort. Dick Clark began welcoming such surprising guests as James Brown onto his show and although the Orlons could still move the dancers with a mechanical revival of Bobby Freeman's oldie "Shimmy Shimmy", Philadelphia's white-owned, white-run record companies' attitude to black artists began to appear increasingly compromised and anachronistic. Chubby Checker, for instance, who two

years before had indeed been the "biggest recording artists in the world", was now reduced to dire, sing-a-long novelties like "Hey Bobba Needle" or imitations of soul singers' dances such as "She Wants T'Swim" which only crawled into the Top 50.

The Philly labels' attempts to bolster their vanquished rosters of white teen idols were failing too. Chancellor's the Fabulous Four — Fabian's back-up group — didn't make it without the "Tiger"; Swan's Mickey Lee Lane only had one sizable hit, the derivative "Shaggy Dog", despite his repeated, and potentially commercial, attempts to ape Negro styles; and Cameo's the Vanderbilts and Pete Antell sank with hardly a ripple. What was to hit the Philadelphia music establishment hardest, however, was the emergence of the four Liverpudlians who were beginning to turn the world's music industry inside out. Yet for a while it had looked as though one Philadelphian record company was going to have the luckiest break in music business history. Frank Virtue graphically describes how Swan Records "found" and lost the Beatles.

"Bernie Bennick, the head of Swan Records, called me one day in '63 and asked if I'd come over and mend one of his machines, one of his record decks which was broken. I said sure, so I went over with a buddy and we took the thing apart and pretty soon we had it going again. So to test it out I picked up a record he had lying around and played it. The machine seemed to be working okay. But I thought the record had something . . . I played it a couple of times and when Bernie came in I said 'listen man, I don't know who they are but you should put it out.' Now I don't think Bernie had liked it too much when it had been sent to him but he seemed to pay attention to what I was sayin'. Cause he released it . . . and that was 'She Loves You' by the Beatles."

Bernie Bennick tells a somewhat different version about hearing of the Beatles, flying to England and picking up the rights to the group's second album, in an impressive display of music-biz acumen. However, no matter how it came about, the end results were finally as destructive as they were beneficial.

The Fab Four broke through to the American charts on Capitol Records after a massive publicity campaign to duplicate their meteoric rise to stardom in Britain. As Beatlemania swept the American continent in hysterical waves, several American companies were delighted to discover that through individual licensing deals scattered around by Britain's EMI Records before they'd begun to realize the potential of their act, several companies had the rights to issue early Beatles discs. So Chicago's Vee Jay, New York's Tollie and Philadelphia's Swan labels all flung out

Beatles discs and helped themselves to a couple of million sales each. It was, of course, a short-term project. Capitol had the rights to all the future material and though Swan milked their Beatles tracks for all they were worth (even making the Hot 100 with "Sie Liebt Dich"), by mid-1964 the market place was clear for Capitol to make a billion.

But Swan had tasted the *big* big-time. Where before they'd relied on a tiny staff, now they appointed promotion men in all parts of America. Such unwise expansion was eventually to have a disastrous effect on Swan's resources, though Bernie Bennick believes that the Beatles had in themselves heralded an end to the small, independent record label. "In a sense they were the kiss of death. They were a great group, one of the most talented groups the world has had. But after the Beatles it seemed that a small company couldn't exist . . . unless they were prepared to be controlled and distributed by a major corporation — like Gamble and Huff and CBS today." But more immediate in its effect on Philadelphia's record companies was the Beatles' image — the lads themselves. Overnight Dick Clark's *Bandstand* with traditional flexibility became a vehicle for whipping up Beatlemania with a constant stream of Beatles discs and contests to win George Harrison's soda pop bottle or Paul McCartney's pillow case. And as the Pacemakers, the Hermits and dozens more British groups

solidified Britain's challenge to the most American of all institutions, the popular music world, Cameo/Parkway *et al* — once so secure with their perfect *American Bandstand* back-up — now began to back-pedal frantically, desperately trying to compete as wave after wave of groups from Liverpool, Manchester and London threatened their once invincible stronghold. They had but one hope — aside from moving the base of their operations two thousand miles. They had to move further into the only American musical movement which didn't wilt under the Liverpudlian big beat heat, rhythm and blues.

Not that it was called that any more. Weldon McDougal sums up what happened in the early sixties. "It was a kinda revolution. All the old styles of R&B . . . the blues things and the doowop things had died away. Instead a lotta singers were comin' outa the church. And their styles were taken by guys, producers, in New York and Detroit and they were makin' it into a new kinda thing. It was a new R&B, so they called it soul music. Around 1964 and 1965 all the labels like Cameo and Swan started getting into a soul music thing. But they blew it man. They'd left it too late. You see Bernie Lowe had kicked Kenny's (Gamble) ass out of Cameo Records once . . . so when the big Philly labels needed guys like him, Kenny was somewhere else . . . Kenny was beginning to do it for himself. . ."

Five: Beat concerto; Philly to New York

"When I first met Solomon Burke he was a raggedy cat. He used to play guitar but nobody wanted to hear him sing. Then one day Solomon did this talent show and he just tore the place up. He'd been around the gospel circuit a long time singing in the churches and all that stuff, but he had an ambition to be more than just another gospel singer. Solomon had to scuffle for years. But he made it in the end. He was the guy who really started soul music off in New York . . ."

Weldon McDougal is right in his assessment of Burke. But it was not only in New York, but everywhere else for that matter. There had been a considerable number of singers performing non-religious songs with the vocal inflections and style of black church music before Solomon. Roy Brown had shouted gospel blues in 1947. In the fifties Little Willie John had wailed spiritual ballads. Ray Charles had fused gospel, blues and jazz. James Brown had screamed his charismatic way to the R&B charts. And Sam Cooke had warmed the mass audience with his smooth resonance. By 1960, the year Solomon Burke began to make his mark, the ex-lead singer of the Mount Lebanon Singers of New Jersey, Clyde McPhatter, was America's bigges R&B act. But the New York producers with whom Solomon Burke worked saw that gospel music didn't simply have to be a subsidiary colouring to blues-based R&B styles or a device to make bearable schmalz pop ditties, but could be extended to become the basis of a new music form in its own right. Solomon Burke was the first singer promoted initially as a "soul" singer and as the "King of Rock and Soul"

played a crucial role in the development of soul music. It seems only right that Solomon Burke — the man who took the gospel spirit and committed passion of the storefront church into New York studios crowded with rock'n'roll rhythm sections, renegade jazz hornmen and Polish Jew violinists and saw it blended into a new concept of popular music by visionary record producers — was from Philadelphia.

As gospel disc jockey Louise Williams remarks, "Solomon learned his music in Philadelphia and he learned it in the church. Then he took a different path." The path was of course to New York, fame, acclaim and riches as a grandiose show-biz personality. But before then, even before Weldon McDougal's memories of the raggedy talent-show guitarist, there was yet another totally different existence for Burke.

In 1945, at the age of nine, Solomon was appearing in his own church, "Solomon's Temple", and on local radio as "The Wonder Boy Preacher". The Temple, founded by Solomon's grandmother, was packed every Sunday and though the Wonder Boy's fame never extended beyond the East Coast, the gimmick of a kid with a soprano voice saving souls and "getting happy" was popular. Then Solomon's voice broke and the Wonder Boy Preacher was wondered at no more. By the time he was nineteen, Solomon was enormously fat, sported a natty process and, after his talent show success, was ready for compromise. The wife of Philly disc jockey Kae Williams got her husband to take Solomon up to New York where he recorded the first of a series of discs with Apollo Records. The result was not the gospel music in which the company often specialized, but a strange kind of soft-centred music — part syrupy crooning, part boisterous rock'n' rolling. Only on the one or two religious numbers he recorded — such as "You Can Run, But You Can't Hide" — did the music show any of the soaring passion and gritty fervour of his church background and Solomon's seven or eight insipid Apollo discs didn't sell. By 1959 Solomon had begun to recognize that the strength of his style and its potential commerciality lay in displaying, not hiding, his hard-won gospel music roots. But inexplicably, Solomon's recordings for his next record label, Singular Records, were derivative. "Be Bop Grandma" was a fiery rock' n'roller, three years too late. "It's All Right" quite clearly borrowed from Ray Charles gospel stomp hits and didn't sell well either. But by 1960 Solomon was moving in the right direction — the offices of Atlantic Records.

Weldon McDougal: "I was in the waiting room at Atlantic and Solomon came in and said 'what are you doing man?' So I said 'I'm waiting here to get somebody to listen to my masters'. So Solomon said he was writing some songs that he hoped to get on some artists. Then Jerry Wexer came through and asked us what we wanted. When he realized who Solomon was he was knocked out — he'd been trying to get hold of him. So they went in the back and the next thing I know Solomon was on Atlantic Records."

What Atlantic did with Solomon was to be repeated ad infinitum over the next half decade. The company would encase a singer's gospel style in enveloping cushions of "beat concerto" productions. At the beginning Atlantic and Solomon sometimes faltered commercially — his debut Atlantic disc "Keep The Magic Working" flopped; or artistically — "Just Out Of Reach (Of My Two Empty Arms)" had the singer swamped in a sugary choir on a flaccid country ballad. But the latter became a major Top 30 success in September 1961 and the pairing progressed from strength to strength. Despite the use of a different arranger at each session Solomon conquered all. His rich, vibrant, baritone voice brought the full majesty of the gospel tradition to a series of intense, moody ballads and laid down the solid groundwork of the soon-to-follow soul music explosion. Hits like "Cry To Me" and "Down In The Valley" in 1962, and "If You Need Me" and "You're Good For Me" in 1963 hit the R&B and pop charts and made previous black singing styles seem limply drab compared with the rabble-rousing emotion of Solomon. And coupled with his records, Solomon evolved a fervently demonstrative stage act. "He

turned theatres like the Apollo and the Uptown into churches, he had folk running down the aisles to be saved by his music", recalls Weldon McDougal. In *Black Music*, April 1975, critic Cliff White described a show where "with head thrown back and one hand cupped to his mouth like an Alpine yodeller he cried out with such overwhelming passion that he left the spellbound audience wrung out and exhausted like so many limp rags."

The discs rolled on. Searing testifications like "Goodbye Baby (Baby Goodbye)", "Everybody Needs Somebody To Love" and possibly the quintescence of Solomon's style, "The Price" all sold well. And all were brilliantly produced by Bert Berns, a roly-poly white New Yorker with a deep love and empathy for black music despite a formal music education at the Juilliard School of Music and a music background far removed from the searing soul in which, by 1963, he specialized. Fellow producer Jerry Ragovoy tells the story: "I was doing a little bit of arranging at Chancellor, who had people like Frankie Avalon and Fabian. Bert was a publisher's representative at that time and he used to drop by trying to sell songs to the label. I was the screener; it was my job to see people submitting material. I got to know Bert then." . . ."

Luckily, neither Berns nor Ragovoy got sucked in by the pretty-boy banality of Chancellor. After a successful spell with Wand Records, Berns joined Atlantic as a staff producer in 1963. In addition to Solomon, Bert hit with the Drifters working closely with sympathetic arranger Gary Sherman. But it was Solomon who made Bert's reputation. Cliff White has written: "From '61 through to '65 Solomon was the main man in and around New York. Indeed across the States several nationwide hits made him one of the first major black acts of the sixties when his intense performance of a mixed bag of songs brought together the elements that were to be synthesized as 'soul' music. Even when younger, more aggressive men like Wilson Pickett and Otis Redding stripped away the subtler edges of the 'soul' sound, Solomon still managed to hang on, gaining two of his biggest hits in the mid-sixties at about the same time as he was ceremonially crowned on stage 'The King of Rock'n'Soul'.

Although the king's crown began to slip a little over the next decade, Atlantic records like "Got To Get You Off My Mind" in 1965 and "Take Me (Just As I Am)" in 1967, Bell discs like "Proud Mary" in 1969 and now, in 1975, Chess records such as "You And Your Baby Blues" have kept one of black music's supreme innovators in the charts where he belongs. It is, however, very ironic that in 1975, in order to find a mass audience, Solomon has had to adopt a derivative form of the style of someone else — namely Barry White. It is also ironic that the artist considered by many to be the daddy of all soul singers has never recorded in the city that spawned him, despite Philadelphia's soul music ascendancy. Perhaps that will come in time — though with Solomon now established as a major West Coast recording artist the need isn't urgent. A singer who today *does* need some of Philly's current hit magic is one who, like Burke, played a key roll in taking a gospel-orientated style to New York and became a first generation soul singing star: Garnet Mimms.

On July 15th, 1958, Philadelphia's Red Top Records recorded a disc by a group whose sound was distinctly at odds with the wurbling doowahs which were making a few bucks for the company. Red Top were able to lease the tape of the Gainors' "Follow Me" to the pop label, Cameo Records. For although the Gainors showed some of the stylized harmonies of the golden group era, their material seemed to be conceived with more than one ear on the catchy ditties of mainstream pop music, while the lead voice sang with richness and warmth, rather than doowop's coolness, and showed a more direct descent from black gospel music than the modified barbershop harmonies of the street corner. The lead singer of the relatively unsuccessful Gainors was one Garnet Mimms.

Garnet had been born in West Virginia in 1933 and had moved with his family to north Philadelphia as a young child. His family were intensely religious. Garnet describes his background: "I spent half my childhood in church; my brothers and sisters, my parents, we all sang in church. When I left high school in '54 I worked in a laundry and began singing with gospel groups. We played all the churches in the area. I was in the Evening Stars and also the Norfolk Four. We did a few records for Savoy Records in Newark. Then I sang with the Harmonizing Four for a little while. Around '56 I went in the Army for two years. When I came out I decided to get a little rock'n'roll group together, that was the Gainors . I'd known most of the guys all my life. The Gainors were me, Sam Bell, Howard Tate, Willie Combo and John Jefferson. Sam was writing a lot of songs and we did some recording for Red Top and Talley-Ho Records. But we never got very far, so we broke up."

While the break up of the Gainors was the end of one story, it was also the beginning of another. In 1961 a new group formed, Garnet Mimms and the Enchanters, consisting of Mimms, Bell, Charles Boyer — who'd worked previously with the Ambassadors — and a girl, Zola Pearnell, one-time member of the Paul

Roberts Choir. The group scuffled, knocked on dozens of New York music-biz doors, and hoped for a break. They got one. Jerry Ragovoy: "When I hit New York one of the first people I called was Bert Berns. He'd signed Garnet Mimms and the Enchanters and been working on this song for him called 'Cry Baby' for six months. He was disgusted; he couldn't complete the song nohow. But one day, over at Berns' house, we got the thing finished. I used the name Norman Meade."

When released on United Artists Records, "Cry Baby" was an immediate smash. By August 1963 it had sold a million. The record was a masterly production, a milestone in pop history with a superb blend of orchestral sophistication and Garnet's lead voice moving from tremulous poignancy to exultantly shrieked passion without ever losing control. Part R&B, part pop, part gospel, it was the archetypal "Uptown Sound" dubbed "soul" by a rapturous industry.

Ragovoy — for almost a decade — and Garnet Mimms — for considerably less time than that — continued to pile on the symphonic pop hits. "Baby Don't You Weep"/"For Your Precious Love" came from a glorious album, *Cry Baby And Eleven Other Hits*. Then Garnet split from the Enchanters. While the group gave the lead mike to Sam Bell and signed a contract with Warner Bros. Loma Records, Garnet continued to hit as a solo with "One Girl"/"A Quiet Place" in 1964, "A Little Bit of Soap" in 1965 (a revival of the Jarmel's 1961 classic) and "I'll Take Good Care Of You" in 1966. Sadly, Mimms then faded from the big time. Despite Ragovoy continuing to produce and write sympathetically for the rich warmth of Garnet's style, the singer seemed trapped in another musical era. By the seventies Garnet was down to constant tours of small British clubs (where he had a tiny but faithful audience) and recording spasmodically and unsuccessfully for New York record companies. Ragovoy, on the other hand, continued his musical conquests throughout the sixties. Working closely with Bert Berns until Berns' death in 1969, Ragovoy hit with productions, songs or both on artists like Irma Thomas ("Time Is On My Side" in 1964), Erma Franklin ("Piece Of My Heart" in 1967) and Dionne Warwicke ("Sure Thing" in 1974). In addition to these singers, two other Philadelphian artists were to benefit from Ragovoy's unique ability to make instant pop classics. One had once sung with Garnet Mimms.

Howard Tate was born in Macon, Georgia, but had settled in Philadelphia by the age of seven. He'd sung in various gospel units around Philly and been given advice and instruction by veteran jazz/R&B organist Bill Doggett. Then Howard joined the Gainors and worked with the team in the clubs at weekends, driving a cab for food money. As Frank Virtue of Virtue Studios tells it: "Bill Fox had an agency just across the road from us. He and Jerry Ragovoy picked up on Howard and brought him in and did a little recording here. Howard Tate had a real interesting style, very soulful but also into a blues kinda thing."

The "blues kinda thing" was supplied by Tate's torrid, B. B. King style guitar. But Ragovoy correctly realized that the role of gospel-blues shouter was far too restricting for the possessor of such a passionately emotive voice. He took the singer up to New York, wrote one of the most haunting songs of the whole

Howard Tate at the Virtue Recording Studios

soul genre and proceeded to envelop Tate's eloquent style in a lilting mid-tempo blanket of undulating rhythm and wistful horns. "Ain't Nobody Home", released on MGM's Verve subsidiary in 1966, became a sizable R&B and pop hit. For two years Ragovoy continued to make Tate one of the most distinctive soul singers of the sixties. Sometimes he used a chunky blues-based background as on "Look At Granny Run Run" in 1966 and sometimes a passionate Memphis influenced whoop-up as on "Stop" in 1968. Tate then split from Ragovoy, but after a handful of unsuccessful discs, including a session in Jamaica, returned to Ragovoy's sympathetic guidance in the seventies with discs on Atlantic. But by then the soul music world had forgotten the name of Howard Tate.

Tate wasn't the only singer based in Philadelphia, recorded in New York, produced by Ragovoy and linked with Garnet Mimms. There was also a Phila-delphia-born gospel singer called Lorraine Ellison, for whom Sam Bell began writing songs after taking over from Mimms in the Enchanters.

In 1963 Lorraine was involved in an attempt to commercialize her gospel music style. But unlike the astute modifications conceived by New York's "beat concerto" record producers, it was an attempt which retained religious lyric content and was an attempt doomed to failure. Author Bill Millar described it in his book *The Drifters*: "The phrase 'pop gospel' was coined in New York in May 1963 to describe the entertainment featured at a newly opened nightclub called The Sweet Chariot. The management booked little-known gospel musicians and stocked a supply of tambourines for leading socialites to shake. A typi-cal evening's proceedings were recorded by CBS, who hoped for an epidemic of twist-like proportions. The sub-standard groups heard included the Golden Chords . . . Thankfully pop gospel, albeit much pub-licized, was a nine day wonder."

The Golden Chords were led by Lorraine Ellison. When she broke up the group in early 1964 she and Sam Bell — her manager — decided it was time for the exit of Lorraine Ellison, gospel singer, and the entrance of Lorraine Ellison, soul singer. She explains: "Soul was what was happening in New York and all the big labels were looking for gospel artists who could cross over. I auditioned for Mercury Records and got a con-tract with the company. Sam had written a song called 'I Dig You Baby' and he produced me on that. It was a small kinda hit."

Lorraine made 22 in the October 1965 R&B chart with the song, which was revived as a much bigger hit by Jerry Butler in 1967. But Lorraine wasn't happy at Mercury — "they just didn't know what direction to take" — and her follow-up, "Call Me Anytime You Need Some Lovin' ", went nowhere. But in the summer of 1966, Lorraine Ellison was to record her classic, a disc which was not only the artistic highpoint of her singing career but possibly the zenith of the whole New York symphonic soul movement.

Lorraine Ellison in 1966

"Sam Bell got me with Jerry Ragovoy who was working with the Enchanters on Warner Bros. I signed a contract with them. Jerry called me up and told us we had the studio for three numbers because Frank Sinatra had cancelled one of his sessions after all the musicians had been booked. I thought wow, a huge orchestra like **that**. No one told them that Sinatra had cancelled. I sat in the booth and watched these guys lay down the tracks with the arranger Gary Sherman. It was a real *big* sound, there were so many musicians. Anyway, when the time came for me to go out and do the vocal the guys just fell apart — Frank sure had changed!"

Anything further from the modulated blandness of Sinatra's contemporary style would have been difficult to imagine. Ragovoy had written a song with George Weiss which lyrically was a startling cry of desperation. "Stay With Me" didn't just tell the truth, it

swore it. The lyric drifted with the rise and fall of a poignant melody until, with a tumultuous crash of timpani and cascading strings, Lorraine shrieked and sobbed and moaned and wailed in the most frenzied climax ever heard in a New York recording studio. It was a soul music landmark instantly recognized by the connoisseur but less easily so by the mass market. "Stay With Me", with its unrestrained passion, appeared to some as a histrionic wallow in self-pity and it was only a small hit. Lorraine and Ragovoy were never again able to capture the magic formula. A 1966 album, *Heart And Soul*, was a confusing mixture of gospel-styled frenzy and lush, easy-listening vapidity. She had a string of small soul hits for Warner's Loma subsidiary including "Heart Be Still" (an adaptation of gospel's "Peace Be Still"), "I Want To Be Loved" and "Try Just A Little Bit Harder". There was also a brilliant, but underpromoted 1969 album, *Stay With Me*. Lorraine often seemed directionless, caught between the raw emotion which constituted her style and the lush settings in which Ragovoy uncomfortably placed her. Lorraine, with a new producer, made a come-back in 1974 with a critically acclaimed album, *Lorraine Ellison*, on Warner Bros. but has now left the company. It remains to be seen whether she will find the stardom the connoisseurs have wished for her.

"After *Stay With Me* everything was somewhat of an anti-climax", muses Lorraine. "Material has been my problem. I write songs. I used to write a lot with Sam Bell but he's quit now; he's a preacher back in Philadelphia. I'm always working on new songs myself. But finding the right things is very difficult. Like 'Stay With Me' was a once in a lifetime song . . . perhaps I'll do some recording in Philadelphia, where it's all happening now. When I started out soul music was just getting together and New York and Detroit were the only places who were hip to what was happening. That's why producers like Jerry Ragovoy had to go to New York to make it. Maybe if Jerry had stayed around in Philly he'd have been the guy who made the Philly sound . . . maybe . . . "

Six:
The birth of the sound

"Getting Dick Clark behind your record" was, by the late fifties, an obsession of the American music industry — or the bulk of it. Although random black acts were sometimes picked up by *American Bandstand*, a chance of white teenage exposure was a bonus the small, independent rhythm and blues companies couldn't rely on. So, in a continuation of a situation that had not radically altered since the end of World War Two, small labels tuned in, or tried to, on the melting pot of popular musical styles — the ghettos of America.

Meanwhile the wave of doowop groups that had risen to national R&B popularity had all but ebbed and the small companies who had recorded the street-corner harmonizers either stopped or paid the price in the bankruptcy courts. Also waning was the raunchy fusion of blues and jazz which had originally earned the "rhythm and blues" name tag. By 1959 R&B lay in a strange state of limbo, uneasily assimilating more and more performers whose roots lay in gospel music but lacking the clear direction that was shortly to crystallize as soul.

Yet in 1959 a new rhythm and blues label was formed in Philadelphia, and one which enjoyed some real success. Lenny Caldwell ran V-Tone Records out of a tiny office on Ridge Avenue. After an ill-considered doowop debut (Little Jimmy and the Tops) and unsuccessful discs by the Fashions and Nelson Dupree, Caldwell stumbled across his first major seller. Although the Bobby Peterson Quintet from Chester, just outside Philly, had a local reputation playing the small

clubs around town, when Caldwell took them into the studio he could have been forgiven for feeling apprehensive. Pianist Peterson played in a ragged boogie style with more enthusiasm than musicianship and came on like he'd just stepped out of a late forties time warp. Yet a repetitive, mid-tempo instrumental called "The Hunch" was an East Coast hit for the Quintet. Unfortunately, V-Tone had few resources to follow up their potential smash and when a cover version by Paul Gayten on Detroit's Anna label appeared, Peterson's chart chance disappeared. The artist's next instrumental, "Piano Rock", did moderately well locally but when Peterson took the Tin Pan Alley standard, "Irresistible You" and added a bawled, exuberant vocal he gained a surprise national R&B hit.

By that time (October 1960) V-Tone had extended their artist roster, but the vocal groups they signed, the Dreamlovers and the Cruisers, both sang doowops for a diminishing market — though both teams subsequently attracted other record producers, Jerry Ross and Gamble/Huff respectively. V-Tone's eccentric signings weren't limited to vocal groups. In mid-1960 they also signed a Texas singer/pianist, Big Al Downing, who was adept at performing accurate musical impersonations of a bewildering variety of styles. The previous year Downing had recorded a disc in New Orleans with the Fats Domino Band, and, encouraged by its moderate success, proceeded to duplicate for V-Tone every vocal inflection and nuance of the New Orleans giant. But Downing's three unsuccessful V-Tone discs convinced the label and the artist that one

Louisiana big beat drawler was enough.

At the end of 1960 two new singers travelled up from the South to record for V-Tone. If the label had only realized it, the styles of the new artists, based firmly in the intense passion of gospel music, could have established the company with the new kind of R&B. Instead, both were allowed to slip through V-Tone's net. Ruby Johnson, on "Calling All Boys", was drowned out with a girly chorus and quickly returned to Memphis, where it was six years before Stax/Volt Records gave her a fleeting moment of "soul" success. But it was the disc jockeys, not inept V-Tone production, which was to blame for Bobby Parker's sales failure. Parker had recorded previously in Chicago with Vee Jay but nothing like the two screaming, frenzied numbers he made with V-Tone. The topside, "Watch Your Step", was a frantic driving rocker, with Parker's over-amplified guitar pounding a torrid riff as he whooped and howled and a girl group song back-up in Raelets mock-gospel style. The flip, the anguished "Steal Your Heart Away", was even closer to Ray Charles' gospel soul style, being based on Uncle Ray's "I Believe To My Soul". Inexplicably the disc jockeys didn't give much play to Parker's V-Tone disc, and the singer returned home to languish in obscurity, though "Watch Your Step" eventually attracted an "underground" British following, with Parker making a brief British tour.

Parker's distressing lack of chart success, and the failure of Bobby Peterson to come up with another big hit, didn't daunt V-Tone. At the end of 1961 they recorded a disc the equal of "Watch Your Step", though again the label lacked the distribution to see it into the best-sellers. Two years previously the West Coast R&B bandleader Big Jay McNeely had had an R&B hit with a gospel-tinged blues song called "There Is Something On Your Mind". A year later an even more successful version of the song hit the R&B and pop charts by Bobby Marchan extending over two parts and featuring a dramatic monologue. V-Tone decided to try for a third hit with the number and recorded a version by the Jolly Jacks. As their eccentric name implied, the Jolly Jacks had a decidedly quirky approach, loosely covered by the description "comedy", though the group's extended recitation on "Mind" must have been the *blackest* comedy heard that year, full of gruesome images about what the lead singer would do to his cheatin' girl with a razor. It sold well and kept V-Tone ticking over. But competition for R&B airspace was beginning to come from elsewhere in the city.

"Billy Arnold had a company here in Philly. I was writing songs and I was trying to get them recorded",

says Bobby Martin. Martin decided to settle down in Philadelphia in 1961 after two years on the road with the Billy Hope Band. "He said he would record some of my tunes, so, after six months I just happened to be in Arnold's office when a guy called Harold B. Robinson from a new record company called Newtown Records called up. They were getting ready to do a thing called 'Mother-in-Law'. They were trying to out-run the one by Ernie K-Doe. They needed an arranger and he asked me did I know how to do arrangements. Well, I had done the charts for the bands I had been working with. It wasn't hard, because there were only seven pieces. So I said yes and I did the record. After that the man hired me as an arranger. I did production and arranging. We did a tune called "I Sold My Heart To The Junk Man" on the Four Sportsmen, but it didn't come off. We had different labels up there, one was called Bluebelle Records. So when we signed this new girl quartet we called them the Bluebelles, and we ended up putting them on the 'Junkman' track."

Girl groups were all the rage by 1962. From being a considerable novelty in the doowop era, with Richard Barrett's Chantels almost alone in the pursuit of ethereal harmony, the rise of New York's Shirelles heralded a virtual flood of female foursomes. Two young girls, Philadelphian Patricia Holt and New Jerseyite Cindy Birdsong, viewed the girl-group explosion with particular interest. "We used to listen to records on the radio and think, hey, we could do that", Patti reminisces. "So we got together with this high school group called the Ordettes. We's sing at parties, things like that. That was around '59 or so. The other girls in the Ordettes weren't serious about music. Anyway in about '60 this promotor called Bernard Montague took two girls from the Del Capris, another local group — that was Sarah Dash and Nona Hendryx — and we formed a new group. That's when we met Bobby Martin — and became the Bluebelles."

Patti's lead voice was distinctive even then, as Bobby Martin notes. "Patti had a strange kinda voice, very shrill and nasal but it seemed to work on that 'Junkman' song. It was just a catchy novelty kinda thing but it was a big hit. It got the company away."

For the Bluebelles there followed two years of energy sapping touring. "We played the Uptown and the Apollo", says Patti. "We mainly did R&B package shows. We'd come on, do two numbers and leave. We enjoyed recording with Bobby. He tried to show us how to get a professional attitude to our music, but we were just young kids. We did a pile of records for Newtown and we worked real hard trying to get another hit."

Sporting a revised name, Patti LaBelle and the Bluebelles, the group tried with other discs conceived on the lines of "Junkman", including Frankie Laine's "Cool Water" and attempted to out-twist the Orlons on "Decateur Street". They didn't click. Then, in 1963, the group turned in one of the most stunning discs of the emergent "soul age". "Down The Aisle" was a tribute to the solemnity of marriage with shrill, grating harmony sung over a mournful beat accompaniment of quasi-church organ, before Patti's nasal lead rose to a shrieking, ear-bursting climax. The blend of cloying sentimentality and impassioned fervour was to become the group's standard style for half a decade.

It was beginning to become patently obvious that the floundering V-Tone couldn't achieve chart success on the scale of "Down The Aisle", even though the artists they signed were undeniably talented. They included Bobby Bennett, a fiery bluesman from Rayford, North Carolina, who today still plays out-of-town clubs slaying audiences with his tough, B. B. King-style blues. There was also Jerry Williams who as Swamp Dogg has evolved into one of the seventies most important West Coast producer/writers. And there was a twenty-one-year-old singer born Walter Sigler and known to his buddies and the Philadelphia club audiences as Bunny.

"They called me Bunny right off because I was born two days before Easter. The first singing I did was in church — Sunday School. I wouldn't say it was very funky, just straight . . . 'our Father which art in Heaven'. But then I started going to my mother's church, that was a Baptist Church, the Emmanuel Baptist. Now *that* was funky. I really dug the way people got down in church.

"I sang in school, all the kids did, you know the group kinda thing. I would get home at six in the morning and have to get up in a couple of hours and go to school. I had a little group called the Opals, me and my brother and two other guys. One was called Murphy who looked just like Nat Cole. We did quite a few shows. But a couple of times the group didn't show up and I had to do the show all by myself. A disc jockey called Cannonball heard me and got me to leave the group and sign a contract. I recorded a thing called 'Come On Home', a Junior Parker song, for a company called Craig.

"They called me Bunny 'Mr. Emotions' Sigler, that's a name I had given to me when I first started singing supper clubs. I used to get on stage and start crying with my songs and going down on my knees and so on. I'm still that way, I guess. But now I don't cry on stage.

"In about '59 I did a thing called 'Promise Me' for a label called Hilo, a subsidiary of ABC. I used to play at a place in Philly called the Music City, 26 Columbia Avenue, where a lot of the entertainers used to go to be discovered. I met this group there called the Cruisers and they backed me on 'Promise Me' for V-Tone Records, but I was never a member of the Cruisers. Those early days were really exciting, though I was just a raw kid. I used to try and stay clean on stage, my suit was always pressed, even if it was the only one I had!"

While Bunny Sigler sang around town hoping for his discovery and the Bluebelles continued coast-to-coast tours as part of big-time R&B caravans, the first releases were appearing on a tiny local label called Harthon. The formation of Harthon was in a sense the single most important event of the early sixties in the eventual evolution of "the Philly sound" of soul. In Canada in 1961 the little jazz-cum-R&B band, the Manhattans, who for more than a decade had been touring the small clubs of America, decided they'd had enough and split for home. Yet despite the seeming insignificance of the Manhattans' disintegration, the band's leader Johnny Styles, with his Harthon partners, was one of the first men to spot the city's rhythm and blues potential within the context of the newly emergent soul music.

"I had no intentions of quitting music when the Manhattans broke up", comments Styles. "But I had every intention of changing my direction. I got a couple of jobs to do around town and I needed an organ player and I got hooked up with Luther Randolph. I had no intentions of starting a group right away." Luther explains further: "Jerry Ross asked me to do a session with the Larks. He said if I could get a band he would prefer that, so I told Johnny and he said all right. So we did the record, and after that, I said to Johnny, why don't we do some more things together."

The resulting Larks disc, the doowop "It's Unbelievable" on Sherryl Records, was a national hit, despite its considerable resemblance to the Flamingos' New York classic "I Only Have Eyes For You". Johnny and Luther continued their partnership. "Me, Luther and a drummer, Norman Collins, formed a trio," says Johnny. "First we were playing with a big group then we decided we weren't going to play any more jobs. We had the organ sitting there, so we decided maybe we should go to the studio and cut a record. We practised for a few days. No one knew what we were going to play, we just jammed and came up with a little blues. We called it 'Crossroads'. The studio we used was where Sigma is now, Reco Arts. I played guitar, Luther played organ and Norman played drums. We

Luther Randolph (left) and Johnny Styles — key Philly producers

took two cuts on a two-track. We didn't even listen to a playback because we didn't have enough money to go into time for one. We said 'Look, we'll pick it up the next day'. So we didn't hear it 'til we got the cut home. I had had some experience messing around pressing records but I didn't know anything about publishing. We wanted to press the records ourselves but we didn't know what to do about publishing, so we put it with a friend of ours called Pancho Villa. We didn't have a publishing company so we went to him and said 'will you please let us put our tune with your publishing company so we can put it out?' And he of course accepted and got fifty percent. Pancho had an agency and a label, but we didn't put it out with him, we wanted our own label. So we started this company called Harthon. Pancho was working with Sol Ramberg. He introduced us to him and we gave him the record to distribute. He was doing the pressing. I took the record to the guy that used to work for the deejay Georgie Woods, Herb Stratton, to get it on the air. He liked it and he liked us so he said he'd see what he could do. Well, we had been out of town and my mother told me Georgie Woods had called us up. So I called him back at the station and he told us we

had a hit record. So he asked us to come out and see him."

Sol Ramberg took the hot master to Cameo/Parkway Records and soon "Crossroads" was being shipped from coast to coast. Although it's difficult to define why the simple, bluesy organ jazz of "Crossroads" should have hit home, it became an East Coast R&B hit. Johnny continues: "We did a lot of working and travelling . . . Philly had a lot of good jazz organ trios — that was back in the days when organs were 'in'. We played mostly to R&B audiences. I guess because of the record we didn't attract the main-line jazz audience. There was a little girl singer, Jo Ann Jackson, that we wanted to record and she wanted us to record her. Well, she wasn't a great singer but the main thing that hit us was she had a connection with Georgie Woods. So we cut the record in the vein of 'Can I Get A Witness' called 'Georgie Porgie'. That was on our own label, called Harthon. But Georgie Woods didn't like it. That was our first venture with an artist other than ourselves."

Johnny Styles and Luther Randolph drove to New Jersey to cut a follow-up, "Criss Cross", for Cameo, but it was their little Harthon Records which took up

Producer/writer Weldon McDougal III

as many sessions as we could afford. Some things came out on Harthon Records which meant they were only distributed in the Philadelphia area, and some things we managed to lease. I remember about the first thing we got a major label to take was a girl group called the Tiffanys. Atlantic took a record by them ("Gossip"). It didn't really move but that advance kept us pushing. Anyway, in '64 I said to Johnny and Luther, 'Why don't we get Jimmy Bishop to come in with us'. Jimmy had just come in from St. Louis and was just making it as a big disc jockey. We thought with him plugging our records we'd get somewhere."

A second production company was formed by Styles, Randolph, McDougal and Bishop — Dyno-Dynamic Productions. Records continued to churn out from the green young record producers. Johnny Styles describes what they were aiming at: "The sound we were trying to get was that Motown sound. The Detroit thing was what was happening so we just tried to get as near to it as we could. Our things were

Left to right: Luther Randolph, Nella Dodds, Wes Farrell, Luther Dixon, Florence Greenberg

most of their interest. They contacted Weldon McDougal, then leader of the Larks, and went into partnership. Soon the three naive young record producers were booking studio time at Frank Virtue's studio over on North Broad Street. Weldon: "We did done in a small time kinda studio but we got the sound we wanted. And we'd found some *fantastic* musicians. We were using a regular bunch of musicians on all our sessions; they were the guys who backed the Larks on gigs — that was Norman Harris, Ronnie Baker, Earl Young and Bobby Eli. We had our first chart record with a thing by a girl called Nella Dodds. That was 'Come See About Me' (74 in the Hot 100 in November, 1964). Man, that record sounded more like Motown than Motown.''

Styles isn't exaggerating. In fact the song, written by Holland-Dozier-Holland, was pure Motown and had already been a hit for the Supremes. Nella Dodds' version had all the ingredients of Hitsville U.S.A., the same relentless echo-filled beat, the same thickly-textured layers of strings and chorus, and the same shrill Diano Ross-like vocal. "Come See About Me" and its equally Motownesque follow-up, "Finders Keepers, Losers Weepers", were both leased to Florence Greenberg's Wand/Scepter New York set-up.

By 1964 Cameo's Bernie Lowe was also making a few painstaking efforts to catch up on black artists with "cross over" potential. But Cameo's efforts were decidedly out of touch with the roaring Motown beat. Earlier they'd failed to recognize the potential of a fiery soulman like Don Covay, who went on to hit with Atlantic. Treating him with a contempt that should have been reserved for Chubby Checker, they had Covay performing such ditties as "Do The Bug" and "The Froog". By 1964 they'd completed a take-over of an independent label only to fail in recognizing the potential of its main arranger, Bobby Martin, or its chief act, Patti LaBelle and the Bluebelles. Patti: "We weren't getting very far with Newtown, though we made some albums — a Christmas one and an Apollo Theatre one — so we were pretty excited when Newtown got taken over by Cameo. But they didn't seem interested in us. They re-issued some of our things . . . and 'You'll Never Walk Alone' and 'Danny Boy' were pretty big hits for us. But they just ignored us! If it hadn't been for our shows at the Apollo and the Uptown we'd have been nowhere.''

Probably the group just got lost in Cameo's change-around. For Philly's biggest record company was in a state of trauma. With wave after wave of mop-haired British beat heroes sweeping away Brylcreem quiffs and dancing-string rock-a-ballads, Swan, Chancellor and Cameo either had to get with the British beat boom, home in on the fast-rising production-domi-nated soul music or crash out of the music biz as spec-tacularly as they'd entered it.

Bernie Lowe chose to face up to none of the alter-natives. Having made a massive financial killing with

Cameo's twistin' whimseys, and suffering from general ill health, Lowe had decided by mid-1964 to sell Cameo/Parkway Records. The buyer was a veteran record distributor, Alfred Rosenthal. He moved Cameo's head office to New York, appointed some additional A&R staff, went in search of British record rights and left the staff of his studio in Philadelphia to come up with the hits as of old. They couldn't, of course. Yet, ironically, a couple of musicians who'd pushed their way into the South Broad Street session men clique had, if Cameo had realized it, the potential to right Cameo's waning fortunes. One was a black, formally trained pianist who played in a small-time group called the Romeos. His name was Thomas Bell.

"I went over to Cameo for an audition when Chubby Checker walked into the room. I was working on my tunes to make sure they were right before pre-senting them to the people at Cameo. Chubby was in the habit of walking in on anybody — he likes to see what's going on, he's a real nosey guy. So he says 'let me hear your song'. So I played the song and he liked it so he says 'would you like to write for me?' Oh yeah, Big Chubby Checker. Yeah, sure Mr. Checker. A week later I get a contract. But I didn't write any songs for him. I wrote a couple of raggy little tunes. But they weren't so hot, so I guess we were even.''

Thomas Bell was twenty-three when he first strode through Cameo's door. Yet he already possessed a knowledge of music decidedly more sophisticated than the average black musician. Born in Philadelphia of West Indian parents ("I made it to the United States before I was even a gleam in my father's eye") Thom was insulated from the roughest aspects of ghetto life.

"We were middle-class I guess. My father was an accountant. We couldn't eat steak all the time but we didn't eat beans all the time either. When I was five I studying . . . I mean in order to survive in my house if you were gonna learn something you had to learn it You were gonna learn something you had to learn it the right way — there was no way out. Then I took to drums also. So when I was eight I was studying piano *and* drums at the same time. I took that for about a year but I didn't like the drums that well and by the time I was nine I took the flugelhorn and piano. I heard my first music other than classical when I was about fourteen. The first things I dug were by the Flamingos — they had 'Where Or When'. But really I used to look down on rock'n'roll then. It seemed so simple when compared with classical music. Then I met this guy Kenny Gamble. Kenny went to school with my sister Barbara. She was my twin, we were two of a family of ten. Anyway Kenny went to school with Barbara. I think he was a little sweet on her at the time, if my memory serves me correct, and she was a little sweet on him. He didn't play any instruments at all, he was a singer.

"The doors weren't open to get in to Cameo at that time. But Jerry Ross was a guy who was also in the Schubert Building on the sixth floor. Me and Kenny went to see the guy in 1959. We were singing together as a duet, Kenny and Tommy. We recorded a record on Jerry's label, Heritage Records. It was a bomb, it went nowhere."

It did lead somewhere, though. Guitarist Roland Chambers takes up Kenny and Tommy's story. "I had a guitar but I couldn't really play. I was in the gymnastics team and I was learning how to play on the side. I was coming home late, walking up the street, and that's when I met Kenny. Him and Tommy Bell had just cut a record together, it was called 'Someday', it was nice. Kenny strolled across the street, and said can you play that thing? So I said 'yeah, a little bit.' So he invited me over to his girlfriend's house as her mother wasn't home. We sat in her kitchen all day and we just sang and played, and that was like the beginning of me, Kenny and Tommy. Then we started playing together. Karl (he's my brother) was playing drums with groups like the Flamingos, out on the road. Well, we got him to join us and then we found this bass player who was from Baton Rouge living right here. That was Winnie Walford."

Winnie continues the tale. "I was playing locally around Philly with groups, the last one was King James, which was a very popular group locally. Anyway I auditioned with the group, which were called the Romeos, and got the job. When I got the job we worked every day, working on songs, the whole bit. And on the weekends we would gig in clubs. That went on for quite a while 'til eventually we got our foot in the door at Cameo."

Thom Bell explains: "Cameo had been into good-looking Italian boys who really didn't have to sing. But around '64 when Motown got big, things changed. The Romeos became a Cameo house band. But we were just the second-string rhythm section. We weren't on any *hits* there at all, because we were just up and coming, and you see, were just the younger guys. But the Motown situation was so big that Cameo had the bright idea of getting an all-black rhythm section to play that kind of music."

The Romeos played on a few Cameo sessions, but not many. Then Kenny Gamble had one of his songs accepted for a session scheduled for a new Cameo signing, a girl group, Candy and the Kisses. The song was in Cameo's favourite style — a new dance called "The 81" — and Kenny had written it with record producer Jerry Ross. Kenny comments: "I worked a lot with Jerry Ross. We had a nice relationship. He actually showed me around, showed me what was happening in the record business. He took me to New York and the big publishers. I only worked out of Philadelphia, but I went to New York a lot. I think Hill and Range was the first publisher I had anything to do with — they were publishing all the earlier things that I did with Jerry Ross."

On "The 81" Candy and the Kisses wailed in a similar bluesy-gospel style to Detroit's Martha and the Vandellas. The "Detroit sound" was heightened by a mock-Motown, brass and stomp-stomp-rhythm arrangement conceived by Jerry Ross. The pianist who added weight to the disc's dance appeal was a music-biz veteran called Leon Huff. He had learned his music on the streets of his hometown, Camden, New Jersey, a bridge distance away from Philadelphia. "There used to be a little guy around Camden", says Leon, "called Sugar Child Robinson . . . long time ago. He was a teenager when I was a young kid and he played a thing called the boogie woogie at the Earl Theater, off Market Street . . . I used to go there when he was playing. Not too many people know this guy, but he was big back then. That's when I started playing — listening to the radio, records — playing what I heard. You know that's when I developed an ear . . . wasn't really no schooling involved. I used to play at local talent shows in Camden. I wasn't thinkin' about no record business then."

By the late fifties Leon Huff could play a mean boogie himself — and *was* thinking about the record business. He caught a Greyhound to New York. By "sitting in peoples' offices 'til they listened" Leon scuffled some session work and began to gain a hefty reputation as a top R&B pianist. Soon he was hauling his ass around every studio in New York.

"I worked as a studio musician. That was out of Leiber/Stoller's office in New York and I was playing piano on most of the dates. Those sessions I'm still thrilled about. Phil Spector being one of the musical giants of the industry and me having an opportunity to work with him — playing on the Ronettes' things was one of the real highlights of my career. And I'll never forget Leiber and Stoller because they helped me get the knack of the studios, and find out what it was all about. They gave me the opportunity to play on the dates and we just developed a good relationship. Jeff Barry, Ellie Greenwich, Carole King . . . I worked with all the top New York people, it was just a fantastic situation for me."

But there were some hassles. "The Union there is so strict, you know, you had to do whatever you had to do in a certain amount of time. To me, trying to cram a head-full of ideas into three hours is pretty rough. They really didn't give you enough time to express your mind. In fact the way we do things here in Philly is we might cut a track two, three different ways before we decide which one has more commercial value to it, but in the New York situation you had to do whatever you had to do right then . . . and be satisfied . . ."

Leon was commuting regularly to New York but also doing Philadelphia sessions — for Cameo and Swan of course. At Swan, Huff led a group of assorted session men, dubbed the Locomotions. Their name came from Little Eva's Goffin and King penned dance hit of 1962, so the Locomotions' first disc was jokingly titled "Little Eva". But the Locomotions' stomping boogie instrumentals didn't make it.

Then in 1964 Leon teamed up with the veteran producer, Leroy Lovett. Leroy's background had been, up until then, a jazz one. Born in Germantown, Pennsylvania, Lovett had led his own band around Philadelphia before touring with Noble Sissle and Lucky Millinder and organizing bands for Cat Anderson and Johnny Hodges. During the fifties he produced albums for Al Hibbler in California, directed a swing band for Ted Weems and did A&R work for the small Wynne Records. But by the sixties soul music was the name of the game. So the fifty-four-year-old leader joined forces with Leon: "Leroy Lovett and I did a record with this group I'd found, Patty and the Emblems. I saw Pat Russell working by herself in a club. I took her and combined the three boys. We cut this song I'd written called 'Mixed Up Shook Up Girl' and it was a pretty good hit."

Patty sang in a lowish voice not helped by decidedly suspect pitching, while the blaring arrangement of "Girls" seemed clumsy when compared with the subtleties of New York or Detroit. But its catchy chorus line and the general vogue for girl groups saw the record, released on New York's Herald label, into the Top 40 by June 1964. Patty and the Emblems, despite two or three more shots, never attained another hit ("they weren't really that good man", Leon laughs) and with Herald/Ember Records folding — one of the final casualties of the doowop age — Leroy Lovett decided to take up Motown's offer of a production job in Detroit. He left Leon Huff to return to session work. "When I met up with Kenny around the time of 'The 81' " — which made 51 in the Hot 100 in November 1964 — "we just hit it off real good. I was doin' work with Swan, Cameo, whatever I could get, and Kenny was singing around town with his little band the Romeos."

Kenny Gamble also hung around Frank Virtue's studio where Harthon/Dyno Dynamic Productions were trying for another hit. In the end of 1964 Harthon got ready to record a new soul sister. As Weldon McDougal tells the story: "One day Bill Oxydine, who was in the Larks, told me about this girl called Barbara Mason who was living next door to him and had a little high school group. Now although we had a recording thing it was still strictly a small-time operation. Johnny and Luther would play gigs at weekends, Jimmy had his job with WDAS and the Larks would play the clubs. Anyway, the Larks had a little bit of a name and when we'd give a show we'd let this little group do a song or two. And Barbara really got over with 'Moon River'. So I said, 'wow, I'd really like to record you all', but the other girls weren't that interested. I couldn't get them together to rehearse. So Barbara said, 'listen I'm interested, I really want to do something'. So I stuck with her."

Weldon took Barbara to the Virtue studios and cut a single with the young soul sister. The vocal back-up for Barbara's "Trouble Child" was supplied by the Larks, while the Tiffanys trilled an accompaniment on the flip. Harthon got the record leased to Crusader Records, soon to hit with Dobie Gray on "The In Crowd". But it didn't break out. "Barbara was a little Catholic school girl but she was writing some heavy songs. The first line of 'Trouble Child' was 'My life, my life, is all messed up, every child has got his own cup'. Anyway, she wrote this thing called 'Yes I'm Ready'. Me, Bobby Eli and Barbara got it together. There was one line in there — 'When I lay with you, I get up and I feel good' — which we had to cut out. In those days you couldn't talk like that. Anyway, we got the song ready to record."

A session was booked at Virtue's which began as a shambles and ended as a milestone in the evolution of the Philly sound. "We got all the musicians together, Norman, Earl, Ronnie and Bobby, but Barbara never showed. So eventually one of us had to go out and find her. She came in real mad. She wouldn't even take her coat off, she just sang the thing one time and split."

The poignant, bitter-sweet ballad caught the ear of everyone. Kenny and Weldon dubbed on a little vocal backup and Jack Faith put on the strings. ("He did the thing for nothing, he just wanted to do it because he loved the song so much"). The production was a masterly work by McDougal; it captured perfectly the little-girl innocence of the tremulous teens, and even if Barbara's voice was occasionally pitched flat ("she had a strange style, you never quite knew *what* note

The good ol' days at Virtue's: (front row) Paul Johnson (disc jockey Fat Daddy), Jimmy Bishop, Cal Rudman (writer of influential record tip "sheet"), Bill Fox; (back row) Frank Virtue, Weldon McDougal, Kenny Gamble and Johnny Styles

she was trying for"), that added to the faltering, pubescent mood.

Paradoxically, Barbara Mason's "Yes I'm Ready" was the song which effectively broke up the promising Dyno Dynamic Productions. Weldon looks back on what happened sadly, though without bitterness. "Jimmy Bishop took the tapes of Barbara and went behind our backs. He got a special deal set-up with Harry Lipsius of Jamie Records and formed his own label, Arctic. Before we knew what was happening, Barbara Mason was in the charts with 'Girls Have Feelings Too'. Jimmy Bishop was credited as her producer and Dyno Dynamic Productions were nowhere . . ."

Jimmy Bishop, not surprisingly, remembers it rather differently. " 'Girls Have Feelings Too' was the first hit I produced on Barbara. Then in 1965 we had 'Yes, I'm Ready' which was a monster and we never looked back."

Jimmy Bishop was born in Alabama. He got into radio in the late fifties and worked for two St. Louis stations, KXLW and KETC. After a brief spell in New York, he went to Philadelphia and in 1962 landed a job as a disc jockey with station WDAS, the *big* Philly R&B station. Radio, however, wasn't Jimmy's only interest. "When I first made it East in '62 I messed around the studios. I produced a couple of things for groups. The Starfires, that was one of them, and the Cordells. But the records didn't do anything. I look back now and I see they were lousy. I cut them at a studio in the north east of Philly, a couple of brothers owned it . . . Tony Lucie. Anyway in '63 or so I'd got friendly with Weldon McDougal. He'd come out to the station to get me to play things by the Larks. Anyway, I went into partnership with Weldon and Johnny Styles and Luther Randolph and we produced some things. But in '64 I decided to start

Yes I'm ready . . . Barbara Mason

my own label and I went to Harold Lipsius at Jamie Records and told him about my idea. We got something worked out — they were national distributors and I had total control. The label was Arctic Records. I got the name because at that time I was very impressed by Atlantic and I thought I'd get something close to that, I thought about Ocean. The first record out on the label was by the Tiffanys, 'The Happiest Girl In The World.' I cut that in a studio over a hotel. Luther Randolph and Johnny Styles were the musicians so we'd get together and they'd write down the bass figures or whatever . . . and we'd work it out from there."

It was Arctic's second release that became a R&B chart entry. With Jamie supplying expert coast-to-coast distribution and Bishop liberal with the radio plugs, Mason's "Girls Have Feelings Too" made 31 in the R&B chart. Then Arctic's fifth release was the classic "Yes I'm Ready" which smashed its way into the American Top 10, selling a clear million. Barbara's style was set; ballads, gentle, coy but with a subtle suggestion of earthy sexuality in her strange flatly modulated voice. After her million-seller she pursued her little-girl-in-a-woman's-body sound mercilessly

Jimmy Bishop, one-time owner of Arctic Records

with self-penned songs like "Sad Sad Girl", which made 27 in the Hot 100 in August 1965.

Meanwhile, Styles, Randolph and McDougal, with considerable disgust, were back trying for a breakthrough. In Styles' words, "We learned from the Barbara Mason situation. We realized that we'd been a little slapdash with contracts and things. Anyway, we reactivated Harthon and really started working around the clock. We were Virtue's best customers. We recorded every good soul act we could find. Everyone was getting into soul in Philly."

Even Cameo — but then, they needed to. The company had invested heavily in the British beat boom only to find that it didn't bring in millions. "Cameo picked up all the wrong things", Joe Tarsia points out. "They had a reciprocal agreement with Pye Records in London and they put out all those things by English acts, a lot of which hadn't even made it in England. They had a couple of hits like Sounds Orchestral and the Ivy League, but some real bombs like the Breakaways and Screamin' Lord Sutch. Man, they even picked up on the *wrong* Kinks records . . ."

Cameo had a small novelty hit with the Swans' "Boy With The Beatle Hair". But the decision to counter the departure of one plastic pop idol (Bobby Rydell) with the new signing of an old faded one (Mark Dinning of "Teen Angel" fame) showed a remarkable lack of perception. Cameo had a whole lot of headaches. And one of their major ones was what to do with Chubby Checker. It didn't seem feasible to re-launch the fat man as Philly's answer to Marvin Gaye, yet Chubby's dire pop novelties like "Lovely Lovely" weren't selling. Ironically, though, in April 1965 Chubby had a fair hit with perhaps his crassest disc of all. Dave Appell noted the massive U.S. success of Liverpool's Freddie and and Dreamers, with Freddie Garrity indulging in particularly ludicrous jump-about stage routines, and came up with "Do The Freddie". Possibly apprehensive that the disc might be too silly even for teenagers obsessed with things British, Cameo slipped a Motownesque "At The Discotheque" on the flip. Amazingly, "Freddie" sold quite well. But even that wasn't the Top 10 hit Cameo hoped for.

And so it was with lumbering deliberation that Cameo at last began moving into soul. By mid-1964 the Orlons were shifted from performing shrill teen-beat to performing Vandellas soundalikes. As the Orlons' Rosetta Hightower remembers: "Like everybody else we were trying to keep pace with Motown. They brought in producers like Jerry Ross and Kenny Gamble and we had musicians like Thom Bell or Leon Huff playing on our records. We were into the soul thing by then but we weren't accepted as a soul group and none of the records really sold and we just got released from the Cameo contract." The discs included "Come On Down Baby Baby", "Don't You Want My Lovin'," and "No Love But Your Love".

Cameo's other black *Bandstand* stalwart, Dee Dee Sharp, also made the transition to soul, with marginally more success. After realizing that a soul approach didn't simply mean dumping Cameo's artificial dance crazes in favour of more authentic, but hardly less stylized ones ("Let's Twine" in 1965), Dee Dee had a chart record with an attractive, heavily orchestrated ballad called "I Really Love You" in 1966. She at least sounded comfortable in the soul idiom.

Other companies like Chancellor Records found soul impossible to come to terms with. After the quick sales demise of Claudine Clark — who, rather mysteriously, was recording for Swan Records within a year under the pseudonym of Joy Dawn — Chancellor struggled to find a major black act. It might have been Baltimore's Royalettes who featured the strange nasal lead of Sheila Ferguson and who Russ Faith produced for Chancellor in 1964 at the peak of girly group popularity. But the Royalettes' "No Big Thing" was just that and with the group moving up to New York to begin a string of smallish hits with producer Teddy Randazzo, Chancellor's president Bob Marcucci decided he'd had enough. Chancellor, the company who had given the world Fabian, disappeared. It was mourned by very few.

Swan Records were *trying* with soul, if not always succeeding. Lillie Bryant of Billie and Lillie had a couple of solo shots, and they even put out something by veteran New Orleans R&B man Ernie K-Doe. And in January 1964 the Sapphires took "Who Do You Love" into the Top 30. The Sapphires were black and included two males in their line-up, but their harmony was considerably removed from the mainstream of church-based soul music while the men in the group were generally as inaudible as the Orlons' Steve Caldwell. In fact the Sapphires trilling female sound was even more pop-inspired than New York's Shirelles and Chiffons. "Who Do You Love" was produced by Jerry Ross and Joe Renzetti. But although the teaming tried for more hits with a similar formula, it had been the prettiness of the song rather than any distinctive vocal quality which had made "Love" successful and follow-ups flopped. Another songwriter/producer was called in, one who's reputation had been made with the sound of doowops — Richard Barrett. But he too was unable to give the Sapphires another hit. Barrett had returned home from New York at the beginning of 1964 and had launched a small independent label, Landa Records. Landa tried with a toned-down version of the Jolly Jacks' "There's Something On Your Mind", which was infinitely less interesting than the V-Tone version, and had a "near hit" with the one-time doo-wopers the Blue Notes.

Harold Melvin says, "We did this thing with Richard in '64 called 'Get Out' which sold a few (making 125 in the pop charts!). There'd been some personnel changes in the group and that was the first record we had out as by Harold Melvin and the Blue Notes. But really at that time records weren't the most important thing for the group. Martha Reeves of the Vandellas had introduced us to some people in the William Morris Agency and we began getting bookings in all the big nightclubs, Las Vegas, Lake Tahoe, Miami, all over. We did a lot of standards, show tunes. We were heavily into a cabaret thing. . . . We weren't concentrating on records."

But Barrett was of course. Landa disappeared from view and the veteran producer/songwriter joined Swan. There he hit. A month after Barbara Mason's "Girls Have Feelings Too" had slipped from the R&B chart, a disc produced by Barrett for Swan called "Gee Baby (I'm Sorry)" crawled into the Hot 100. The artist label credit read, the 3° Degrees. "The two lots of degrees was a gimmick to catch people's attention". It was the group's first record.

"We were all born and grew up in Philadelphia", begins Fayette Pinkney, the only member of the current Three Degrees who started with the "Gee Baby" group. "The original Three Degrees were Linda Turner, Shirley Porter and me. One day I was playing around on the piano at one of the girl's houses and I'm just singing at the top of my lungs not knowing that it's a producer sitting there on the couch. After we'd finished messing around he got up and said 'I'm Richard Barrett' and immediately I sat down with my mouth closed, nothing else to say. He sat at the piano and he played all his hit records. My mouth went 'Oh you wrote that!' Then he asked us if we would seriously like to sing. We said yeah, sure, but he said 'Look, music's no game.' And it sure wasn't. Our first recording was arranged and "Gee Baby" was a hit. Over the next three years or so there were various girls in the group. In all about six to eight different ones. At the time to some girls it was just a fad. To other girls it was just something to do. But in show business you have to be very, very serious about it. It's very difficult for girls on the road. Guys can go from one city or country to another and just take it over by storm but ladies can't do that, you know. It is a little more difficult."

The problem of retaining a consistent personnel wasn't their only worry. When "Gee Baby (I'm Sorry)"

hit the charts in March 1965, the girl-group explosion had run riot. Any bunch of pretty black chicks who could wiggle their bums and approximate a melody line were herded in their hundreds into America's recording studios. "Like black girl groups were about the first kind of R&B act to cross over to pop *en masse*", says Barrett. "Now a group like the Chantels had been a bit too black to make it big in pop music. But once chicks like the Shirelles came along, who had a kind of 'churchy pop' sound, all the New York producers recognized that as a R&B style, a soul music style, which, with the right production, would appeal to the white kids."

While Richard Barrett, Swan and the Three Degrees were battling to find a distinctive note in the stereotype girl-group scene, Kenny Gamble and the Romeos had landed a recording contract — ironically, with Arctic Records. As Jimmy Bishop recalls, "I recorded Kenny and the Romeos 'Down By The Sea Shore' and 'Ain't It Baby', that was recorded in Detroit". Roland Chambers adds, "We were recording for such a short period that we never got the time to make anything. We went on tour for a year with Little Anthony and the Imperials as Kenny Gamble and the Romeos, and we did concert tours, it was great. There wasn't much money though. Tommy Bell had left the Romeos to get married."

"We had never wanted to make it so big", Mr. Bell continues. "We just wanted to make a few hundred dollars a week doing what we liked to do . . . which was playing . . . We were always smart enough to get paid in *advance*. Have to attribute that to Kenny Gamble, he was always the businessman, and he's smart to this day. But a lady named Sybil, from Newark, New Jersey, came along and swiped me from the band. Sybil and I got married. So Leon Huff came in."

Roland Chambers describes how the Romeos dissolved. "We came back from touring with Little Anthony. I went on the road with Stevie Wonder, but no one believed that I had got the job. He was like, too big a star! Winnie wanted to get into acting and modelling, and Kenny, he teamed up writing with Leon Huff. Arctic wasn't doing anything with us so the group just split up."

Throughout 1965 and into 1966 Philadelphia's frenetic bout of soul music recording continued unabated. Among the new signings made by Swan Records were a group from Norfolk, Virginia, who'd had one taste of chartdom four years previously, the Showmen. Consisting of General Norman Johnson, Leslie Felton, and Milton, Dorsey and Gene Knight, the quintet had in Johnson one of the most distinctive lead voices in black music, a wheezing baritone capable of sobbing passion. Unfortunately producer Richard Barrett, under strict instructions from Swan, tried to duplicate the sound of Detroit's Four Tops and Temptations. Although "You Are Everything" (not to be confused with the Stylistics' song in the seventies) picked up a few sales, none of the Showmen's sadly derivative Swan discs sold very well. General Johnson had to wait another three years for fame when, based in Detroit, he made it with the Chairmen of the Board.

Ironically, the artist and producers who got nearest to duplicating the compulsive Tamla Motown dance beat, or at least those who had the most success doing it, were white. Leonard Borisoff had finally split from the Bristol stompin' Dovells — "We hated each other come the end, we used to have our meals in different rooms when we were out on the road" — left Cameo,

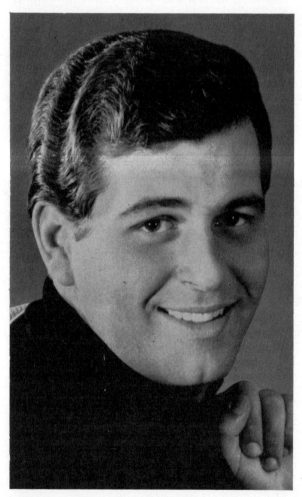

Len Barry, one-time leader of the Dovells

changed his name to Len Barry and teamed up with producers John Madara and Dave White, once a member of Danny and the Juniors. Madara and White took Len in the studio and recorded "Lip Sync", which was a small hit when released on Decca. But it was a song they'd written called "1-2-3" which became the smash Len needed. The song's wistful lilt was beautifully counterbalanced by a pungent brass arrangement. And with Len's high wavery lead in front of the band's undulating rhythm it was obvious what Len was aiming for. Interviewed in 1965 he admitted: "People thought I was black when the record came out — it got a lot of play on the black radio stations . . . I suppose you could say we were trying for a soul kinda sound."

So white boy Len Barry shot to the top of the charts, sold about three million world wide, and proceeded to record another smash, "Like A Baby", with almost identical tune and arrangement. Predictably the American pop establishment made little of the *basis* of Barry's musical style. Blue-eyed soul was still relatively new in 1965. But the lead shown by Barry in assuming an essentially black stylistic approach was to become one of the recurrent sub-plots in the next decade's development of Philadelphia soul music.

Madara and White also produced *black* soul singers for Decca. Bunny Sigler, for example. "I was into a ballad kinda thing and I played supper clubs in Philly, Springfield . . . oh yeah, and Montreal. When I was with Decca, Madara/White/Borisoff had this company and I did some things with them. I did 'Everything Is Gonna Be Alright' and I did a tune which had been a big hit for the Shirelles, 'Will You Love Me Tomorrow'. But Decca weren't that hip a company and I just got kinda lost . . ."

Sigler would have to wait two more years for his link-up with John Madara and Dave White to pay off. A couple of modern Detroit-sounding soul discs did give Bunny a chance to play the Uptown Theater however, and the Uptown was going from strength to strength with the rise in soul music's popularity. As Weldon McDougal puts it: "It was like one of *the* theatres in the country. Every big soul act played there. It was almost as big as the Apollo. In '64 Atlantic Records came down and recorded a whole show." The album was *Saturday Night At The Uptown*. "There were the Drifters, Patty and the Emblems, the Vibrations, Wilson Pickett, the Carltons, Patti LaBelle an' Barbara Lynn."

Singer/guitarist Barbara Lynn was the artist who kept Philly's Jamie Records firmly in the soul stakes. Her full name was Barbara Lynn Ozen and her style, a delicate balance of understated bitter-sweet vocal,

Where the rock'n'roll legends were made: the Uptown Theatre

poignant, self-penned songs, and chunky guitar rhythms, fully captured the earthiness of her Alabama origin. Producer Huey Meaux had begun recording Barbara in the early sixties and discs like "You'll Lose A Good Thing" in 1962 and "Oh Baby (We Got A Good Thing Going)" in 1964 were big successes on Jamie who continued with their preferred policy of leasing the bulk of their music from outside producers, rather than recording it themselves.

As a result of the Atlantic Uptown recording, the New York giant snapped up the contract of Patti LaBelle and the Bluebelles who were by then disgruntled with Cameo. As it was to turn out, the group's move to the New York recording scene was only a marginal improvement for them.

At the end of 1965 the Sapphires, their Renzetti and Ross productions now leased to the major ABC Records, got another hit, a catchy piece of Chiffons-style ephemera called "Gotta Have Your Love". The

flip-side of the disc was a song called "Gee I'm Sorry "Baby" (not to be confused with the Three Degrees "Gee Baby (I'm Sorry)"). It was written by Kenny Gamble and Leon Huff. Says Kenny, "I suppose we started writing together because we just had the feeling — the second sense — that told us we had something special to give each other. Once we wrote together we just knew we had to produce together. We had to take the initiative. Nothing much else was happening for us."

Kenny's Romeos were disbanded. Leon Huff was tired of doing random session work with the Three Degrees for Swan, Anthony and the Sophomores for ABC and Pervis Holder for Jamie — the latter's flip being an instrumental "Soul City" credited to Leon. So the duo decided to take a risk. "We formed a plan to start our own label. We scuffled around trying to raise some capital to start the venture off and eventually this clothing manufacturer Ben Krass put up a little bit of money. But we *had* to be right on the first shot. We called the label Excel Records and the act we recorded were the Intruders."

The Intruders (Sam "Little Sonny" Brown, Eugene "Bird" Doughtry, Phil Terry and Robert Edwards) are in 1975 still the very backbone of the Philly sound. Their history reads like page one of the doowop book of clichés. Phil Terry tells the story:

"We began back in '60 or so. I sang on street corners with a bunch of kids and I got to know the Intruders 'cause they were doing the same thing. We were just hoodlum kids singing a little bit of music. The Intruders — they were a quintet then — began to do a few gigs. They had a manager who'd get them a booking or two. Then they broke up and I joined three of them. We did a recording, nothing substantial, in '61. It was for the same people that were responsible for making the Hearts successful; the only difference was they had been out of business for almost two years. The Hearts were no longer happening. A younger member of their family who was about 19 decided that he wanted to go off into the record business. That was Michael Gowen. Barry Gowen was instrumental in the Hearts situation. Michael discovered the Intruders, and he laid out the bread and we recorded from that. We had a two-sided local hit for Gowen Records. When I say a local hit, on the Top 10 survey it was Number 1 for two months. With us being so young, that local hit was like being Number 1 in the world. I can remember the excitement of being Number 1 for almost two months; I always felt that if it could happen on a local scale it could happen nationally also.

"We met Leon Huff around that time. That was

Kenny Gamble at the breakfast table

about the time he began to do session work in New York. He was connected with a local group, he backed them up. They were called the Lavenders. We used to do record hops together. Throughout the year we used to run across each other's paths. Strangely enough it wound up that the Intruders and Leon Huff had the same manager, Leroy Lovett. This is where he got his studio experience from."

Leon Huff agrees. "Yeah, after I got back from New York Leroy was the first guy to show me how to produce. He taught me quite a bit. He did a record on the Intruders in '64, it was leased to Musicor Records in New York. It didn't take off though."

But Leon was convinced that the group had something. They booked a session at 290 South Broad, and in mid-1965 went in to record "All The Time", a doowop-cum-soul ditty with no pretensions at greatness. "It was no big thing", laughs Leon, "but it got us away. We sold about 20,000 to 25,000 records — it was a local Philly hit. It enabled us to go in and record some more things the following year. But we only had the one release of Excel, there was another organization who claimed the name. So we switched names to Gamble."

While Gamble and Huff were taking the first falter-

ing steps at getting a local group off and selling, another ex-member of the Romeos was doing a similar thing in the same studios. Thom Bell: "In '66 I was doing a little work with Cameo Records. And I came to England with Chubby Checker as his musical director. And I even did a session with a new singer they'd signed called Bobby Sherman." He later found fame as a teen idol. "Then a fellow called Stan Watson came to me with a group called the Delfonics. He knew nothing about recording, and I really didn't know anything about producing but it was something that I wanted to learn. I had an idea that I could produce records. So when Stan Watson brought the group to me I listened to them. Stan asked, 'Can you do anything with them?' and I said I thought I could do the job. So I did a thing with the group called 'He Don't Really Love You'."

Stan Watson had fleetingly been a member of the Pittsburg doowop team the Del Vikings ("I left before they recorded") and the Delfonics were his protégées. He discovered the group — William Hart, his brother Wilbert, Randy Cain and Ritchie Daniels — when they were performing a local gig or two as the Four Gents. Hart, the Washington-born lead singer, comments: "We used to sing things by the Imperials and the Teenagers. People reckoned I sang in falsetto but it's my natural voice, it's always been high."

In fact William's high, soaring tenor was startlingly similar to that of Little Anthony Guordine, though a little less nasal than the tone of the Imperials' lead. Stan Watson took the group under his arm and changed their name. William explains, "I had a liking for the Orphonics but Stan was still hung up on that Del Vikings thing, so we settled on the Delfonics. That first session with Thom Bell was kinda strange, we were all feelin' our way, but I think it came out pretty good. But when Thom played it to Cameo they didn't like it. They were looking for Motown kinda dance sounds an' our thing was a slow harmony ballad. So they took our record an' sold it to another company called Moonshot Records, who were distributed by Calla."

Cameo showed a decided lack of judgement. For the disc's subtle, delicately orchestrated lilt with William Hart's voice drifting and soaring around timpani made it a record of true distinctiveness. William continues, "With better distribution 'He Don't Really Love You' could have been a big hit. But it *did* do well in Philadelphia and Cameo said, 'we'll take over from here' and the next record we did with Thom came out on Cameo."

Thom's talents, particularly as an arranger, were suddenly in demand, especially by Harthon Productions who were still chasing the Detroit shadow. They did it with considerable skill. The Larks, with Weldon McDougal's wife Irma singing lead, moved from doo-wop into churning Motown style rhythms and with McDougal handling production and Bell doing the charts, came up with numbers like "Rain" and "Groovin' At The Go-Go", leased to Los Angeles-based Tower Records and released under the name the Four Larks to avoid confusion with the L.A.-based Larks group. More successful for Harthon was Ruben Wright whose "I'm Walking Out On You", arranged by Luther Randolph and produced by Marvin Holtzman, became a Top 30 R&B hit for Capitol in May 1966. In July, the Volcanos compulsive dancer "Storm Warning" made the R&B charts.

The Volcanos featured the rich, virile lead voice of Gene Faith. Their disc — "It's Against The Laws Of Love", "Storm Warning", "Lady's Man", "The Loss Of Love" and "Help Wanted" — were far more important than their mainly regionalized sales might have suggested. As Weldon McDougal observes, "The Volcanos records were really like when Philly started developing their own thing. Up until then most up-tempo Philly records were based on the Detroit things. But Norman Harris, Ronnie Baker, Earl Young, all the

musicians who later became the MFSB band — were getting into their own thing by then. The vibes sound, the way the strings sweetened things without getting in the way of the beat, all the rhythm sounds started coming together on those records. The songs were pretty good too. Kenny and Leon wrote some of 'em. Gene Faith was a pretty good singer, he just never had the breaks. The Volcanos never got pushed by Jimmy Bishop like Barbara."

The Volcanos, like Barbara Mason, were on Bishop's Arctic Records. The brittle-voiced soulstress had done reasonably well since "Yes I'm Ready" — "Sad Sad Girl" hitting in 1965 and "I Need Love" in 1966 — without gaining another really big smash. Her discs under Bishop's supervision seemed to be becoming increasingly sugar-coated. But for all their problems, Arctic Records made out considerably better in the soul stakes than the majors. The Three Degrees' re-recording of the Chantels' "Look In My Eyes" was about the last chart record Swan had. Producer Richard Barrett comments: "Bernie Bennick at Swan was just callin' all the wrong shots. I discovered this really fine singer called Sheila Ferguson." She had previously recorded on Jamie. "After I'd cut her as a solo I put her with the Three Degrees. But all Bernie wanted me to do was copy the Motown sound. And people weren't buying copies . . . who needed 'em? The last couple of Three Degrees records, 'Tales Are True' and 'Love Of My Life', bombed out. Bernie had over-extended himself and the company just folded up. That was that, Swan were finished."

Although not yet bankrupt, by 1966 the giant Cameo had problems too. They had escalated their release schedule to an unprecedented eighty in a year but their success rate was shamefully low. After a flurry of British flops with the John Schroeder Orchestra, the Ivy League and even Pete Best, they tried a string of Nashville-recorded discs by New Orleans veteran Bobby Marchan. They were rich slices of Joe Tex-style Southern Soul, but didn't sell. The Marchan discs, from producer Buddy Killen, weren't the only recordings leased from outside Philly. Wailing blue-eyed soul (Evie Sands) and plastic punk-pop (3½) were also picked up by a Cameo exec-cum-singer who warbled as Neil Scott and wheeled and dealed as Neil Bogart. But Bogart did pick up one master that broke out — "96 Tears" by ? and the Mysterians. Originally released on the Pa-Go-Go label out of McAllen, Texas, the disc featured a hypnotic organ riff with Question Mark (a Texas Mexican, Rudy Martinez) hollering a lyric of compulsive banality.

American fanzine *Who Put The Bomp* described it like this: "Question Mark and the Mysterians fulfilled the dreams of every punk band — a national Number 1 hit (Number 2 in total sales for the year) — and with a home recording at that! On paper '96 Tears' is nothing; songs don't come any simpler. But the performance was perfect, and the record became an instant classic."

The immense sales of Question Mark helped make up for Chubby Checker's spectacular demise. His only Cameo hit in 1966, and his last, was a noisy Motown derivative "Hey You Little Boogaloo". Just as stereotyped and even less successful for Cameo were the ancient duo Billy And Lillie. They were now thankfully free from the vapid rhumba novelties once conceived for them by Bob Crewe, who'd quit Philly and throughout the sixties and seventies enjoyed a constant stream of production hits. But the weak soul that replaced them, "Nothing Moves" and "You Got Me By The Heart", failed to excite or sell.

Ironically, Cameo were being shown the art of selling soul by some of the labels on which they'd picked up distribution rights. The New York-based Calla hit big with J. J. Jackson, while Curtis Mayfield's Windy C and Mayfield labels had Chicago soul hits with the Five Stairsteps and the Fascinations respectively. One Cameo distributed label that didn't make it was Winchester Records. Billy Jackson recalls, "John Madara, Dave White and Leon Huff got together with the Tymes and formed a record company. The group did one thing 'These Foolish Things' — Leon played piano on that — but Winchester never got off the ground".

Another irritation for Cameo was that while they struggled with white singers performing essentially black styles — Johnny Maestro, the ex-lead singer of the multi-racial Crests harmony group; Bobby Paris, a quasi-soulman later to gain a little success on Tetragramaton Records; and even a group called Blue Eyed Soul featuring Billy Vera — ex-Cameo artist Len Barry continued to hit for Decca. Barry's "Somewhere" from West Side Story, "It's That Time Of The Year" and "I Struck It Rich" made the Hot 100.

But Len had problems. A music-biz executive who worked closely with the singer observes, "He couldn't really come up with anything as good as '1-2-3' and he couldn't really decide whether he wanted to be a soul singer, or a pop singer like the industry treated him. Also he had quite a hefty ego and annoyed a lot of industry people. A shame cause he's a great talent."

Another ex-Cameo act, the Orlons, were having a really bleak time of it. They cut a record with Calla, one side produced by Richard Rome and Jerry Williams and the reverse by Thom Bell and Billy Jackson. Then they had a couple on ABC accompanied by a band directed by Joe Renzetti. But their blaringly orchestrated soul didn't make it, the group disbanded and Rosetta Hightower split to England for a new career. Perhaps she should have checked out Gamble Records first. For by 1966 Kenny and Leon were really getting it on.

Phil Terry of the Intruders mused on the steady growth of Gamble. "We were Gamble Records. Our first Hot 100 record was 'United'. Then we had a thing called 'Devil With An Angel's Smile'. To a degree they were primitive compared with what we have today, but the sound was coming together. We were singing ballads with a little bit of the old doowop sound but with a kind of slickness in the production that the public wanted. But what really got the Intruders and Gamble away was Little Sonny's voice — his voice is unique. Little Sonny is the only one of his kind. Musically it doesn't make any sense, because his whole conception of vocal effort and the way he delivers it is just different. It sounds flat, but it's not really flat. It's that difference that made us successful."

Little Sonny Brown sounded flat all right. But his erratic pitching and bizarre bleating delivery only added to the effectiveness of the ballads which were the group's speciality. The intricate harmonies oohed and aahed around Sonny's broken-down vocals were partly influenced by the old doowop sound and partly by the all-powerful sound of Motown's gritty stars. But the arrangements and productions were different again. Kenny Gamble sees it like this: "We were feeling around, looking for own sound. We knew the kids weren't buying the old primitive kind of R&B anymore, they wanted something more sophisticated. So we were using strings, vibes, big orchestrations. But it took us some time to find the right blend. When we started we just used whatever session men were available. But by '67 we'd begun to settle on a regular bunch of musicians. They were the guys who were beginning to mean something in Philly, they were cutting hits over at Frank Virtue's . . ."

The musicians Kenny was talking about were Norman Harris, Roland and Karl Chambers, Ronnie Baker, Earl Young and a veteran pianist and arranger who in 1967 was to give the Virtue Studios possibly its two biggest-ever hits — even bigger than the Virtue-produced "Who Stole The Keeshka" by the Matys Brothers — a purported million-selling polka! Cruelly however, Bobby Martin was to receive no credit for his work on the two gold discs, as he explains: "There was an independent producer called Jesse James who used to book quite a lot of studio time at Virtue's. It was a real cheap operation, he used to find local singers, rehearse them on a couple of songs and take them down to Virtue's and do a session as quickly as possible. Then he'd hawk the tapes around and maybe get them placed with a label. He found this singer called Johnny Corland. He wasn't the world's greatest singer but then Jesse wasn't the world's greatest producer. Half the time Jesse would foul up the balance

Fantastic Johnny C (left) and producer Jesse James

so you could hardly hear the singer, stuff like that. Well, anyway, in '67 there was this big dance thing called the 'Funky Broadway'. So Jesse wrote a tune called 'Boogaloo Down Broadway' and Johnny went down and recorded it. It was just a little funky riff, but it seemed to work. Jesse got the record placed with Jamie (on their Phil L.A. of Soul subsidiary). They put it out as by Fantastic Johnny C and man, the record smashed. It sold a million, everyone was dancing to it. As soon as that started to happen Jesse did a thing with another local singer called Cliff Nobles. Cliff had done a little recording before. He was from Alabama."

Mobile, Alabama. Cliff was twenty-one when he moved to Philadelphia sporting an appropriate soul singer's background — gospel music — and anxious to break into something more lucrative. He got a break and landed a contract with Atlantic Records but his three releases during 1965 to 1966, "My Love Is Getting Stronger", "Let's Have A Good Time" and "Your Love Is All I Need", showed him to have a rich, meaty voice but no direction, and no sales potential. Atlantic dropped him and Jesse James picked him up. His first release on Phil L.A. of Soul, "The More I Do For You

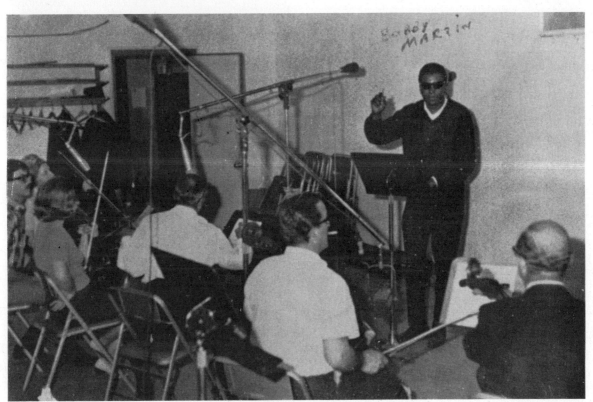

Bobby Martin and session men at the Virtue Studios, *ca* 1967

Baby" meant nothing. But he was about to get a break no singer had a right to expect.

"Jesse did this song on Cliff called 'Love Is Alright'. I did the arrangement, worked out the whole thing. When we had a take Frank asked Jesse about a flip-side. But Jesse just said, 'I don't give a shit man, use the backing track'. Then he left the studio and Frank and I worked out the flip-side. We brought the guitar up which was playing a repetitive figure and had a hypnotic kind of beat to it. When Jesse took the tape away and gave it to Jamie, they called the flip 'The Horse'."

The record was released under the name Cliff Nobles and Co., but the reaction to the jaunty bounce of "Love Is Alright" was cool. After a couple of months, however, a lady disc jockey in Tampa, Florida flipped the record over. The response was overwhelming and within seven days the repetitive, mindlessly churning "The Horse" had sold ten thousand in the city. It began to break coast to coast and Cliff Nobles, a non-instrument-playing singer, had a two-million-selling instrumental hit. The stroke of incredible luck was to turn sour, though.

Bobby Martin again: "I tried to get some bread from Jesse James for 'The Horse'. After all, the band were the guys who did it, Cliff and Jesse weren't even there! But he wouldn't give me anything. So we all swore we wouldn't work with that guy again. He made a lot of money of course, and he's started his own studio now, but he made a bad mistake 'cause instead of sticking with him we went with Gamble and Huff who dealt straight."

In the long term the failure to "deal straight" with the brilliant session men who'd so effortlessly presented him with a massive smash was to cost producer Jesse James infinitely more than he gained. In the short term, however, James and Phil L.A. of Soul flourished. The strangely named label had been started by Jamie/Guyden Records in 1967. The first things the company released were masters purchased from Henry Stone's Miami studios. But despite coming up with a soul hit first time out with Helene Smith's "A Woman Will Do Wrong", producers Willie Clarke and Clarence Reid were disappointed with the money they got for their efforts ("Jamie gave us peanuts man" notes Willie Clarke) and Phil L.A. of Soul turned to local product.

While Jesse James was (mis)using Martin, Baker, Young and co. to make million-selling hits, Johnny Styles, Luther Randolph and Weldon McDougal were booking as much Frank Virtue studio time for humbler projects. Johnny remembers, "We did sessions on lots of people. Like there was a blind guy, Lee Garrett. He later wrote songs for Motown. We tried leasing them

to labels or putting them out on our own label, Harthon. We made a few dollars on some of our records but really every penny we got we fed back into the company. 'Round '67 or so Eddie Holman began to work with us."

Eddie Holman was born in Norfolk, Virginia in 1946. He'd moved to New York and attended the Victoria School of Music. By the early sixties Eddie was singing around town ready for a record contract. His voice hadn't broken — "It never really did, I was always still able to reach the notes I could when I was twelve" — but Eddie's strict musical training ensured that his natural tenor voice possessed a strong, resonant tone pitched from the diaphragm and capable of near-operatic note holding. The teenage supper-club singer cut three records in New York, for Leopard and Ascot Records. Then he drifted down to Philly. "Harhon had this little office on Chestnut Street", says Weldon McDougal. "One day Eddie Holman came by and said he could write songs. He began writing some things for us. Eventually we thought it'd be good to record him. Jimmy Bishop didn't think he was shit but Harthon went in the studio and cut a thing called 'This Can't Be True'. It came out real well and we

Eddie Holman in London, 1974

were able to lease it to Cameo/Parkway Records."

"This Can't Be True" on Parkway was significant not just because it was Eddie's first hit record (Number 17 in the R&B chart) but because it was unarguably the archetype on which much of Philly's "sweet soul" sound was based, as well as being one of the most beautiful records of the era: a slow, haunting ballad with a spiralling chorus building falsetto patterns around the lyric of Eddie's realization of his lover's infidelity.

"The hit gave me a chance to play in other cities. I was still learning the business. And man, did I learn! But those Harthon guys were pretty good. You see the records I'd done in New York, they'd been recorded live, but the Harthon sessions were done piece by piece. We would start with the rhythm track, then we would add vocals, then we would add strings. Now you take all those things for granted, but back in '66 it was a new way to do things. Anyway, we had another hit with 'Am I A Loser From The Start' and I cut a couple more, "Somewhere Waits A Lonely Girl" and "Never Let Me Go", the old Johnny Ace standard. And I produced a couple of things for other acts. When I wasn't on the road I was 'round Frank Virtue's."

Jimmy Bishop was using Frank Virtue's too, though with increasing infrequency. "I got a little dissatisfied with Virtue's. So I began shopping around, using other places. I had a big hit with Barabara Mason in '67 called 'Oh How It Hurts'. That made the Top 60 pop. Arctic had other artists of course. We did a thing on Harold Melvin and the Blue Notes, 'What Can A Man Do', and a guy called Kenny Hamber; Kenny Gamble produced him. But Barbara was the singer Arctic was concentrating on."

And the Intruders were the singers Gamble was concentrating on. Over in a raggedy little office in the Schubert Building, Kenny and Leon worked nonstop trying to run a national record company by themselves. They got more Intruders hits with "Baby I'm Lonely" and "A Love That's Real", and began auditioning for new acts.

"We used to come in on Saturdays", remembers Leon, "and do auditions all day. We had a beat-up old piano in there and artists used to line up, waiting their turn. Man, it seemed we had the whole of Philadelphia up in that office."

Gamble Records signed an act or two – the ex-V-Tone doowoppers, the Cruisers, a girl group, the Baby Dolls and the oddly named Madman – and the producers looked around for some outside production work. A new Philadelphia independent, Crimson Records, had been formed in 1967 which offered them just that. Crimson signed up a mouldie oldie (Lee

Andrews), a great unknown (Damon Fox — whose shrieking "Black Widow Spider", amazingly produced by "sophisticated" Thom Bell, was one of the *soul*full-est flop flip sides ever) and a group of white street punks who wanted to be Philly's Mitch Ryder and the Detroit Wheels. The group were called the Soul Survivors. Kenny Gamble and Leon Huff got the job of writing/producing for them.

"We got together with the band, they had two singers Charlie and Richard Ingui. Now they'd just opened the expressway in Philadelphia and like everyone was talking about it. So we wrote this song called 'Expressway To Your Heart'. We did it with the group. It wasn't soul, it was like soul-influenced pop. It did good, it was a big, big, hit (Number 4 in the Hot 100). That really got us noticed as producers in the whole industry and not just the soul market. We had another reasonable hit on the group called 'Explosion To Your Soul'."

Neither the Soul Survivors in their original form nor Crimson Records were to last past 1968 and the group's irritatingly thin thump-thump sound was certianly no masterpiece of musicianship. But the Soul Survivors' success did show Gamble/Huff's flexibility, something which was to become one of their major assets.

While Kenny Gamble was drinking the wine of success with the Intruders and the Soul Survivors, his old songwriting partner Jerry Ross was giving Philly another look and reactivated his long defunct Heritage label. For almost two years Ross had been a regular producer for Mercury Records and had had a string of chart records with a mechanical clockwork pop group, Spanky and our Gang, and an equally mechanical, two black-five white band from Allantown, Pennsylvania, Jay and the Techniques, who specialized in gross pop-soul like "Apple, Peaches, Pumpkin Pie" and "Keep The Ball Rollin'". Now Jerry Ross decided to give Heritage another chance and a first Philly soul release was scheduled – but not one Jerry Ross had produced. Back in 1966 a group of Philadelphian teenagers calling themselves the Showstoppers were working a gig or two around town when they were spotted by Bruce Weinroth. The Showstoppers consisted of two sets of brothers, Timmy and Earl Smith and Alex and Laddie Burke, the latter younger brothers of the illustrious Solomon Burke. Bruce Weinroth took them to his father Irv who was forming an independent label, Showtime Records. A session was arranged and with Bruce producing, the group emerged with a piece of raucous, Motown style dance music called "Ain't Nothin' But A House Party". It was released in 1967 and sold well around

Ain't nothin' but a houseparty . . . the Showstoppers

Philly but Showtime had neither the expertise nor the resources to distribute the disc nationally.

Then a freak event occurred. The record was heard by Milton Samuel, the head of a small independent label, Beacon, who were just commencing operations in England. Samuel picked up the master, released the disc and by March 1968 "Houseparty" was a major British hit. The near incredulous Showstoppers were bundled off to Britain for a tour while Jerry Ross, encouraged by the U.K. success, picked up the disc for national American release on Heritage. It didn't do quite as well as Ross had hoped, making the 80s in the charts, and, as it turned out, the subsequent discs Ross produced on the group, like the inane "Eenie Meenie", flopped. Heritage Records continued to release discs until the early seventies.

While Heritage were beginning operations and Gamble were continuing theirs, Cameo clanked to a halt even though Thom Bell was still hard at work with the Delfonics. "After 'He Don't Really Love You' Cameo said they wanted in on the group. So I said

okay, I'll produce another one — that was 'You've Been Untrue' and that one came out on Cameo. And that one got a little bigger — but then they lost it again. And then a buzz started going around that the company had real problems."

Problems indeed — and not simply musical ones, though the lack of sales by pop artists like Jimmy Velvet, the British Walkers and Bob Seger didn't help. In mid-1967 Alfred Rosenthal sold Cameo/Parkway to Allan Klein, the wheeler-dealer lawyer who'd made millions of dollars and almost as many enemies with his managership of the Beatles. Shortly after the sale, the Securities Exchange Commission commenced investigations of alleged stock manipulations by Cameo. And, when Cameo issued a single by Ed McMahon which received an inordinate number of plugs on the *Tonight* show, the Federal Communications Commission took an interest in Cameo too. Klein blustered on for a few months but Cameo's general manager Harry Chipetz must have spent a fortune in aspirins.

Chipetz, once the owner of the legendary East Coast, Chips Distributors, and today the general manager of the Sigma Sound Studio, recalls: "Yeah, we had problems but that's the record business. But we had a hit or two as well. Like there was a guy I'd always respected. Bunny Sigler, he had a *smash* in '67."

Bunny himself explains how it came about: "John Madara took me to Cameo after the Decca thing petered out. The first song I recorded with Parkway was called 'Girl Don't Make Me Wait'." (This was eventually available on Bunny's Parkway album). "They couldn't find anyone else to sing it in that key, it was too high. But I could reach the notes with my natural voice. It sold pretty good, locally. Anyway, John had this idea for getting a very modern, Motown groove behind a couple of real old Shirley and Lee songs. And we worked out this arrangement with a drum intro and all. Of course 'Let The Good Times

Roll and Feel So Good' was a nice hit."

Nice indeed — Number 22 in the Hot 100 of June 1967. John Madara record some more tracks with Bunny for a *Let The Good Times Roll* album, and even did a couple of lectures at American colleges on the anatomy of a pop hit. The same hit 45 formula worked when the medley "Lovey Dovey and You're So Fine" hit the Hot 100 with Clyde McPhatter and Falcons' oldies placed in a sixties soul setting. But the next single, the stomping "Follow Your Heart", never made the charts.

For in early 1968 came the final Cameo bombshell. Three records, a quasi New Orleans jazzband the Village Stompers, a wind-em-up pop group the Ohio Express (who'd had a reasonable hit in '67 with "Beg, Borrow And Steal") and a blue-eyed soulstress Evie Sands, were Cameo's final releases. Allan Klein announced that the company were shutting up shop. As an ex-Cameo employee comments: "It wasn't a

Gamble and Huff's old reliables, the Intruders

big surprise really. Like the investigations into their
activities were the final thing, they were going under
before that. They'd just been calling the wrong shots
too often."

Klein absorbed Cameo's massive back catalogue of
masters into his ABKCO corporation, and the staff
scattered, Neil Bogart taking the Ohio Express and
starting a New York record company, Buddah Records,
who with producers Kasenetz and Katz hit really big
with a shrill new form of plastic punk rock dubbed
"bubblegum".

One thing Cameo didn't wind up was their 290
South Broad studio. It still remained open for hire to
any independent producer wanting recording facilities.
Like Gamble and Huff.

"In '68 we had our first monster smash with the
Intruders", Kenny muses, "our first million-seller.
That was 'Cowboys To Girls' and that really kind of
established everything we'd achieved so far. At last
people began to hear our records and say 'yeah, but it
don't have the same groove as Motown'. Now they
accepted what *we* were doing."

It's difficult to assess why "Cowboys" was quite
such a massive hit. But the rather silly lyric about pro-
gressing from childhood activities ("I remember when
we used to play shoot 'em up") to the wonderful world
of hearts and flowers romance was decidedly novel,
while the clever counterbalance between the mellowly
harmonic chanted title, the complex, almost fussy
orchestration and Little Sonny's eccentrically mean-
dering lead was as special a sound as heard in soul that
year. Other Intruders hits followed, "(Love Is Like A)
Baseball Game" and "Slow Drag". On these the
increase in the "depth" of sound, the precise way in
which strings offset rhythm, and the usage of electric
piano brilliantly played by Leon Huff showed that
Gamble and Huff had achieved their aim of creating
something different from the other major soul music
sounds. The precise balance of pungent rhythm, silken
strings and warm soulfulness showed the industry and
the world that a Philly soul sound had emerged.

Seven: Philly ascendant

With Cameo gone, Philadelphia was ready for some brave new ventures. Thom Bell was involved in the most successful. "When all the contracts were handed back to the artists at Cameo, Stan Watson said 'Listen I thing we should try again, but this time we should try with our own label.' So Stan formed Philly Groove Records and asked me if I'd go with them and I said sure . . . I had nothing else to do . . . Philly Groove Records was a little raggedy office on 52nd and Spruce Street. We didn't have any air-conditioning or anything . . . it was hot . . . Boy, I used to rehearse in my tee-shirt and my bermuda shorts and sandals . . . if it was a hundred outside it was a hundred and five inside."

Ritchie Daniels had left to go in the service and the Delfonics had become a trio when the group gathered in the Cameo studios on 5 March 1968 to record what was to be Thom Bell's third production/arrangement and the Delfonics' first hit. William Hart had written "La La Means I Love You" without particularly believing in it. Certainly, in its rudimentary form, the oddly old-fashioned song structure and sugary sentimentality of the lyric must have sounded pretty unpromising. But around William's beautifully mellow vocal, Thom wrapped a swirling cushion of strings and woodwinds to create a mood of anxious innocence.

Stan Watson tells the story: "When we put out 'La La' it got picked up by radio and pretty soon it was the hottest new record around. We couldn't handle a national distribution thing so Larry Uttal of Bell Records, who at that time picked up piles of soul labels for distribution, got in contact and Philly Groove

became a Bell-distributed label. Then it *really* started to happen. It was a coast to coast smash in soul and pop."

"I was tickled, once I realized what I'd done", laughs Thom Bell. "On it I played all the keyboards, and also played the timpanies. I play most of the instruments we couldn't afford to have anybody else play. The other musicians on the disc were the same guys we use now. Ronnie Baker on bass, Norman Harris on guitar, Roland Chambers on guitar, Earl Young on drums and Vince Montana on vibes."

With "La La" Tommy officially became Thom and with the nation's Number 1 song to his credit no one was arguing. Thom had somehow mixed an unlikely combination of pure falsetto lead harmony singing, tight rhythm section and lush quasi-classical orchestrations into a hit-making formula. And hit after hit followed. "I'm Sorry" made Number 42 in the Hot 100, "Break Your Promise" 35, and even a re-issued "He Don't Really Love You" gave the reactivated Moonshot label a small national hit. When the lush ballad sound became jaded, Mr. Bell gave the group an infectious dancer "Ready Or Not Here I Come". "The french horns and fugelhorns and things surprised some folks. In fact on all the sessions I do — even today — the instrumentation is strange. That's the classical training. I wrote songs with the Delfonics' William Hart. He wrote the lyrics and he was pretty good. I didn't do many sessions with Philly Groove and I cut the whole of each track at the same session. I carried forty pieces into the studio."

That was Cameo's old studio. But Joe Tarsia, the veteran engineer on so many of Cameo's old hits was about to offer an alternative. "Around the end of '68 I decided to make the gamble of my life. There was this studio over on North 12th Street where Cameo had done all their early sessions before they got their own studios on South Broad. It'd changed its name a lot. It was called Reco Arts, then Recording Arts, then Sound Plus. Tony Lewis, the guy who owned Sound Plus, was a musician but he didn't like people much and didn't like the hassles of a studio and wanted to get out. So I put up everything I had on the line, my house, my car, the shirt off my back. And I took over the studio. I changed the name to Sigma Sound. It was a real chance I was taking. But Thom Bell was coming off hits . . . and Kenny and Leon were doing real well with the Intruders. I had really fine relationships with those guys. I respected their creativity. I just hoped they'd give me a shot. They did, it worked out great and there was no lookin' back. Things really started happening for Kenny and Leon . . . and for Sigma, when the major labels started coming to them wanting them to produce their acts."

One of the first major label representatives to call on Messrs. Gamble and Huff in early 1968 was from Columbia Records. On the artist roster on Okeh, the corporation's black music subsidiary established right back in the twenties, was a R&B vocal group, the Vibrations. The veteran team, consisting of James Johnson (lead), Richard Owens (first tenor), Carl Fisher (second tenor), Dave Govan (baritone) and Don Bradley (bass), had a history of quite startling complexity. Originally formed in Los Angeles in 1956 as the Jayhawks, they'd had a R&B hit with "Stranded In The Jungle" for Leiber/ Stoller's Flash label before changing their name to the Vibrations and cutting doowops for Bet and Checker Records. In 1961 they had a hit on *American Bandstand* with a dance disc, "The Watusi", and while doing a little moonlighting under the name of the Marathons they recorded a big seller, "Peanut Butter", for Arvee Records. A lawsuit ensued over their contract violations and the Vibrations stayed with Chicago-based Checker. In 1964 they were in New York hitting with the Bert Berns production of "My Girl Sloopy" and the following year sold a few with "Misty", recorded in Chicago. But the Chicago soul producers weren't able to come up with another Vibrations hit and eventually Columbia decided to see what the new Philadelphia producers could do with the much travelled group.

The record Gamble and Huff wrote and produced for the Vibrations was one of the best dance discs of the era. "Love In Them There Hills" had everything: a wickedly infectious Leon Huff propelled rhythm, some superbly tongue-in-cheek lyrics — "bless my soul, mama you gotta go, there's love in them there hills" — and a rich vibrant lead from James Johnson. Disappointingly the record barely crawled into the Hot 100, though the quality of "Hills" encouraged a hit revival of the number in 1974 by the Pointer Sisters. Musically, however, it was an impressive start. Other major labels soon followed Columbia's lead. Mercury brought along Jerry Butler who, like the Vibrations, was based in Chicago and badly needed a big hit.

Born in Sunflower, Mississippi, Butler had grown up in Chicago. After singing in various gospel units, he formed a vocal group who began recording as the Impressions in 1958. Their first disc, "For Your Precious Love", was a brilliant fusion of old-style doowop and new style "soul" and over the next decade gained the status of "classic". Butler quickly left the Impressions, who eventually fell under the extremely successful leadership of Curtis Mayfield. His next step was a solo career with Chicago's Vee Jay Records. He was successful mainly because of brilliant airy songs and productions that Mayfield conceived for him, and hits like "He Will Break Your Heart" in 1960, "I'm A Telling You" in 1961 and "Just For You" in 1965 followed. But Vee Jay went bankrupt — another possible Beatles casualty — and Butler signed with Mercury Records. Then his problems started.

During the period when soul was just beginning to develop, Jerry's rich, vibrant baritone voice was the perfect compromise for people who wanted something more virile and emotionally interpretive than drooling doowop singers but felt uncomfortable with the screeching exhortations of Wilson Pickett or James Brown. Because Jerry's mellow tone also appealed to the Billy Eckstine end of the supper-club market, he frequently recorded creaking show-biz schmalz and in that way skilfully hedged his bets for quite a while. By the mid-sixties, however, the singer's lack of a single direction, coupled with his decidedly old-style image, meant that he was not the red-hot property Mercury had hoped for. They farmed the soulful crooner out to various producers in various cities trying to find a formula to make him big. Although they got a little chart action, the noisy, often over-dramatic productions seemed at odds with the subtle qualities of Jerry's poignant vocal style. Mercury had just about given up hope when they approached Gamble and Huff. Kenny Gamble comments: "Jerry was a great singer. But he was cold, man. The guy I used to write with, Jerry Ross, had written a fairish kinda hit on him in '67 but guys like Jimmy Wisner and Joe Renzetti

Chicago soulman Jerry Butler

Bobby Hebb . . . six years on from "Sunny"

weren't really getting anywhere with him. We sat down with Jerry and we wrote some songs together. Then Bobby Martin did the charts, we took our regular guys over to Sigma Sound and we gave the guy hits, real hits man."

"Never Gonna Give You Up", "Hey Western Union Man", "Are You Happy" all smashed in 1968 and *The Ice Man Cometh* and *Ice On Ice* became two of the biggest soul albums of the year. With a superb blend of wistful orchestration, slinky vocal back-up and vibes and strings encouraging but never enveloping his soulfully mellow voice, Jerry Butler's "new" sound was truly hypnotic.

Mercury/Philips weren't so successful when they brought Gamble and Huff the singer Bobby Hebb, languishing after his classic hit "Sunny" in 1966. However, Mercury weren't the only label coming to the

production duo. Atlantic Records also had a project for them.

In 1967 a Houston-based soul band called Archie Bell and the Drells had a cut a record produced by their disc jockey manager, Skipper Lee Frazier. It was sent to Atlantic in New York who released it, but nothing happened. Just when it was at the point of being forgotten, the flip-side, a funky dance track of maddening repetition called "Tighten Up", took off and over the next few months went on to sell close to four million. By then, however, the group's leader, Archie Bell, was in the Army earning $126 a week instead of the $30,000 he would have received on the road. Bell was still stationed in Germany when he and his Drells — Lee Bell, Willie Parnell and Jamie Wise — got together with Gamble and Huff. The resulting disc was "I Can't Stop Dancing" and while it didn't sell on the scale of "Tighten Up", it did pass the million mark and its infectious joy was infinitely better in quality than the crude drive of their first effort. When they followed up with a double-sided hit, "Do The Choo Choo"/"Love Will Rain On You", Atlantic were very impressed with the guys from Philly.

"Yeah, '68 was a good year", laughs Kenny. "One of my disappointments, however, was that I couldn't get a hit on my wife". Kenny Gamble's lady is none other than Dee Dee Sharp. Kenny and Dee had married in 1967 and, after Kenny took over her production, the soulstress, having mashed her last potato, sang some poignant, bluesy soul. "My Best Friend's Man" was leased to Atco but no promotion meant no sales, so Kenny and Leon transferred her to Gamble

Records. In 1968 Dee Dee cut a powerful dance item, "What Kind Of Lady", but somehow radio play again escaped her.

During that year radio play was always a certainty for Arctic Records. Dee jay Jimmy Bishop continued to spin Barbara Mason's wistful ditties and the label also made the R&B charts with a couple of new acts. One of them was Della Humphrey, a soulstress with a brittle vocal style pitched between Barbara Mason and the up and coming Betty Wright. Della (like Betty) was recorded in Miami under producers Clarence Reid and Willie Clarke who then leased the tapes of her Hot 100 hit, "Don't Make The Good Girls Go Bad", to Arctic. Ironically, when Della recorded follow-ups in Philly with Jimmy Bishop and Bobby Martin she flopped. Another soul hit for Arctic were the Ambassadors, the veteran ex-gospel team. The subtle mixture of sweet harmonizing and the fiery twin leads of Curley Johnson and Bobby Todd deserved more than their one success, "I Really Love You."

Arctic and Philly Groove and Gamble weren't the only labels entering the charts with Philadelphia soul in 1968. Jamie's Phil L.A. of Soul label also did. Fantastic Johnny C hit with "Got What You Need" and "Hitch It To The Horse" while Cliff Nobles and Co. made the charts with "Switch It On". Anxious to cash in on "The Horse", Nobles went out on the road with Bobby Tucker (guitar), Benny Williams (bass) and Tommy Soul (drums), but his appeal quickly faded. Producer Jesse James, the man who made the real killing from "The Horse", pursued the dancing public's taste for repetitive ephemera and the James Boys took "The Mule" backed with "The Horse" into the charts.

More melodic if only marginally more original than the funk excesses of Jesse James were the Formations, a new vocal group who scored a Hot 100 hit for MGM. Victor Drayton tells their story: "Jerry Akines and me were solo artists. We didn't do any recording, we just did local club things while we were at school. Then Jerry and I formed a group with Reginald Turner and Ernie Brooks. First we called ourselves the Extremes and then in '65 Johnny Bellmon came into the group and we called ourselves the Formations. We ventured out to Detroit to try and make a record but it didn't work out. Then Thom Bell did a couple of demos with us at Cameo/Parkway. But we didn't finally get into recording until '68 when we went to New York and John Madara and Dave White produced us on a song Leon Huff and Jerry Akines had written called 'At The Top Of The Stairs'. Vince Montana — now MFSB's vibes player — was on it. It did okay. It made the eighties in the chart."

When "At The Top Of The Stairs" was released its gentle melodic lilt made up for the distinctly Motown-style orchestration. And even though a follow-up recorded in New York failed, more would be heard in time from Messrs. Akines, Bellmon and company.

Over at the Virtue Studio, Harthon Productions struggled on. Producer Johnny Styles chuckles wryly, remembering the tough competition. "Once the Philly thing really got under way the musicians we had been using almost exclusively were being used by everyone . . . Gamble, Philly Groove . . . We had to line up and wait our turn. Harthon kept with Eddie Holman. When Cameo closed down we did a record on him called 'I'm Not Gonna Give Up' and we got the master with Bell Records. But they lost it. Eddie got a bit disillusioned."

So did Weldon McDougal. Fed up with the bad deals that had gone down in the past, he left his production job at Harthon for a while to work as a promotion man for Motown Records. Johnny Styles and Luther Randolph continued to book time at Virtue's, but thoughts of the big-time suddenly seemed a little pie in the sky. "We had a chance to sign Aretha Franklin back in '66", Johnny recalls. "She came to us when she'd split from Columbia. It would've taken all of our bread but we coulda done it. But we turned her down and she went to Atlantic and became a superstar. We recorded a singer called Lois Lane instead of Aretha. She had a record on Wand and it sold about five copies . . ." One can only wonder what Gamble and Huff or Thom Bell would have done if they'd had a chance to work with Aretha.

Over at Philly Groove Mr. Bell and the Delfonics continued to hit. "You Got Yours And I'll Get Mine" was followed by "Didn't I (Blow Your Mind This Time)", the group's first recording at Sigma and a superb departure from the usual ballad formula with a mid-tempo timpani beat and an eat-at-you falsetto chorus, and "Trying To Make A Fool Of Me". As group member William Hart says, "Any way you look at it, the string of hits we had with Thom was pretty great. A lot of people were after our sound . . . then Thom left and Stan Watson took over as producer."

Talking about his departure from Philly Groove, Thom Bell explains: "The Delfonics had a hit with everything I did on them. They had over ten hits. But my mind kept on wanting to lead me somewhere else and where your mind leads your body is going to go. I knew that I had done as much as I could with the Delfonics. So I decided to leave Philly Groove. But I didn't get into no fisticuffs thing with Stan Watson."

Bell moved in with Gamble and Huff. "Gamble asked me if I wanted to come down there with Leon

Huff. I said well, I don't mind, man — I'd known them a long time and they were honest fellows. I said I'd give it a try. At that particular time they were doing independent work for big labels and they were also cutting the Intruders for their own label. They had about three arrangers there but they were looking for one that gave them a different kind of sound. So when I came there the first thing I started doing with them was the Jerry Butler stuff: 'Only The Strong Survive', 'Western Union Man', things like that. I became their arranger down there for about two years . . . Every artist that we had always came to Philadelphia because we were trying to break the Philadelphia scene, the musicians, the Sigma Sound Studios. I really dug working with Jerry Butler."

Atlantic Records, impressed with Jerry Butler's phenomenal chart success, brought more of their artists to Gamble, Huff and Bell. Not just black American ones. Dusty Springfield came all the way over from London. "We had a ball working with that lady on 'Brand New Me'," Thom recalls. "In fact I wrote a hit song for Dusty. That's when Linda Creed and I came into it. That was a tune called 'Free Girl' and it did fairly well — Top 70 I think. We were tickled pink. Again, that was the first time we'd ever written together. Linda was a singer on Philly Groove Records, but she wasn't really that hot. She never had a record out. We just took her in the studio one time and tried her but it didn't really sound very good. For some reason she sang but she didn't quite sing well enough. There are singers and there are *singers*."

Linda, like Dusty, is white. Bell continues, "Linda's a beautiful girl, a French Jew. She was born in the States, but her father's people are from France. One day she had a bright idea of writing songs . . . no, she wrote poetry. Now I wasn't really into the poetry thing. So I said 'can you write songs?' And she says 'I don't know, I never tried'. So I said I'll tell you what I'll do. I'll write a melody and let's hear you put the lyrics to it. She said okay. We've been doing it ever since. I'm writing melodies and she's putting lyrics to them. I write the melodies and the sing-a-long, the chorus, of the song. I tell her what I want the song to be about. I do that eighty-five percent of the time, then sometimes I just write the melody and she comes up with the chorus. After 'Free Girl' Gamble/Huff put her on the staff."

In addition to Dusty Springfield, G&H continued to supply Atlantic with hits on Archie Bell and the Drells. In 1969, shortly after their leader had finally freed himself from the unwelcome attention of Uncle Sam the group cut one of Philadelphia's greatest masterpieces. "(There's Gonna Be A) Showdown"

wasn't, as the title might suggest, another contribution to the growing catalogue of black "social awareness" songs. In standard Drells tradition, it was a call to get up on the floor and dance, and a call which has rarely been bettered. After an opening organ chord, Archie boasts, "They tell me you're pretty fast on your feet, so I want you to meet me down the dancehall on Market Street"; then smack snap smack — a drum beat so crisp it positively leaps with energy — while the group joyously sings the airy wistful line, "Hey-hey, gonna be a showdown". Two thirds of the way through comes the confrontation which the song is all about:

> You've gotta reputation here for the fastest man alive
> So I'm gonna see how good you are when I count to five
> One (smack) Uh man, you're outa step
> Two (smack smack) You can do better than that
> Three (smack smack smack) Man, will you move aside
> Four (smack smack smack smack) And let me get out there and do my jive.

The image of the super slick cat encircled by his buddies for the dance-step showdown of the year remains one of the most vivid in sixties popular music.

"We really were getting somewhere with out independent productions", Kenny muses. "And that was kinda ironic. It was easier to get a hit for an artist like Archie Bell on Atlantic or Peaches and Herb on Columbia than to get a really big record on the Intruders. We were still doing okay with the group." ("Sad Girl" made Number 47 in the pop chart in August 1969.) "But they weren't as big as we wanted them to be. And the other acts we signed were getting lost." Two groups who couldn't break through nationally were Frank Beverley and the Butlers, a tremendously popular soul band around the Philadelphia club scene, and the Panic Buttons, a blue-eyed instrumental group whose "O Wow" was picked up from the tiny Chalom label. "We needed more marketing and merchandising — we were getting hit singles but not albums. Also Gamble had run into the problems that every independent runs into over collections and bad debts. You really need a staff of people and we didn't have a staff to operate Gamble Records for us, it was a very small operation.

"We wanted to try and hook up with a major outfit and we had known Leonard Chess for quite a long time. That was right when Chess merged with GRT and they were expanding . . . looking for producers and more material. So we started Neptune Records." Neptune Records displayed the fully developed Philly

Archie Bell and the Drells

sound in all its pungently rhythmic glory — not to mention an artist roster that today is the backbone of Philadelphia International.

The first Neptune release, in March 1969, was "One Night Affair" by the O'Jays. "When we met Kenny and Leon", recalls the group's Eddie Levert, "we'd been on the brink of makin' it for so long we should have been called the Almosts. We did a show at the Apollo Theater in Harlem and we were on the same bill as the Intruders — they were doin' 'Cowboys To Girls'. Gamble and Huff came up to see the show and got interested in us. We were on Bell Records at the time but that was just the latest in a line of companies who'd promised us the world and given us a parking lot. So

we invited Kenny and Leon to Cleveland 'cause we were doing a show at Akron, Ohio which is about thirty miles from Cleveland. They came to see us and then we sat down and talked business. We'd waited a long time to meet guys like them."

The O'Jays had indeed been patient. Back in 1958 in Canton, Ohio, Eddie Levert and Walter Williams, who'd sang gospel together, teamed up with William Powell, Bobby Massey and Bill Isles and, as the Triumphs, began singing around private parties and the local YMCA. William Powell commented on those days in the August 1, 1974 issue of *Rolling Stone* magazine: "Back then a group of us would just start off singing walkin' home from school, y'know, but now they're taking up the bass or the guitar or something, which is better. The singin' part will come easier if they got any kind of background like goin' to church to know how to sing harmony."

By 1961 the group had been renamed the Mascots by Sid Nathan at King Records, but the eight sides the group recorded, including such gems as "Do The Wiggle", did very badly. A Cleveland disc jockey, Eddie O'Jay, began to help them get bookings for smallish shows in and around Cleveland and took them to a then obscure Detroit producer Don Davis, who later found fame with Johnnie Taylor and the Dramatics. They cut "Miracles" on Dayco, then leased to Apollo. O'Jay also gave them yet another new name — his own. The group "worked the clubs", polishing their sound as well as the cuffs and elbows of their suits. They were suffering from a serious bout of stagnation when they met up with H. B. Barnum, a West Coast singer/pianist/producer. H. B. took them to Los Angeles to cut a record and work as back-up musicians behind Lou Rawls and Jimmy Norman for Barnum's Little Star label. Then H. B. was able to get the group with a major, Imperial Records. A reflective understated ballad backed by a dramatic overstated accompaniment gave the O'Jays a small hit, "Lonely Drifter". The group recorded steadily for Imperial and in 1965 hit with a version of the New Orleans standard "Lipstick Traces", a noisy histrionic "Let It All Out" and a really fine ballad, "Stand In For Love" complete with Tony Williams-like hiccough from Eddie.

The following year, however, was a bad one. Imperial was bought out by the Liberty conglomerate which didn't seem interested in a group that, at the whims of Barnum or Nick De Caro, were buried in echo and often sounded more like the Drifters of the early sixties than the O'Jays of today. Their record for Minit, "Working On Your Case" had virtually no impact and in August 1966 Bill Isles left the group. The disgruntled O'Jays moved back to Cleveland.

In 1967, just as the inactive quartet was prepared to give up, a couple of Cleveland businessmen, Jules Berger and Leo Frank, offered them the chance of a "come-back" appearance. Leo's Casino organized a programme headlined by Chuck Jackson — but it was the O'Jays who stole the whole show. A business "alliance" was formed with Jules and Leo providing the financial backing and Bobby Massey, their long-time business manager, providing the know-how. The resulting company, Prime Enterprises, helped the O'Jays break clean from Liberty/Minit and, when the time came, got them a new contract.

The group had been playing the Apollo in Harlem

when disc jockey Rocky Gee persuaded them to cut some demonstration records with producer Richard King. Gee took the results to Larry Uttal of Bell Records who liked them, signed them and astutely placed them with arranger Richard Tee and producer George Kerr, one-time Motown producer who later found success with Stang/All Platinum Records. With a subtle blend of rhythm and harmony and with some really memorable ballads by the Poindexter Brothers, and Kerr himself, Bell got three fairish soul hits with the group, "I'll Be Sweeter Tomorrow", "The Choice" and "Look Over Your Shoulder". A Bell album came out, but dubbed-on audience noise ruined it and when the next couple of Bell singles didn't do very well, the O'Jays seemed to be at the bottom again.

Then Gamble and Huff moved in. "One Night Affair" was a masterpiece of highly charged energy, with Leon Huff on electric piano dominating a rolling accompaniment to Eddie Levert's wheezingly soulful voice wailing his need for a one-night stand. As the singer admits, "We *knew* Gamble and Huff were great after that record". The disc did well enough in the pop charts, reaching Number 68, to establish Neptune as an ongoing company.

It's next release was by the Corner Boys. The group's Victor Drayton tells the story: "We didn't get too far as the Formations and Ernie Brooks left the

The Formations (also known as Silent Majority, the Corner Boys and Hot Ice)

group. But the other guys — me, Jerry Akines, Johnny Bellmon and Reginald Turner — decided to stick together as a songwriting team. We did a few things that got recorded. Then we signed with Gamble and Huff and did a record with them. We called ourselves the Corner Boys and the song was 'Gang War (Don't Make Sense)'. It was about all the gang wars that have been goin' on in Philly. Kids fighting, maiming, killing each other for no real reason." The record had a good backing track as well, used as the flip and called 'Take It Easy Soul Brother'. " 'Gang War' just about sneaked into the soul charts. But it was a great record."

Other great Neptune releases followed at regular intervals throughout 1969. Apart from a fine Linda Jones disc leased from George Kerr, all are classic examples of distinctive Philly soul with powerhouse piano, crackling drums, evil bass lines, sympathetic strings and rich, soulful vocals. Records issued that year included the O'Jays' compulsive dance number, "Branded Bad"; Bunny Sigler's raucous angry whoop-up, "Great Big Liar"; the Indigos' O'Jays-styled "Taboo"; a smokily soulful duet by Bunny (Sigler) and Cindy (Scott) called "We're Only Human"/ "Didn't Take Long (For The Word To Get Around)", a double-sided "concept" single; a fiery revival of "Expressway to Your Heart" by the Vibrations who had been plucked from an indifferent Columbia; and a Christmas record, "(Christmas Ain't Christmas, New Years Ain't New Years) Without The One You Love" by the O'Jays. Yet none of these Gamble/Huff classics sold as well for Neptune as a gimmicky one-off hit for United Artists which featured most of Philly's regular session musicians.

Frank Virtue recalls how "Keem-O-Sabe" became a top 20 hit for Electric Indian. "Bernie Bennick had this idea for a sitar instrumental. It was around the time all the kids were into that Indian stuff. So he got together a bunch of musicians, a lot of the guys who're in MFSB now, and they put down this sitar thing called 'Keem-O-Sabe'. It was like funky Indian music. They leased the tape to United Artists Records. It was a gimmick but it was a stone smash."

United Artists weren't the only major entertainment corporation to see a little Philly paydirt. ABC picked up on Eddie Holman and teamed him with Philadelphian arranger/ producer Peter DeAngelis. It seemed an unlikely combination — stratospheric falsetto wailer joining forces with an apparently bland old symphonian who specialized in "easy listening" and comedy novelties such as Guy Marks' 1968 hit for ABC, "Loving You Has Made Me Bananas". But the teaming worked — artistically and commercially. DeAngelis took a good part of the Philadelphia Orches-

tra into the Virtue Studios to put down lush tracks for a song Eddie had written (though for contractual reasons it was credited to his wife Sheila) called "I Love You". The mixture of expressive, impassioned singing with only hints of falsetto, billowing strings arranged around the favourite instrument of "classical soul" — a french horn — and a beautifully simple lyric ("I love you, what more can I say") made the disc's release on ABC records a successful one.

Eddie continues the story: "After that was a hit I did an album called *I Love You*. One of the things I recorded was a song Ruby and the Romantics had cut called 'Hey There Lonely Boy'. We changed it around a little and when everyone heard it they freaked out — they said 'man that's a smash'. And it was!"

The beautiful lilt of "Hey There Lonely Girl" made it Eddie's biggest ever hit and it reached Number 4 in the soul charts in December 1969. ABC then pulled two more successful 45s from his superb album: a stratospheric version of the Skyliners' oldie, "Since I Don't Have You", and a lovely Holman composition, "Don't Stop Now". Then it suddenly began to appear that DeAngelis didn't realize the secret of the success formula onto which he had stumbled. After his first fusions of lushness and soul, DeAngelis' next efforts took Eddie too far into the barren wastes of easy listening. "Kathy Called" was a smallish hit in November 1970 but that was due solely to the memorable melody and not to the inappropriately syrupy accompaniment. DeAngelis was beginning to uncover the problem which another Philadelphia record producer, Billy Jackson, was also discovering: putting black singers in front of massive unwieldy orchestras could as easily lead to musical emasculation as to the production of a hybrid "symphonic soul" form.

Billy Jackson still worked first and foremost with the Tymes. In 1967 he had taken them to MGM, where they had two flops, "Touch Of Baby" and "Pretend". The following year he moved them to Columbia Records and there Jackson at last came to terms with the fact that the record world didn't really need another Mills Brothers and he told the Tymes to play down the finger snapping, on records at least, and get moving with "soul". A Motown-style dance arrangement was conceived for the veteran group though it was peculiarly ironic that the song George Williams and his fellow Tymes warbled across the stomping beat was the histrionic standard from *Funny Girl*, "People". Still it was a hit of sorts — big enough, anyway so that Jackson couldn't resist saddling the group with a whole album of standards.

Billy Jackson then landed a job as a staff producer with Columbia in New York and was assigned to the duo Peaches and Herb. Peaches was Francine Barker, though Marlene Mack replaced her for a short spell. Herb was Herb Fame. Their vapid twee harmonies, which earned them the title "Sweethearts of Soul" made them the direct musical descendents of Mickey and Sylvia — and in fact Peaches and Herb even hit in 1967 with a re-recording of "Love Is Strange".

Peaches and Herb — the sweethearts of soul

However, Jackson's sound for the couple was just plain dull. (In fairness, Gamble, Huff and Bell had also failed to make Peaches and Herb musically interesting, even though they consistently hit on Columbia's Date subsidiary from 1966 through 1970.) In fact, Jackson's production work was the epitome of blandness, even when he worked with a promising artist like Ronnie Dyson. Born in Washington and raised in Brooklyn, Dyson was a warm-voiced singer who had been plucked from the cast of *Hair*. Jackson seemed unable to stop the massive New York orchestras who accompanied Dyson on such hits as "(If You Let Me Make Love To You Then) Why Can't I Touch You", "I Don't Wanna Cry" and "When You Get Right Down To It" from sounding noisily fussy and hopelessly overblown. Neither the producer nor the New York musicians seemed to possess the deft Philly touch.

Such deftness continued to give Neptune a continual stream of often brilliant soul discs throughout the first half of 1970. The Vibrations recorded their happily bubbling "Smoke Signals". Bunny Sigler had

the expressively moody "Where Do The Lonely Go". And the O'Jays released one of their finest ever, "Looky Looky (Look At Me Girl)" with an incredible piano-driven beat featuring Leon Huff spiralling off into lurching finger-flying runs like a drunken bar-room boogieman. In addition Neptune issued discs by the Three Degrees and Billy Paul.

Richard Barrett had done a pretty impressive job of managing and producing the Three Degrees after the fall of Swan Records. Fayette Pinkney recalls: "Richard took us to Boston to build up our stage work. After a while we were getting bookings in prestige venues and worked our way up to the largest night-club in Boston." As the girls' supper-club bookings grew the group, now firmly settled as Fayette Pinckney, Sheila Ferguson and Valerie Thompson, signed with Warner Bros. Records. The stay (one single called "Contact") was brief, as was their stay with Metromedia, where they cut "The Feeling Of Love" among other flaccid recordings.

"I wasn't happy with the way record companies were handling the group", continues Richard Barrett. "The sessions I was producing weren't very satisfying. Well, by '69 Gamble and Huff had really blown the Philly thing wide open. Everyone was interested in them — it was like my vision of what Philly could become was really coming true. So I thought it'd be nice if we teamed up."

"They saw us at the Latin Casino in New Jersey", says Sheila Ferguson, picking up the story. "And they liked us. We did one track, just the one track. They released it and we didn't even know they were going to put it out — a deal was going to be negotiated. But by the time it came out we had already signed with Roulette in New York." As it turned out, the group's failure to sign with Neptune wasn't a serious lapse.

Another act whose first Neptune release appeared in the early months of 1970 had been recording with Gamble/Huff for a while. Kenny Gamble describes how he first produced Paul Williams, otherwise known as Billy Paul. "In '67 I got talking to Billy about coming to Gamble Records. Billy had gone and recorded a few things on himself and he brought them to me. I told him he wanted three more sides to make an album. So we went in the studios and cut three things and we put out the album *Feelin' Good At The Cadillac Club*." The LP featured show-biz standards sung with a tight jazz trio. But then, jazz was originally Billy Paul's musical direction.

"Jazz music was where my head was for a long, long time", says Mr Paul. "My mother used to play 78s of all the jazz greats and I grew up in north Philly with guys like Lee Morgan, McCoy Tyner, Sam Dockery

Billy Paul

and a very great musician, John Coltrane. While I was still a kid I listened to people like Nat Cole to learn phrasing . . . you see, I was always singing, like I was doin' radio broadcasts when I was twelve. I went to the West Philadelphia Music School and the Granoff Music School. When I was sixteen I played the Club Harlem in Philly and I was on the same bill as Charlie Parker. He died later that year (1955). I was there with him for a week and I learned what it would normally take two years to pick up. Bird told me if I kept struggling I'd go a long way and I've never forgotten his words."

Billy formed a trio which included Sam Dockery on piano and Buster Williams on bass. With jazz giant Tadd Dameron he then cut his first record, "Why Am I", for Jubilee before being drafted. On his release from the army he made a recording for the New

Dawn label and then, surprisingly, sang for a while with the Blue Notes in early 1961. "Me and Harold Melvin had been friends for years, so when one of his fellows got sick I stepped in. But I'm kind of an individual singer, so eventually I left to continue as a soloist."

Throughout the sixties Paul played the jazz clubs, but when he finally got to record his first album for Gamble, he found that there wasn't a very big market for sophisticated finger-snapping jazz renditions of "On A Clear Day", particularly with Gamble Records' difficulties in distributing albums. "We decided to do something with a more up-to-date sound, with more musicians . . . something that would venture a bit into R&B but without me losing my sound. We spent a lot of time working it out and then we came up with the album called *Ebony Woman* which came out on Neptune. It was a chart album and they pulled a single from it, 'Mrs. Robinson'. But then the Neptune thing just folded up. . ."

Kenny Gamble succinctly sums up how Neptune dissolved in July 1970. "Unfortunately Len passed away three or four months after we had made the deal with Chess. And then it seemed that everything went haywire . . . they had to re-group Chess Records and GRT and like we were pushed to the side . . . it was an unfortunate thing for us . . . and as it turned out, an unfortunate thing for them."

In retrospect, of course, the massive GRT corporation blundered as badly as the Decca executive who said no to the Beatles. GRT had taken over an independent label and proceeded to get rid of what was transparently its most valuable asset.

Kenny and Leon, with no money to pay off their disgruntled artists had to let some of them go. But as Leon Huff says philosophically, "We knew there'd come a time when GRT would realize what they'd blown . . . so we just regrouped with what we had already. That was the Intruders. We had three hits on them in '70; 'Tender Was The Love We Knew', 'When We Get Married' — that was the old Dreamlovers' thing — and 'This Is My Love Song'. They kept our hand in, so to speak. Things went a little haywire after that Neptune thing. We knew we could give artists hits if they'd have a little confidence in us . . . like Jerry Butler stopped working with us and he slumped right away . . ."

In an interview in the April 2—15, 1971 issue of *Blues and Soul* Bill Yale Matheson, Jerry Butler's manager, was quoted as saying: "They (Gamble and Huff) wanted Mercury to pay them more for producing Jerry's recording sessions. Mercury agreed to the first raise since the partnership had been very successful for all concerned. But Gamble and Huff came back again and asked for another raise and Mercury refused." Whatever the situation, Jerry's production for himself lacked much of the dynamic duo's magic and a lot of their sales power. And Archie Bell and the Drells weren't quite the same monster sellers when Atlantic passed them over to producer Dave Crawford.

While Gamble and Huff were "regrouping" their faithful, arrangers Bobby Martin and Thom Bell were having a little production success with a new act, the Intrigues. The trio's sound was falsetto, harmonic and rather derivative, but the happily bubbling "In A Moment" in 1969 and the lushly mellow "The Language Of Love" in 1970 were soul chart records in between Akines, Bellmon, Drayton, Turner penned flops like "I'm Gonna Love You" and "Just A Little

Bit More". When the Intrigues faded, so did their label, Yew Records.

Yew weren't the only new Philadelphia label as the seventies began. Jerry Ross started Colossus Records, though most of its material was recorded in the studios of New York, and a third company, Vent, were bubbling around the soul charts. Vent, like Yew, were more or less a one-act label with a hot group called the Ethics.

Ronald Presson, otherwise known as Tyson, was the lead singer of the Ethics, now known as Love Committee. "We started just like all the other groups started, I guess, singing around town, going for auditions with record companies — we sang for Richard Barrett at Swan, people like that. But there were so many groups then with that high tenor sound, so many groups . . . Finally I met this guy called Thaddeus Wells who wasn't really in the business but who had a group called the Philadelphians. He hooked up with us and we got a record contract through him. We went with this company called Vent Records, run by Ed Kaslow and Butterball, the disc jockey. Around '69 we began recording. We did our things at Sigma Sound with all the musicians who are famous now — Norman Harris, Bobby Martin — we did mainly ballads: "Think About Tomorrow", "Farewell", "Tell Me", "Standing In The Darkness". A couple of them made the charts." ("Farewell" and "Tell Me".) "But nothing too big. Little labels weren't makin' it like in the old days; only big companies had the bread to get big hits."

Jimmy Bishop had made the same observation and wound up his Arctic label. Bishop explains: "After taking Barbara Mason off the Arctic label, I was offered this deal with a new label for Barbara that had a hook-up with motion pictures. So that was the direction we took. But it didn't work out for the best. We hoped that she would end up doing a picture with them but she ended up doing one with some other people — she did a soundtrack. The film was called *The Last Cowboy*."

The only seller Barbara experienced with National General Records was in fact a rather pointless version of Bacharach's "Raindrops Keep Falling On My Head" from an album that proved once again that the line between sweet soul and string-filled vapidity was infinitesimally fine. At the beginning of 1971 a Sigma-recorded girl trio from Washington were to emphasize the point further. Sheila Young, Barbara Gilliam and Val Williams called themselves the Passionettes until they met disc jockey Carl Henson. Henson changed their name to Fuzz, rehearsed the trio in a studio in south-east Washington and in late 1970 travelled with

the group to Sigma Sound to record a song Sheila had written called "I Love You For All Seasons".

Fuzz sang the wistful song in cloying three-part harmony and with layers of violins swirling fussily around the twee sound, the disc relied on the prettiness of the melody for its effect. When Nate McCalla released it on his Calla label it became a massive hit, staying in the charts for over three months. Joe Tate was called in to produce a whole album for the group, an ambitious "concept" project with romantic monologues and huge dramatic orchestrations. Despite minor hits with "Like An Open Door" and a skipping, hand-clapping "I'm So Glad", Fuzz quickly disintegrated.

In 1971 another group broke through with a sweetly delicate sound conceived in the studios of Philadelphia. Unlike Fuzz, the Stylistics had the durability and the unquestionable talent to benefit fully from their achievement of chart status. The group had waited a long time for success to come, though not

always as the Stylistics. From 1965 to 1968 the Monarchs and the Percussions played the tiny Philly clubs and when both groups disbanded for lack of any big breaks, a hybrid sprang up. From the Monarchs came Russell Thompkins Jr., Airron Love and James Smith and from the Percussions, Herbie Murrell and James Dunn. The new group dubbed themselves the Stylistics and things began to look up when they toured Pennsylvania with a six-man backing group, Slim and the Boys.

In 1969 the Boys' guitarist, Robert Douglas and the Stylistics road manager, Marty Bryant, wrote a song which belonged more in the age of baggy-pantsed doowoppers than the sixties sounds of soul. It was called "You're A Big Girl Now". The Stylistics' Airron Love looks back on how the song was recorded. "We cut 'You're A Big Girl Now' for a guy called Bill Perry. Bill ran a label called Sebring Records. It was our very first record but we weren't nervous. In fact we produced it ourselves, though the label says it was Bill Perry. 'Big Girl' was played by the local jocks. You know, they'd always give a lot of spins to group sounds — like that thing in the fifties started in Philadelphia. I guess 'Big Girl' was a bit like those old sounds. Anyway, soon it was the biggest record in Philly, that's when it was picked up for national release."

The Avco entertainment conglomerate, at first known as Avco Embassy, had launched itself belatedly into the heady world of records and brought in two music-world veterans, Hugo Perretti and Luigi Creatore, to run the Avco label. It was Avco who put "You're A Big Girl Now" out to a national audience. It was a captivating sound of innocence with Russell Thompkins' strangely nasal falsetto soaring sweetly, broken up by a ludicrous bass voice monologue: an "unproduced" sound in an age of production. "Big Girl" was a reasonable soul hit and made Number 1 in New York.

Avco, who'd bought the group's contract as well as

the disc's master, patted themselves on the back and looked around for a way to cement the Stylistics' modest success. Thom Bell remembers only too well the result of Avco's deliberation. "A black promotion man I know called me early one morning. I blew that guy out, too, boy! I said 'Hell, what do you wake me up at seven o'clock in the morning for?' I had babies man, running all over the house, I wasn't getting much sleep anyway. He told me Avco were after me to produce a group they'd just signed, the Stylistics. The money looked kinda nice . . . Their first hit . . . was on the chart . . . so I said 'I think I can do something with the group, they sound pretty decent.' About 'You're A Big Girl Now': that kinda music doesn't knock me out. So when I got the group the first thing I did was lower Russell Thompkins' voice. When you start singing that high and loud you don't make sense, you just make noise. Now that boy sings *UP THERE* — he goes *WAY UP THERE*. But it's not singing. It's what they call a monotone — monotone means you can sing up or down but you always sound the same. So far I hadn't failed with anything I'd done so Avco were willing to take that chance. The one thing about Russell is that he has a fantastic memory, he can do an album in three hours. He'd sing a song almost the exact way you sang it to him. Fantastic memory. So you don't have to rehearse him for a long time. I rehearsed them ten tunes in four hours. For their first session the Stylistics needed an hour a side. The first thing was 'Stop, Look and Listen'. And when that did well I said all right, now we have to do an album. So the second time I recorded them I did 'Betcha By Golly Wow' and 'You Are Everything' . . ."

No group in the history of popular music had ever sounded like the Stylistics. With the Delfonics, Bell had taken a vocal group whose deft harmonic blend focussed around a breathy high tenor lead and developed orchestrations that gave sophisticated embellishment to the vocal mood of trembling romanticism. Without jarring he managed to combine the seeming contradiction of a black vocal style in a lavish orchestral setting. With the Stylistics the producer/arranger went one stage further. Russell Thompkins had a voice of such unique tonal pitch and sweet, almost effeminate, purity that an accompaniment of just strings and woodwind would have produced a sound of cloying sickliness. So Bell, in addition to orchestral instrumentation, utilized electric pianos, more emphatic bass and drums and, on "You Are Everything", even an electronically phased introduction. The result was captivating: soul music that neither excited the listener with deep intensity, nor left him marvelling at his mellow coolness, but soul music which came from a

Working on a new song . . . Thom Bell

remote etherial world of love, sadness and purity.

While the Stylistics triumphed the Delfonics — without Maestro Bell — began to falter. Randy Cain had left the trio in late 1971 to be replaced by Major Harris and the group's work without Bell was erratic, ranging from the beautifully mellowed "Hey! Love" to the theatrically mawkish "Walk Right Up To The Sun". But as Stan Watson says, "Success is kinda relative. Nobody gets Number 1 records *all* the time. There were some real nice things on the *Walk Right Up To The Sun* album and it sold pretty good. But people were *expecting* a slump after Thom Bell left and they tried to make out the Delfonics and Philly Groove were finished . . . Now it'd be true to say we couldn't break another act in the early years of the company." Discs by both Billy Bass and Mary Holmes failed to sell. "But the Delfonics were still a big, big group. And Philly Groove were probably doing better than a company like Jamie despite their resources."

By the seventies Jamie/Guyden's hits weren't coming as thick as they once had. The label was unable to find a pop act who could provide a consistent string of hits a la Duane Eddy, and their move into soul seemed oddly fragmentary in its conception. A record producer who wishes to remain anonymous comments: "It was a funny thing, Jamie was a big label in Philly all through the sixties and they had had plenty of opportunities to get with all the happening things in soul music. But they're run by a white lawyer and their whole attitude towards soul music seemed to be — get in there, make a killing and get onto the next thing, the next record. They never *built* acts, like really got artists *careers* going. There's a lot of musicians in Philadelphia who don't like that company."

About the only act that broke big for Jamie was Brenda and the Tabulations, who had a consistent string of soul hits from 1967 right through to 1972. Brenda Payton had been singing around Philly since 1965 with a local group, the Joylettes. When they split up, sixteen-year-old Brenda formed the Tabulations with Jerry Jones, Eddie Jackson and Maurice Coates. The group were spotted by Gilda Woods, wife of deejay Georgie Woods, and cut their first record in December 1966. It was one of the most haunting sounds ever to find its eerie way into the American Top 20. Over a sombre organ Brenda's shrill voice wailed "Dry You Eyes", a ballad similar in sound to the Chantels hymnal dirges. The sound of purity was almost cloying in its intensity. The disc, produced by Bob Finiz, was released on Dionn Records, distributed by Jamie. That hit was followed by a string of excellent, mainly slow discs such as Smokey Robinson's "Who's Lovin' You" in 1967 and "The Price You Have To Pay", the latter produced by Gamble and Huff and arranged by Martin and Bell. By 1969 the Tabulations had been supplemented by Bernard Murphy, the group had begun recording on a new Jamie distributed label, Top and Bottom, and their first hit, "The Touch Of You", was in the charts. Although Brenda's voice retained its desperate quality, her accompaniments changed from the uncomplicated directness of "Dry Your Eyes" to string-heaped orchestrations. In 1970 Brenda dumped the old Tabulations, brought in a new set — Dennis Dozier (lead guitar), Donald Ford (piano), Lee Smith (Bass) and Kenneth Wright (drums) — and added two female vocalists, Pat Mercer and Deborah Martin. The hits on Top and Bottom, like the billowing "Right On The Tip Of My Tongue", continued, but Brenda was losing musical direction. The girls' harmonies tended to clutter her vocals and by the time she joined producer Van McCoy at CBS' Epic Records, her approach was disappointingly stylized.

On Jamie's Phil L.A. of Soul, Cliff Nobles and Co., Fantastic Johnny C and Jesse James had faded from national prominence by the seventies. The label's subsequent soul sellers — such as the anguished wailer Tyrone Ashley or the fiery gospel dancers the Soul Brothers Six, featuring the torturous lead of John

Ellison — were leased from producers outside the city. About the only exception is Peoples Choice, a Philly-based act which hit with Phil L.A. of Soul and is still very much part of the recent soul chart scene. In July 1971 the group were in the soul Top 10 with a piece of compulsive dance funk called "I Likes To Do It". And their lead singer's story goes back quite a long way. Frankie Brunson was born in Buffalo, New York in 1931. He learned piano and organ as a child, but it wasn't until he reached his mid-twenties and moved to Ohio that he began working full-time in music, playing and singing with the local Dukes of Rhythm band. In 1959 he made his first record under the name Little Frankie Brunson (he stands about five foot four) for RCA and was subsequently placed on their subsidiary Groove. By 1962 Brunson was managed by the famed Nat Tarnapol and recorded an album *Big Daddy's Blues* for George Goldner's Gee label. Not much was happening in New York, however, so Frankie moved to Philadelphia. There he sang with the boogie-blasting Lynn Hope Band, cut a single with Cameo produced by Billy Jackson and released on their Fairmount label, and eventually joined a group, the Fashions. "The Fashions were mainly into the show bag, singing Broadway numbers, stuff like that. There were two girls and three guys in the group. The guys were a bass player, Roger Andrews, and a drummer, Dave Thompson, who I got on with real good. Anyway, we worked together for awhile. But then we split and called ourselves Peoples Choice." They added Stanley Burton on guitar and Leon Lee on congas. "This independent producer called Bill Perry decided to record us in 1971. We did a session with him at Virtue's. And he got the record placed with Phil L.A. of Soul. That was 'I Likes To Do It'."

Frankie had an extraordinary voice, a deep, resonant baritone which boomed and rasped and roared a mixture of dance instructions and unmetaphorical sexual joy. The People's Choice were "funk". "I can't tell you what *funk* is an' I don't know who started it. Somebody said it was James Brown, but it was going before him. It's just the hard beat, the beat which *makes* you move. When you hear it you wanna shake your stick or whatever you do . . . But you just *can't* sit still."

Neither the dancers nor the record-buying public did. Three-hundred thousand people bought the most swaggeringly aggressive dance disc of the year. For a while the group enjoyed the benefits of their "I Likes To Do It" hit. "The Staple Singers recommended us to do the Al Green Show at the Apollo and that was held over one week. Kenny Gamble came to see us there and he said he was sorry to have let our first

Peoples Choice, featuring veteran Frankie Brunson

single get away from him. He said 'As soon as you're free of your contractual obligations you come an' look us up.' "

Perhaps Kenny Gamble sensed that Phil L.A. of Soul would allow the group to fade quickly, even though "The Wootie-T-Woo" follow-up made the soul charts. As the record producer said, Jamie never "built" any careers. On the other hand, building something much, much bigger than Phil L.A. of Soul's "one-off hits" was by 1971 an obsession that dominated the thinking of Kenny Gamble and Leon Huff. Kenny explains their reasoning: "We'd been really brought down by the Neptune situation. We'd said to them, here's a new kind of music, something which has the ingredients to appeal to all audiences, black and white. All we want you to do is use your expertise to market it and get it into the shops. And they'd like slapped us in the face. But when we recovered we thought 'hell man, they're the ones who've blown it, not us'. We *know* the music's good, we *know* it's what the public want. So we began talks with another company, another big corporation who had the financial resources to get the sound we'd nurtured and nursed and developed to the mass public. A few people said, you're crazy considering going with Columbia, what do *they* know about soul music? But

things had changed. They had a lot of hip people in the company. It wasn't that old establishment Tin Pan Alley thing. And anyway we wouldn't be presenting them with records that only had black market potential. Philly soul records had the ability to break big big pop if only a company could recognize that situation."

Columbia Records, an arm of the immense CBS conglomerate, recognized it. A deal was signed and the American music trade papers announced the start of a new label, Philadelphia International. Leon Huff comments: "It took a few releases to get Philadelphia International sorted out. And the first few releases went nowhere." In fact the initial release — a confused pop ditty by one Gideon Smith produced by Lenny Pakula — deserved nowhere. "But, things began to straighten up and fly right. Our third or fourth release was a hit."

On April 24, 1971 *Record World* announced the release of Philadelphia International 3503, "You're The Reason Why" by the Ebonys. Within a month it had climbed into the Top 10 soul sellers. It was a near masterpiece with the production and song by Gamble and Huff, a Thom Bell arrangement and an introduction which *demanded* attention. A cymbal clashed and strings hovered on a dramatic chord before a female voice wistfully doodled "ba ba ba" 's for several seconds. Then a tortured voice sounding as though it had been torn from a tormented soul rasped "baby, baby, baby, baby" while a shrieking falsetto wailed "yeah". Each component had been expertly conceived. The expressive lyric was the final touch.

"I feel like a king sitting high on top of the world If my heart could sing I'd sing a love song to you girl"

As a final bonus to the shattering "Reason Why", Gamble/Huff tossed in a flip-side, "Sexy Ways", which showed more guts, joy and unadulterated drive than a million Cameo dance crazes. Philadelphia International were off and running even though the Ebonys didn't catch the spotlight of superstardom.

The Camden, New Jersey group had been formed for about three years when they were discovered by Gamble/Huff. "It was very exciting growing into what we are now", enthuses the Ebonys' Jenny Holmes. "With all of us being from the same general area, it was easy for us to get together. Our biggest break came when Leon Huff caught our nightclub act and signed us. What would be great now is a real *smash*." David Beasley, James Tuten, Clarence Vaughn and Jenny Holmes are still waiting for that big hit. Their second Philadelphia International release, the fiery "Determination", barely made the charts, while

Heavy soul wailers, the Ebonys

their 1972 releases, "Without The One You Love" and "I'm So Glad You're Me", tended to get lost.

"I don't think even Columbia realized the package they were buying at first". says a Philadelphia International employee. "I think they saw Gamble/Huff and Bell as a means to break into R&B, the black market, but for a year or so they didn't really think in terms of the pop market. It was just a black audience venture to them at first. The only guy they really worked on at the beginning was Dick Jensen, and he was white."

And he didn't make it. Jensen was a swarthy Hawaiian who sang in a rich, reverberating baritone with more than a nod in the direction of black vocal style. But Jensen was in no way a soul singer. He in fact appeared to model himself closely on the discs and stage act of Britain's Tom Jones. Jensen's singles and album failed to find sales even with those who went for vocal histrionics linked with hairy-chested sexuality. The singing and recording might have appeared an odd move for two black record producers. But Gamble and Huff had no qualms — or hang-ups — about such things. Kenny Gamble remarks: "We've never thought along the lines of a black music thing. We work mainly with black artists, sure, but we're quite capable of working with pop acts. Like we did an album with Barbara Streisand . . . and we've worked with several other white acts."

In truth, the album Gamble and Huff recorded with Streisand — and particularly the medley track

from it "Where You Lead"/"Sweet Inspiration" —
was extraordinary for the way it made the queen of
showbiz melodrama sound so close to soul music. It
was so close that it unsettled both her fans, though
it was a sizable hit, and those who felt "soul" was a
question of skin pigmentation as much as an inherent
feeling for projecting emotion and truth through
music. An even more startling example of how adept
Gamble and Huff were becoming at turning the un-
likeliest of white artists into something which
"sounded just like soul" was the Jaggerz. As pre-
packaged pop stars, the group had scored a string of
hits on Kama Sutra. When G&H produced some singles
for them on Gamble Records — "Baby I Love You",
"Gotta Find A Way Back Home" and "Need Your
Love" — their sound was an absorbing one of soulful
moodiness.

The Jaggerz weren't successful on Gamble. For that
matter neither were the black Brothers of Hope or
B. K. Marcus. In fact, the only group who continued
to hit on Gamble and Huff's brave first venture were
the Intruders. Although the unthinkable had happened
when Little Sonny Brown had left (to get married),
his temporary replacement Bobby Starr was able to
keep most of the group's distinctive sound on their
hit "I'm Girl Scoutin' ". It wasn't long before Sonny
returned to sing more soul hits like "Pray For Me"
and "I Bet He Don't Love You" in his cracked is-he-
flat, isn't-he-flat voice.

1971 was also a good year for Gamble and Huff's
"outside" productions. Among the soul acts who
made the trek to Sigma Sound to sample Philly funk
was a soul music superstar who was in serious danger
of falling over his crown, Wilson Pickett. Wilson had
seen it all, heard it all and done it all. The problem
was it sounded like it. Born in Prattville, Alabama,
Pickett had replaced Joe Stubbs as lead singer of a
Detroit vocal group, the Falcons, after four years with
Detroit gospel outfits. His screeching testifying was
soon heard as a solo and in 1964 his R&B hits on
Double L led to a contract with Atlantic. There he
was sent to Memphis to record with the Stax Records
house band and produced a series of startling discs,
including "In The Midnight Hour" and "Ninety Nine
And A Half", which were massively successful and
unquestionably innovative. From then on Wilson's
style was firmly set. The locations and backing musicians changed — with Atlantic cutting Pickett in
Muscle Shoals and New York — as did the material,
which moved from Covay and Womack through to
Hendrix and Steppenwolf. But the Wicked Pickett was
always required to rasp and scream over fat funky

rhythms and swaggering raunchy horns. Slowly, what
had been an immensely exciting style of attack, able
to enrapture a mass audience, became a rigid set of
clichés. Pickett became the very embodiment of the
clockwork soul singer screaming "sock it to me" 's
and "Lord have mercy" 's until everyone was either
quite frankly bored or simply amused or bored.

Sending Pickett to Gamble and Huff seems to have
been a desperate measure for Atlantic. Pickett's tor-

The wicked Wilson Pickett

tured style was unsophisticated, instinctive and the
very essence of the Southern soul style which brought
Stax Records so much success. It appeared to be light
years away from the thoughtful, precise sophisti-soul
of the City of Brotherly Love. But with Pickett,
Gamble and Huff were to gain one of their greatest
triumphs. "It was a real trip working with Pickett",
comments Huff. "He needed a hit when he came to us
and we gave him a gold record, 'Don't Let The Green
Grass Fool You'. An' the album *In Philadelphia* was a
monster. We got a different sound with Pickett . . . "

The "different sound" involved playing down the
horns, bringing up Leon Huff's pounding electric keyboard and coming up with some really fine songs.
"Green Grass" was a mid-tempo number with a
thoughtfully conceived lyric, so patently right for
Pickett that it made many wonder why the singer had

ever been persuaded to record "Sugar Sugar", "Green Grass" was written by Akines, Bellmon, Turner and Drayton. Drayton: "We still did a bit of singing. We cut a couple of records with Holland, Dozier and Holland in Detroit for Hot Wax Records under the name Silent Majority. But mainly we were concentrating on writing. 'Don't Let The Green Grass Fool You' was like our classic."

Pickett and Atlantic weren't the only people who experienced Gamble/Huff's hit magic in 1971. Joe Simon and Spring Records also got the treatment. Joe was born in Luisiana and moved to Oakland, California in 1959. He recorded a handful of discs for the tiny hole in the wall labels until his "My Adorable One" was picked up by Vee Jay. Then in 1966 Joe signed with Sound Stage 7, a R&B subsidiary of Monument Records of Nashville, Tennessee, and began a working relationship with producer John Richbourg.

Joe Simon during the "Pool of Bad Luck" era

There followed a stream of poignant, understated hits like "(You Keep Me) Hangin' On" and "The Chokin' Kind" which combined the natural soulfulness of Joe's masculine baritone and the orchestrations — and often the material — of country music. Eventually, in 1970, Joe moved on to Spring Records and had a big hit with the mournful "Your Turn To Cry". Under Gamble and Huff, however, Joe's soulful and occasionally languid sound gained added dynamism — and sales. "I really like the set-up down there" said Joe in an interview (*Blues and Soul*, 3—16 March 1972) after his first two Philly sessions. "I was able to communicate with the people and we had a sort of 'together' relationship that made the whole thing very enjoyable for me."

The togetherness showed. A Gamble and Huff special, "Drowning In The Sea Of Love", sold in excess of two million. "Pool of Bad Luck" with it's memorable hookline — "I tripped and I fell in a pool of bad luck" — was another smash. Joe's Philly-recorded album was his biggest ever, with over 150,000 advance orders prior to release.

The Sigma Sound success story had not by 1974 reached its ultimate triumphs, but already the studio's constant gold records must have seemed a little unreal to Frank Virtue. Virtue's studios still hired out to any takers and if the veteran engineer and producer ever felt he'd missed his chance at the caviare breakfast stakes, at least there was plenty of work. Also back in 1969 Frank had started a label, Virtue Records. The discs Virtue released didn't exactly storm the charts — although Willis Wooten's "Your Love is Indescribably Delicious", written by Ronnie Baker, should have done so on title alone — but acts like the R.D.M. Band and the Creations sold fairly well. And one singer, the former Volcano Gene Faith, showed enormous potential. In fact Faith's moody "My Baby's Missing" had appeared fleetingly in the national soul chart (Virtue being distributed nationally by Mercury).

So the big and the small continued in their frenetic efforts to produce quality soul music. But none of them, not even Gamble, Huff and Bell could have envisaged the amazing events of the next twelve months.

At the beginning of 1972 Philadelphia International signed Harold Melvin and the Blue Notes. Throughout the sixties the group had played the supper-club circuit, entertaining middle-American audiences with a mixture of Hilos' style harmony and Temptations take-offs, Broadway show tunes and the Holland—Dozier—Holland songbook. They'd recorded spasmodically in Miami, where they frequently wowed the yacht-in-the-harbour nightclub set. Producer Luther Dixon, one of the first blacks to use "beat concerto" techniques in New York in the early sixties, cut a single (leased to Chess) with the group at the Criterion Studios. Steve Alaimo and Willie Clarke cut a 45 at the TK Studios for release by Henry Stone, and Stone, a legendary label owner and *the* man in the Miami music business, even cut an album on the group.

Then the group underwent a shake-up in personnel — a change that led to a string of recordings which not only equalled but outstripped the success of their live appearances. Blue Note Lawrence Brown continues the story: "When we were on the road — which was just about permanently — we always had our own backing band, maybe five or six instruments. Around '69 we heard our drummer, Theodore Pendergrass, sing something and we thought 'there's a voice the Blue Notes need'. Theodore has a very hoarse, soulful voice. In '70 the group broke up for a while — there were disagreements about what we should be doing and where we should be going — and when we re-formed after a few months John Atkins, who'd been taking on more of the lead work, left and Theodore joined the Blue Notes. So we got our new line-up. Harold Melvin, Teddy Pendergrass, Lloyd Parkes — he joined us about '69 — Bernard Wilson and myself."

Teddy Pendegrass had an abrasive, gospel-derived vocal style, similar to the Dells' Marvin Junior and had worked briefly as drummer-cum-singer with a James Brown Band ("not *the* James Brown"). Lloyd Parkes, on the other hand, sang in a high tenor-cum-falsetto with shades of the old-time harmony groups. He'd previously sung with the Epsilons, a Philly group who had a small hit in 1970 with "The Echo" on Stax. The Epsilons also included John Whitehead and Gene McFadden, later to record as Talk of the Town and to become Gamble/Huff staff writers with hits such as "Backstabbers" and "I'll Always Love My Mama".

Eventually, in 1972, the Blue Notes were ready for some "serious" recording. In Lawrence Brown's words, "When Kenny and Leon had first approached us about recording in the sixties we hadn't been very keen. You see, then we didn't have a very serious attitude towards recording. Sure, we'd record a side here and there but club work was how we *ate*, like working with Kenny and Leon would mean a month with no pay, so to speak! But we rapped and came to the decision that things were gonna change for the Blue Notes. I mean up until then we'd been trying to be a whole group of Sammy Davis Jr.'s. We'd not been selling records — well, not to the kids. But we knew that with Theodore doing that soulful lead and Kenny and Leon allowing us the freedom to express

ourselves we could make it. So we signed with Philadelphia International."

The result was a staggering disc, "I Miss You", released in April 1972. The song was an excursion into self-pity with none of the sunny lilt that permeated much of Gamble/Huff's material.

Ever since you went away, I ain't been doin'
nothin' but thinkin'
You been away so long, I don't think I can carry
on, so I start drinkin'.

Performed by a Southern soul singer, the song would have been simple, direct, passionately intense. But Gamble and Huff managed to retain all the intensity and at the same time used much more than the standard horns and organ accompaniment. They carried the rhythm on guitar and vibes; they brought in an unbelievable Lloyd Parkes' falsetto shriek at the beginning; and, when the full orchestra came in, it featured Leon Huff's piano tinkling over swirling layers of strings, which added depth and drama to the disc's sound. But the key to the record's massive chart success was Teddy Pendergrass' lead — jagged, hoarse, apparently on the verge of break-down, but somehow always winning his struggle to articulate his sorrow. By Part Two, the song had developed into little more than the chant "oh . . . I . . . oh . . . I . . . miss you, miss you, miss you, miss you, miss you" behind a solemn Harold Melvin monologue. A more chillingly desperate sound has yet to be heard.

Despite its phenomenal success with the black market, "I Miss You" didn't "break pop" — perhaps it was slightly too anguished for Top 40 radio. From the *I Miss You* album which quickly followed, however, came a track which finally shot the group into the pop charts. "When we were cutting the album", Lawrence Brown recollects, "there was one song 'If You Don't Know Me By Now' which just seemed so heavy that we just *knew* that'd be the one. It came out in September and by Christmas we were being presented with a platinum record — two million sales."

"If You Don't Know Me By Now" was the equal in quality of "I Miss You". If it lacked the edge of intensity of its predecessor, it made up for it in proud beauty and passionate solemnity. The disc also clearly showed that Gamble and Huff were still capable of absorbing an influence or two. In the late sixties Chicago producer Bobby Miller and arranger Charles Stepney had begun to explore the possibilities of fusing three separate musical concepts. They took the Dells, up until then performers of doowops or supper-club schlock, and put full emphasis on Marvin Junior, whose voice was rough, rasping and quite unlike the

Harold Melvin and the Blue Notes with Teddy Pendergrass (nearest left)

concept. And the effect they had on the audiences was unique. Disc jockey Tony Brown comments, "There had never been a sound quite like it. The first time I heard Teddy Pendergrass sing I felt my whole spine tingle. It's a bit strange, a group who've been into all that show tune and nightclub thing coming on with such a heavy soul thing. I guess it was their first chance to really get into that stuff."

The Blue Notes arrived at soul and pop superstardom in 1972. By then they weren't Philadelphia International's first pop break-through. That honour went to another veteran team who were one of the Gamble and Huff faithful, the O'Jays. The group's Walter Williams describes what happened. "When the deal with Chess Records went bad we went back to Cleveland and did some things with H. B. Barnum but they weren't nothin'. In September '71 Bobby Massey quit to concentrate on production." He had one dramatic success, the Ponderosa Twins + One with "You Send Me". "We decided we'd carry on as a trio. We kept in touch with Gamble and Huff and they kept us informed about the Columbia deal. We got offers from

normal cool mellow sound of the black harmony teams. By giving him full scope to roar and moan and sob across the group's ethereal harmonies and bursts of falsetto, they had the perfect vocal sound over which to introduce massive dramatic orchestrations, with violins, harps, french horns and crashing timpani to emphasize Miller and Stepney's dramatic ballads. It was a stunning sound, one which was duly noted by Messrs. Gamble, Huff and Bell. They also realized how Miller and Stepney were misusing their technique. For the producer and arranger increased the size and noise range of their accompaniments until the Dells' records sounded hopelessly overblown and theatrical. At their peak in 1969, however, Chicago's Dells were among the most exciting sounds in soul and the Blue Notes' "If You Don't Know Me By Now" owed a little of its arrangement to Miller and Stepney's over-all concept. But the Blue Notes, like all Gamble and Huff's groups, sounded in no way derivative. The Blue Notes were an original development of the Dells

The O'Jays, *ca* 1967

And then there were three: the O'Jays today

Holland—Dozier—Holland (Invictus/Hot Wax) and from Motown. But we figured that those people make all the groups sound alike and we wanted our own sound. So we went with Philadelphia International. The day we signed was the day we *finally* came in from the rain."

The shelter they accepted was a gold record for one of the best songs and productions ever to emerge from Philadelphia. "Backstabbers", produced by Gamble and Huff, arranged by Thom Bell and sung by the O'Jays was released in June 1972. It positively raced up the charts. A roll on Leon's piano, a popping bass-drum beat with a Wes Montgomery-styled guitar filin-, a rush of strings and then the voices ask:

"What they do?" They themselves supply the answer — "They smile in your face" — and Eddie wheezes, "All the time they wanna take your place, the back-stabbers".

The sound was so finely conceived and perfectly executed that "Backstabbers" was recognized as a popular music milestone by fans of soul and pop, black and white. Eddie Levert: "In a sense it wasn't *that* different from the things we'd done with Neptune except that it had a heavier lyric." The lyrical theme in fact bore a considerable resemblance to "Smilin' Faces Sometimes" which Motown's Norman Whitfield wrote for the Temptations. "But there we were with a chart-topper and suddenly we were big stars. Our album sold pretty good and we got a couple more hits from that, '992 Arguments' and 'Love Train'. They should have put "Love Train" after "Backstabbers" — it had that beat and that lyric that everyone wanted. But really Gamble and Huff knew exactly how to get us across. We couldn't believe how good the musicians were, the quality of the songs, everything was just fantastic."

"Just fantastic" was also the response of a Columbia record executive when asked by *Billboard* maga-

The "Slow Motion" man, Johnny Williams

zine to comment on the sudden sweep of Philadelphia International discs into the charts. The week he spoke another one was about to make the U.S. Top 10. "Slow Motion" by Johnny Williams seemed to go against the general sound of Philadelphia soul. It featured a vocalist who grunted and "good god"-ed like a Stax Records renegade and the brass played raunchy riffs sounding as though they were right out of the Memphis Horns songbook. But the beat churned with a determined relentlessness that made "Slow Motion" one of the year's most danceable and danced-to discs. Johnny Williams — unlike all of Philadelphia's other chartmakers — has so far had only one Top 20 hit.

Johnny was born in Tyler, Alabama in 1942 and by the sixties was singing around Chicago clubs. He made discs like "My Baby's Good" for Chess, and "Breaking Point" and "Maggie" for Twinight without really getting anywhere. After a spell in Los Angeles, Johnny was back in Chicago where he cut a couple of discs for Brunswick/Dakar's Bashee subsidiary reunited with producer Willie Henderson. Then in 1971 he joined Gamble and Huff. As Johnny tells the story, his manager, Chicago's number-one disc jockey E. Rodney Jones "recommended me to Mr. Gamble and Mr. Huff. I'd always followed their work and never dreamed that one day I'd be working with them. I recorded 'Slow Motion' in '71 but before it could be released Neptune Records closed down. When Philadelphia International started up they put out a thing on me, 'It's So Wonderful', which didn't do anything and then in the summer of '72 'Slow Motion' came out. And it smashed."

The startling thing about Philadelphia International's hits was their diversity. The O'Jays with their undulating rhythms, the Blue Notes with their testifyin' orchestrated passion, Johnny Williams with his unsophisticated call to dance — all had the sound of success and the stamp of quality, each one was unique. And the next act to join the label differed stylistically not only from other acts recorded at Sigma Sound, but from any other soul acts recorded.

"We really wanted to get a big hit on Billy Paul", Kenny Gamble muses. "The problem was finding a balance between his natural jazz style (singing double tempo verses while the band keeps single time, etc.) and what was going down in soul music. The *Ebony Woman* album for Neptune had started getting Billy into a commercial groove and got a lot of favourable reaction from the industry. So for Billy's next album, *Goin' East,* we extended the concept further. We took in outside influences — the Beatles, the Eastern thing — but we kept it rhythmic and we didn't try to smother Billy. We nearly had a hit with "Magic Carpet

Ride" from the album . . . And then we did Billy's *360 Degrees* album and it all came together with "Me and Mrs. Jones".

"Me and Mrs. Jones" with its poignant lyric about infatuation with a rich married woman and its killer line of "I didn't know, I didn't know it would get this strong" captivates both America and Europe. Britain's *Black Music* magazine wrote "Me and Mrs. Jones' is an instant recall disc. When it slides provocatively out of a car radio or a super hi-fi the listener will immediately picture the instant he first heard that slyly insinuating mixture of iced vocal and emotive story line. In a decade's time rock archaeologists will be placing the disc in their list of 'all time great pop records'."

Columbia recovered from their amazement at such a rapid string of million-sellers, and the international acclaim that was beginning to pour forth for their super quality soul "product", and a bright young promotion man thought up the "Philly sound" tag. As Weldon McDougal explains: "When Philadelphia International started to get super hot, the industry at last worked out the significance of the whole thing. That Kenny and Leon and Thom weren't just guys who could make hits but they were offering a sound . . . a new sound, something that was going to be as big as the Motown sound."

Weldon McDougal knew about Motown. After leaving Harthon Productions he'd worked with the legendary corporation, by then based in Los Angeles, as a promotion man. But Weldon couldn't forget Philly — or it him — and in 1972 he returned to the City of Brotherly Love. ("I had a fight with Motown and Kenny said, come and work for us"). Gamble and Huff were expanding their empire. As Leon Huff himself puts it: "When we really started coming off *big* hits we were able to set up the situation we'd always dreamed about. Bring in more staff, promotion men, administrators, and take on some staff as writers. And of course we set up the Gamble, Huff, Bell family."

Thom Bell, the maestro of symphonic soul, had been as active as Gamble and Huff during Philadelphia International's flurry of gold. The Stylistics continued on a fabulous road of hits. "We recorded *Stylistics 2* in fabulous road of hits. "We recorded *Stylistics 2* in April '72", relates Airron Love. "You know, one of those things about Thom is that every track he puts down with us he works on like it's a potential single. So we got some big hits from that album too. 'I'm Stone In Love With You' was a really big 45 for us of course. We came to Britain when that was out. Up until then British radio had ignored our records but

that one they played . . . that one was a hit. That Thom Bell is a brilliant cat, man."

Another group sprinkled with Thom Bell stardust were the Spinners. Group member Pervis Jackson talks about how they finally attained success after more than a decade as everyone's bottom-of-the-biller's. "We'd quit Motown and we shopped around. We went to Stax, Avco and Atlantic. We signed with Atlantic. We played Atlantic some tapes we'd made in Detroit with Jimmy Roach. They seemed to like 'em but like in the same breath they asked us whether we would mind cutting some tracks with a producer of their choice. We agreed 'cause it was obvious they were trying to do something for us."

Thom Bell takes up the story. "I went to Atlantic and they said, here's a list of every artist we have. We'd like you to produce any one you want. So I looked down the list and right at the bottom was the Spinners. Now I'd heard something by them years ago which I liked real well. I couldn't even remember what it was but something made me choose them. Atlantic were kinda surprised that I wanted the Spinners but it worked out real fine. I went and wrote some songs, got some other things together and then went into Sigma and put the tracks down. The voice-overs by the group were done in Detroit. That was 'How Could I Let You Get Away', 'You And Me Baby', 'I'll Be Around' and 'Could It Be I'm Falling In Love'. The first thing Atlantic put out was 'How Could I Let You Get Away', but after that had started going up the charts the radio stations started playing the other side and pretty soon 'I'll Be Around' was Number 1. It sold close to two million."

"I'll Be Around", written by Bell and Phil Hurtt, was one of the warmest discs ever. With Phillippe Wynn singing lead over a mid-tempo thudding rhythm which the industry was to dub "the Thom Bell beat", it became one of the most influential sounds in seventies soul. Its follow-up, "Could It Be I'm Falling In Love", had an even more delicately pretty lyric driven home with resonance and plain, unbridled soul. That was a double million-seller and the Spinners' metamorphosis was complete.

Back in 1956 things had been different. They had formed on the streets of Detroit, as the Domingos. Bobby Smith remembers: "The group was me, Pervis Jackson, Billy Henderson, Henry Fambrough and George Dixon — he was the original lead singer. We all went to Lincoln High in Detroit. Smokey Robinson was there too. It was tough recording-wise back in the fifties because they didn't have any major record companies in Detroit. In '57 we became the Spinners.

Thom Bell opening a present, watched by Linda Creed and the Spinners

We were considered like an amateur group. We didn't know nothing. Around '60 we met Harvey Fuqua and Gwen Gordy. We had our first record out on their label Tri-Phi. 'That's What Girls Are Made For' — Marvin Gaye played drums on that. It was a hit and we thought we had it made . . ."

None of the Spinners' subsequent Tri-Phi discs sold as well as the first and in 1964 Harvey Fuqua joined his brother-in-law Berry Gordy at Motown Records and brought his stable of Tri-Phi and Harvey artists with him.

"We had some hits with Motown but I think it was the thing that they had so *many* groups. Like the Temptations and groups with the big hits got in first and we got the material nobody else wanted."

Despite spasmodic sellers such as "I'll Always Love You" in 1965, "It's A Shame" in 1970, featuring the lead voice of G. C. Cameron, now a solo artist, and "We'll Have It Made" in 1971, it was live appearance that kept the group eating. "We were two years with an act we called the Brown Beatles — we really got across doing that. When we finally split from Motown it was a unanimous decision. We had a settled line-up — Phillippe Wynne, Pervis Jackson, Billy Henderson, Henry Fambrough and Bobby Smith — and a better vocal sound than we'd ever had before. We just wanted a record label who could pay us atten-

The (Detroit) Spinners

tion. So we quit Motown and it began to happen . . . after all that stuff which had been put down, it finally began to happen."

Thom Bell, established by his hits for the Stylistics and the Spinners, linked up under an umbrella company with Kenny Gamble and Leon Huff. And while the giants smiled over the tops of their growing piles of gold discs, Sigma Sound and its dynamic session men continued to service the needs of mere mortal record producers. Stan Watson for instance. In addition to the Delfonics, who had a distinctly cool year in 1972, Stan was trying to build up some more acts. "I did Nat Turner's Rebellion . . . One of the group, Joe Jefferson, is a writer with Thom Bell now. And I did the Broadway Express . . . and a band called Sound Experience." Their "black rock" wah-wah electricism has been heard on albums on GSF — recorded live at the Glen Mills Reform School — and Soulville, a Philly Groove subsidiary. But as Stan says "It was kinda difficult."

Honey and the Bees were also finding it tough. Their 1972 discs on Bell Records were being lost in the general melée over the Gamble/Huff/Bell super soulers. The group had been on the verge of success for ten years. Honey and the Bees began in 1962 when two schoolgirls, Gwen Oliver and Ann Wooten, joined a group, the Superiorettes. By 1964 it was the Yum Yums and by 1965 Honey and the Bees. Honey was Nadine Felder and her little workers were Gwen, Ann and Jean Davis. Deejay and record label owner Jimmy Bishop picked up on the group and from 1966 to 1968 the group had six Arctic discs. From their first, "I'm Confessin' That I Love You" — "It was a silly sound now that we look back" — to their last, "Sunday Kind Of Love", they sang standard bluesy harmony, over interesting Bobby Martin arrangements. None, however, sold too many copies. When Arctic folded manager Bishop continued to produce the group and by 1970 was leasing the tapes to Jubilee/Josie Records in New York. With fine Sigma Sound accompaniments played by Huff, Harris, Young *et al* and with excellent songs, some written by Gamble and Bishop, discs like "(I Want You) To Make Love" and "Love Can Turn To Hate" showed Nadine Felder to be a singer of soulful maturity. Their "It's Gonna Take A Miracle", originally recorded by the Royalettes and including in its structure a medley of several other Teddy Randazzo songs, was genuinely ear-catching and bubbled around the charts for ages. But nothing really broke big. In 1972 the group moved on to Bell Records where an intriguing arrangement by Roland Chambers turned the Spinners' ancient doowop classic, "That's What Girls (Boys) Are Made

Progressive black rock: Philly Groove's Sound Experience

For", into late-night-soul. But neither that nor "Song For Jim" on Bell sold well. As Nadine's brother, songwriter Alan Felder says, "They're still together, still waiting for the right song and the right production, still waiting for their turn."

While they were waiting, in 1973 producer Jimmy Bishop took his beloved Barbara Mason to Buddah Records and her discs like "Bed And Board" and "The Pow Pow Song" were soon bubbling in the soul charts.

Over at Virtue's, one-time president of Swan Bernie Bennick found that he couldn't quite leave the excitement of the record business. Certainly it doesn't appear to have been for the money (he had a valuable "cutout" (deletion) business) that Bennick started up a label or two. In fact if Marmaduke Records' "Hot Pants (Gonna Get You In Trouble)" by Norma and the Fascinators or a monologue by disc jockey Larry Daley didn't do very well, they did show once again that old-time execs don't die, they simply begin again in obscurity. Virtue himself was still turning out excellent, if generally unheard discs by the Creations,

Gene Faith and a mysterious Salome Bey. But the motivation for a big push wasn't really there — "I done pretty good", says Frank smiling, and his car and lovely home prove the point. And the distractions from music were many — "I had a chance to play in the Cannon TV programme. I was gonna be his twin brother 'cause I look just like him." So Virtue's Studio stayed with the small sessions and did fairly well, even though a few new studios were opening up. Jesse James, for instance, founded the optimistically titled Future Hit Studios for outside hire in the early seventies after he found that nobody was buying his singing — "The Sweetest Thing This Side of Heaven" on Buddah — or his productions — who could forget "Yaba Daba Do" by the Flint-Nicks?

By 1973, though, Sigma Sound Studios were the undisputed kings of Philadelphia. As Joe Tarsia puts it, "We only had the one studio then; now we got three. It got to the point we were running seven days a week, twenty hours a day. I was here twenty hours a day. It was almost impossible to service the equipment."

As Tarsia began to build more studios and take on more staff, Gamble and Huff and Bell installed more telephones and took on more staff, and Harris, Young, Baker, Chambers, Martin and the dozen other super sessioners worked themselves around the clock, the Philly sound hits continued to tumble out. Throughout late 1972 Philadelphia International made the charts with Harold Melvin and the Blue Notes' sonorous "Yesterday I Had The Blues", Billy Paul's arrogant "Am I Black Enough For You", the Ebonys' dramatic "It's Forever" and the O'Jays' pungent "Time To Get Down". Columbia hit hit with Thom Bell's masterly Ronnie Dyson productions, "One Man Band" and "When You Get Right Down To It". Atlantic scored with the Spinners' "One Of A Kind" (another goldie) and "Ghetto Child". And funky little Gamble Records, now with CBS distribution, came on with the Intruders' "She's A Winner" and "I'll Always Love My Mama".

1973 saw much more than the maintenance of hit runs however. A whole new set of names were about to be introduced into the Philly scene, both for artists and producers. Weldon McDougal: "What happened was that when the Philly sound broke everyone wanted a piece of the action. CBS had the key guys under contract, but there was a real rush to get with the sound and artists started coming down here to record at Sigma Sound in their dozens, like they were queuing up to get the sound. And as more and more companies got involved, all the session men who were really what the sound was all about got involved in producing and arranging themselves. So guys like Norman Harris and Bobby Martin started coming off hits as well. The whole thing got kinda frenetic, man."

Frenetic but successful, at least for the session men and the studio. The word was out. Philadelphia was *the* place to go to cut soul. Detroit, Memphis and Muscle Shoals were forgotten in the mad scramble by companies to get to Sigma Sound to put a few impeccable tracks down for their artists to wail over. Atlantic Records in particular sent acts to Sigma: the cryingly soulful Percy Sledge, the ex-Cleveland singer Clyde Brown, now in the Drifters, the jazzily smokey Vivian Reed. None were particularly successful. As a Sigma Sound engineer observed, "You can't just come in, do a session and fly out again and always expect a smash as easy as that." But the activity did throw up a whole group of new production talents known as the Young Professionals. They included Phil Hurtt, LeBaron Taylor — who was made an executive at Columbia Records in 1975 — Tony Bell (Thom's brother), Bobby Eli, Vinc Montana, Lenny Pakula.

A young professional — producer Tony Bell

First Choice

And Bunny Sigler. "I really started getting into production on my own records first", says Bunny. "I was about the first act signed to Philadelphia International . . . I tried a whole series of things before trying for a big hit. Versatility has always been my bag."

Legend has it that back in the fifties Bunny was billed in clubs as O'Sigler, De Siglio or Sliglowitz depending on the ethnic group attending. And certainly his records were startlingly diverse. A rock progressive-sounding "Everybody Needs Good Lovin"; a duet under the name David with Dee Dee Sharp on "Conquer The World Together" which he'd originally recorded with Cindy Scott; a revival of the old rock'n'roll classic, Bobby Lewis' "Tossin' And Turnin'"; an exquisite ballad, "Regina"; and even a hilarious Kung Fu movie track, "Theme From Five Fingers Of Death". "But I was producing and writing for other artists . . . I did a lot of things with Phil Hurtt, I did Ike Perkins on Apt Records . . . oh, quite a lot of things. There were a lot of guys doing sessions at Sigma."

One of them was the guitarist on a hundred hits who'd finally turned his hand to production, Norman Harris. As he says, "I got teamed up with this very talented songwriter called Alan Felder. We started writing together and did pretty good. So in about '71 or so we thought we'd give production a shot. We got a production deal with this New York company Argon Productions and we did an album in New York with Linda Hopkins which came out on RCA . . . and we had Jean Wells, she flew into Philly from Florida . . . But we couldn't get that thing off the ground. Anyway, one day in '72 Georgie Woods the deejay called me and asked me to listen to this group he'd found. I said 'not again, not this week' . . . *I* could sing better than most of his acts. But eventually I said I'd give it a try once more. And they knocked me right out . . . that was First Choice." Or the Debronettes as they were known, a little sing-at-weekends trio.

"We were just high school kids", laughs First Choice's Rochelle Fleming, "trying to sing. When Georgie Woods introduced us to Norman Harris he brought in Mr. Stan Watson. The first thing we recorded was called 'This Is The House Where Love Died. It should have been a big hit but it got leased to Wand Records and they didn't promote it and that was that. Then we recorded this song called 'Armed And Extremely Dangerous'. Wand/Scepter turned it down so we got a release from our contract and Mr. Watson put the record on his Philly Groove label which was distributed by Bell. And it became a hit."

Norman Harris' production on "Armed And Extremely Dangerous" was rivetting. Earl Young's zipping cymbals and a thudding Bell-influenced drum rhythm created a mood of high energy. Rochelle's throaty contralto whooped "wow-oh-yeah-wow"'s across the charging rhythm while Annette Guest and Joyce Jones chirped appropriate responses. First Choice were a superb new act to bolster Philly Groove's

The Delfonics during the "Alive and Kicking" era

failing roster. For in 1973, with severe misgivings, the Delfonics cut what was to be their final album for Philly Groove. William Hart speaks about it: "We cut the *Alive and Kicking* album over several sessions in mid-1973. We had some nice arrangements on that by Tony Bell, Vince Montana and Caldwell McMillon and we got a couple of big 45s from it." "I Told You So" an up-tempo lilter, and "Lying To Myself", a lovely introspective ballad. "But there were all kinds of problems inside the group and outside it."

While the First Choice were blooming and the Delfonics were fighting with their label, Norman Harris was helping a friend and fellow session man into the charts in his own right. Drummer extraordinaire Earl Young had stepped in to sort out the flagging remnants of the old Volcanos. After Gene Faith had left to work alone, the group had struggled on under a new name, the Moods. They recorded two discs, both produced by Tom Sellers for John Madara's production company: "Rain Maker", released on Wand, and "King Hustler" a wah wah guitar, funk opus written by Len Barry and released on Reddog. Jimmy Ellis was now featured as the group's lead singer. He had formerly been with the Exceptions, who in 1965 had recorded an extraordinarily dated "Down By The Sea" on Cameo, and he sang in a rich, impassioned baritone-to-tenor. But nobody bought the Moods' discs and they were going nowhere until Earl Young took them under his drumsticks.

Thinking back, Earl comments — "They were kinda raggedy when I first got them together, so the Trammps was a pretty appropriate name to call them. We went in the studio and did this thing called 'Zing! Went The Strings Of My Heart', a real oldie. I sang the lead vocal, the bass vocal on that. We leased the record to Buddah and it was a pretty good hit."

"Zing" was a mischievously conceived piece of dance magic. Producers Harris, Baker and Young had taken the old vocal arrangement of the creaking standard sung in another era by the Coasters. To that arrangement with its hypnotic "dit-did-it, dit, dit, did-dit" chant and booming bass voice lead, they added Jimmy Ellis bellowing passionately across the top. Behind the whole thing they put a track that shuddered and rippled with electrofunk force. The Trammps had two more hits with Buddah, "Sixty Minute Man", which was another oldie, this one by the Dominos, suitable Philly-funkisized, and "Pray All You Sinners" with a delightfully tricky backbeat.

Then came a rather extraordinary sequence of events for which Buddah Records should have been presented with the "dumboes of the year" award. Ronnie Baker tells the story. "The Trammps' contract with Buddah expired in '73. They had an option and, as all the things they'd put out had sold, we waited for them to come along and pick it up. But they didn't. Nobody from Buddah made any contact. We waited for the days to go by and then bang . . . the

The Trammps, featuring Earl Young

Trammps were free. So we decided to start our own label, Golden Fleece Records, and record the group for that. You see we still had a really beautiful relationship with Kenny and Leon, but we felt it was time that we personally had a little more benefit out of the Philly sound. Kenny and Leon said, sure, it's a good idea, and they got us a link-up with CBS, so Golden Fleece got CBS distribution like Philadelphia

Magic of the blue . . . Blue Magic

International. The first thing we put out was the Trammps 'Love Epidemic'. It wasn't a stone smash but it did okay. It got the label away.''

The Trammps, consisting of Earl Young (lead bass singer), Jimmy Ellis (lead singer), Michael Thompson (drums), Dennis Harris (lead guitar), John Hart (organ), Stanley Wade (bass), Ron Kersey (keyboards) and Harold Wade (rhythm guitar) are still right up in the front line of recent Philly soul stars. So are another group with a totally different style who in 1973 first began to slide into the soul charts under the expert guidance of Norman Harris. "I first got to hear of Blue Magic when I was approached by this independent production company called W.M.O.T. Inc. They wanted me to produce them. I listened to them and then I said sure . . . they were real nice."

The "real nice" Blue Magic consisted of Theodore "Ted" Mills (lead), Vernon Sawyer (baritone, second tenor), Wendell Sawyer (baritone), Keith Beatons (second tenor) and Richard Pratt (bass). The group was formed by merging two local units, Mills coming from the Topics and the others from the Shades of Love. Alan Rubens who, with Stephen Bernstein, is the group's manager, recalls: "We went to Sigma in June and cut some tracks. Atlantic were the first company we took them to and they told us to look no further — they really liked our sound. They were more or less buying the group. We were lucky and the first

record (on Atco) took off a little. 'Spell' was a flip-side turnover from 'Guess Who'. It took its time to make it but it sold quite well in the end. Then came 'Look Me Up'. That was recorded at our second session and that was a bigger hit. Then our album came out and things really started happening."

Blue Magic's sound was one of the most beautiful Philadelphia had yet spawned. Although the group's deft, delicate harmonies were in the mode of the Delfonics and the Stylistics, Ted Mills was a lead singer of real individuality. His breathy high tenor had none of the raucous edge often associated with falsetto and was sweetly sensitive, almost vulnerable, in its gentle tone. It was a voice the equal of Russell Thompkins Jr.

The Stylistics continued to triumph in 1973. Discussing their success, Airron Love says, "Stardom was a pretty strange thing to get used to. We'd go on stage and the roar would come up . . . wooah! . . . it always quietened down when we sang though. We were doing all these beautiful slow songs that Thom and Linda were writing and we thought it'd be nice if we could do a fast thing for a change. So they came up with this thing 'Rockin' Roll Baby'. We kinda laughed when Linda first told us the story line, you know, 'got a funky walk in his little orthopaedic shoes'."

Whatever amusement "Rockin' Roll Baby" 's uncomfortably twee lyric caused, Thom Bell's production was the usual serious demonstration of inventive flair. Thom pounded a piano riff which drove relentlessly against Russell's nasal falsetto whine. It was a masterly disc and a brilliant move away from the group's increasingly languid numbers.

Thom was still spreading himself around with an extraordinary display of energy. He took up an offer from Wes Farrell to produce a new group on Farrell's new label Chelsea. Not that the group was really that new. New York City's Tim McQueen explains: "Our background is kinda complicated. Back in '67 I met Ed Shell and Mike Sanford and formed a group, Mark III. Then Mike dropped out and we brought in John Brown and Claude Johnston, became a quartet and changed our names to Triboro Exchange — we got that from the name of one of the bridges that spans New York and Long Island. We played around New York, a gig here and a gig there, and we cut a record with Buddah called 'Lonely Night'. But it never got a play anywhere."

John Brown, whose vocal group background stretches back to the Five Satins (1957 to 1960), the Cadillacs (1960 to 1962) and the Moonglows ("for seven months 'til they worked out nobody was into 'Sincerely' anymore") takes up the group's story.

New York City

The Sigma boards

"When Triboro Exchange joined Chelsea Records in late '72 they weren't goin' nowhere. Then Wes Farrel gave us a new name, New York City, and let's face it, it ain't a name you're gonna forget. When we found out we were gonna record with Thom Bell it blew our minds."

Tim McQueen, New York City's lead singer, continues: "Thom came into Mr. Farrell's office where we did an audition for him. A few weeks later we were heading down to Philly to put our voices on some tracks he had cut for us. We cut four sides with Thom, 'Ain't It So', 'Uncle James', 'Quick, Fast, In A Hurry' and 'I'm Doin' Fine Now'. The session was so easy, so relaxed, everyone just mellowed out down there and when we finished we knew we had a hit."

In fact they had two, both gold. The rich, warm lolloping beat of "I'm Doin' Fine Now" and the happy though rather slight "Quick, Fast, In A Hurry" each sold a million and the Philly sound had its most unlikely named champions. But Thom Bell had an even more unlikely sounding project up his sleeve. "There was another idea I had", he explains. "I'd been trying for three years to get ahold of Johnny Mathis but Columbia must have thought that I wasn't right for him. I think Mathis is a trend setter, not a trend follower. He has a *fantastic* voice, man. I had an idea for him for putting him into today's sound . . . but not *funky*. . . and piece by piece in the course of the year make him a leader again. Eventually, after a long, hard struggle, they let me produce him. So I did an album on Johnny, *I'm Coming Home*."

Columbia's reluctance was understandable. Thom Bell, along with the other kings of the Philly sound, had achieved success with singers working in recognizably black styles. However sophisticated the Philly producers' techniques and however far their artists seemed to stray from the roots, the Philly sound was unquestionably a soul sound with its performers articulating the current black music experience and totally in the flow of the black cultural mainstream. What Thom Bell was proposing seemed to be a contradiction of concepts. Johnny Mathis was black, but his beautifully modulated yet pallid crooning had always been aimed at the white middle-of-the-road audience. What's more, under the directorship of Mitch Miller he had been fantastically successful in reaching them. *Johnny Mathis Greatest Hits*, for example, stayed in the album charts for four hundred weeks. Columbia must have felt that putting Mathis with a "soul" writer/producer, no matter how sophisticated, would totally alienate the staid audience who required endless recordings of Berlin, Porter and show tunes served in a lush cocoon of choirs and strings. At the same time such a move could give more ammunition to those who attacked the work of Bell and the other creators of sophisti-soul as a spineless sellout of "soul" to the tastelessness of "easy listening". But Mathis' record sales *had* been slipping and Columbia finally gave Thom a chance. *I'm Coming Home* worked quite well considering the immense dangers of falling between two stools. Mathis was no soul singer, but Bell was able to bring out a poignancy and a glimmer of involvement on the pretty Bacharach-inspired title track and particularly on the lovely Creed/Bell ballad, "Foolish". Predictably, however, the record did tend to provoke some critics to say "the Philly sound is bland".

In addition to his frenetic production activity, Thom Bell, like Baker, Harris and Young, next decided that he too should have his own "CBS custom label". "Tommy Records was started in '73", says Thom. "There were a few problems at first. Under the contracts I'd already signed I wasn't able to produce for it. We put out a thing by Bobby Taylor which he produced." The one-time Motown hitmaker turned in an excellent, charge-along-rhythm version of a Four Tops oldie, "I Can't Quit Your Love". "But Tommy took a while to happen."

In mid-1973 Atlantic Records, keen to follow up their Blue Magic success, signed another Philly group. Sister Sledge had been around since 1971 when, as Sisters Sledge, they'd recorded "Time Will Tell", produced by Marty Bryant and accompanied by Slim and the Boys for the local Money Back label. But it was when the teenage sisters, Debbie, Joni, Kim and Kathi, began working with Gamble/Huff as background vocalists that they came to Atlantic's attention. Their first Atco discs, "The Weatherman" and "Mama Never Told Me", produced by Tony Bell and Phil Hurtt, were vibrant, neatly made slices of the Philly sound, but without any real distinction. Their Sigma Sound records got little exposure ("our things just weren't heard on the radio" says Debbie) and no big sales, though the group went on to make it recording in New York with Tony Sylvester. "The problem was", observes Richard Barrett, "that after the Supremes and groups like that had started to fall off in popularity, everyone thought girl groups were a thing of the past. So groups like Honey and the Bees and Sister Sledge had a hard time to get too far, to break out of the local club thing. That's why the Three Degrees were something special."

They were indeed. In a time which had seen girl groups move from being one of the dominant forces in popular music to a decidedly *passé* anachronism, the Three Degrees went from strength to strength under Barrett's expert guidance. Sheila Ferguson dis-cusses the group's career: "When we signed with Roulette Records, Richard produced some sessions on us in New York and we had some hits." (These included "Maybe", a stirring re-revival of the Chantels classic done with a long monologue and the heaviest soul arrangement the group had ever tried, "You're The One" and "Ebb Tide", another oldie.) "But nothing really big. We did some R&B tunes, some standards, some rock, just like our stage act. On stage was where things were really happening for us. We played the big nightclubs all over the world. We toured with Engelbert Humperdinck. We were in the *French Connection* movie. We were into a whole lot of different things."

And all of them made money. Barrett had skilfully taken this raw trio from the Swan Records era and rehearsed and instructed them until they emerged as something quite unlike any other act in popular entertainment. Their appeal lay in a series of paradoxes. They were black but their three-part harmony style was fairly far removed from black "soul" sets, with only Sheila's theatrical lead occasionally showing through. They performed soul songs, but for every Motown tune there was a Broadway medley, for every Sly Stone funk opus, a David Gates ballad. They were outrageously sexy, always dressed in slinky dresses clinging to voluptuous bodies in a dazzle of sequins, but their hip-thrusting stage movements had a kind of antiseptic obviousness too deliberate for real sexual allure or suggestiveness. The "rock" writers hated them. One particularly virulent critic wrote, "They are like black Barbi dolls. Posturing and wriggling in a dewey lipped, laquer haired, synchronized dance stepped orgy of visual theatrics. Their singing is shrill and without grace. But their charisma is total. One cannot avert one's gaze. They are a hypnotic tribute to all that is tasteless, the ultimate plastic performers for a plastic world."

Despite their critics, the Three Degrees' nightclub popularity continued to grow and in mid-1973 they rejoined Gamble and Huff. Fayette Pinkney: "We were very excited about joining Philadelphia International. We did an album at Sigma Sound and as soon as we heard the musicians there, we knew we were going to get with the younger fans who buy records. You see, that had been our problem. We would play shows to an adult audience, but it's the teenagers who buy records. We cut the *Three Degrees* album and it was very successful for us."

Philadelphia International were finally coming through with big albums. As Kenny Gamble observes: "When we'd started out with Gamble Records, soul LP's didn't really sell in very large quantities. Soul was a singles market. Albums had a very small part of

the total turnover. But then all that changed and suddenly you could sell 300,000 or more on a really hot soul LP. One of our ambitions was to establish Philadelphia International with hit singles which we did, but those singles were taken from super hot albums. All our albums were the product of hundreds of hours of work and so we made sure they were given every opportunity to sell."

And sell they did. At the end of 1973 record reviewers called Billy Paul's *War Of The Gods* "a superb example of blending orchestral eclecticism, inventive jazz scat singing and probingly searching lyrics." The O'Jays' *Ship Ahoy* was described as "an album with a stunning array of styles from a truly versatile soul group" and Harold Melvin and the Blue Notes' *Black And Blue* was heralded as "a great set which beats their first album". All made the album charts. In 1974 they were followed by *Music Is The Message* by MFSB. When it was released Kenny Gamble was quoted as saying, "The session musicians on our records were absolutely vital to the success of the Philly sound so we decided to bring them out into the limelight a bit."

In addition to Philadelphia International's triumphs in the American singles and albums markets, other countries were catching on to the Philly sound. "It was obvious that what Philly had to give the whole world wanted", laughs Kenny. "So we spread out a bit. We set up a Philadelphia International label in England through CBS and in December '73 we took a show to Europe to get our acts known. It did pretty good."

Disc jockey Tony Brown summarizes a year of hits for the established stars. "It's like they say, when you're hot you're sooooo hot. The Intruders had that slow mellow ballad thing 'I Wanna Know Your Name', Ronnie Dyson had 'I Think I'll Tell Her', the O'Jays had 'For The Love Of Money' (another gold disc), The Spinners had 'Mighty Love' (and another), Billy Paul had 'I Was Married', the Stylistics had 'You Make Me Feel Brand New', Blue Magic had 'Sideshow' (one of Philly's most beautiful gold discs), First Choice had 'The Player' and MFSB had 'The Sound Of Philadelphia' . . . and it sure was."

More labels brought their acts to Philadelphia for a Sigma Sound session or two. Particularly prone to the treatment were vocal groups. GRT/Janus Records, for example, brought in the Whispers from Los Angeles. Identical twins ("yeah we have identical voices as well") Walter and Wallace Scott formed the group with Nicholas Caldwell, Gordy Harmon and

The Three Degrees

Programme of the tour that broke the Philly sound in Europe

Marcus Hutson in 1965. They cut a couple of records for Dore before meeting up with L.A. producer Ron Carson. He recorded them independently and leased the tapes to Wally Roker's Canyon/Soul Clock company. The discs were fine examples of harmony singing. "Planets Of Life" led to an album and the lovely, poignant "Seems Like I Gotta Do Wrong" gave the Whispers their first major chart record. When Canyon folded Ron Carson continued producing the group for Janus Records, but their discs became increasingly patchy, resting uneasily between the bitter-sweet ballads they did so well and over-orchestrated attempts at social comment ("It Sure Ain't Pretty (Hard Core Unemployed)"). Bill Degree came in to the group in place of Gordy Harmon. Then came a new producer. As Walter Scott explained to *Black Music* back in November 1974: "Chess/Janus lost Ron Carsons's contract so they had to find someone new to produce us. So we went to Philly and cut an album with Norman Harris and Bunny Sigler, plus all the MFSB guys of course. We're very excited about it. There's a thing called 'Bingo'. And 'A Mother For My Children'. There's plenty of good stuff."

And so there was, though the swaggering MFSB rhythms tended to stylize what was a unique sound by the Scott brothers. The accusation of "putting acts through the Philly machine" was also levelled at Norman Harris and Alan Felder. In 1974 they produced an album on one of soul music's most beloved groups, the Manhattans, who emerged sounding like shadows of their former, so original, selves. Yet, ironically, their previous album, acclaimed by some as the finest soul LP of 1973, was also recorded at Sigma Sound.

The Manhattans were formed in Jersey City in 1964 and consisted of George "Smitty" Smith, Winifred "Blue" Lovett, Sonny Bivins, Kenny Kelly and Richard Taylor. They entered an Apollo Theater talent contest and, although they only came in third, they were spotted by Joe Evans, owner of a small independent record company, Carnival Records. They signed and commenced to record a stream of successful singles which cleverly varied doowop-style ballads with Motown-derived dance discs. They included "I Wanna Be (Your Everything)" in 1963, "Can I" in 1966 and "I Call It Love" in 1967. In 1968 the group joined King Records' DeLuxe label where they hit with beautiful soulful ballads such as "If My Heart Could Speak" and "From Atlanta To Goodbye". Then tragically, George Smith, who'd shown himself to possess one of the most poignantly soulful voices ever heard in a New York recording studio, died of spinal meningitis. The group were stunned but found a new lead singer, Gerald Alston, whose voice was almost as expressive. When King/DeLuxe Records finally wound down in 1972, the Manhattans signed to Columbia.

Blue Lovett speaks about how this happened: "Sonny Bivins wrote this song called 'There's No Me Without You' and I'd written some things like 'We Made It' and 'The Other Side Of Me'. We ran the whole thing down with our group Little Harlem and then we took the tape to Bobby Martin. Bobby liked the way our band did it so much that MFSB just followed our routine. You would never believe the album *There's No Me Without You* was cut in Philly." Maybe not. But the captivating way in which Martin placed emphasis on Gerald Alston's lead, while at the same time bringing out the full dramatics of the material with punchy use of vibes, horns and strings made the LP, released in mid-1973, a classic of group soul singing. Unfortunately, the next album, *That's How Much I Love You*, in no way reached the highpoints of its predecessor. Norman Harris and Alan Felder seemed to smother the group on the five tracks on side one, while side two was comprised of old re-issued DeLuxe recordings.

But even if the Philly-recorded "Summertime In The City" lacked the magic of "There's No Me Without You", the difference between the two songs did show how much variance there was in the supposedly stereotyped Philly sound. As Blue Lovett comments: "It just ain't true to say all Philly sounds the same. They've got a formula, sure, just like Motown had a hit formula in the sixties. But those MFSB guys and those arrangers and producers are too hip to run a conveyor belt through Sigma Sound."

Another group who found Philly the key to the charts was Ecstasy, Passion and Pain. Their "I Wouldn't Give You Up", a chart bubbler recorded at Sigma for Roulette, was their first disc. Yet their leader, Barbara Roy, had been around a while. "I started out with a duet called Barbara and Brenda. Brenda Gaskins was my niece. We used to sing around Washington. We made some records for the Heidi label in '64 and our first thing, 'Hurtin' Inside', was kind of a hit. Around '67 we signed with Musicor Records on their Dynamo subsidiary and a couple of things, 'If you're Hurt I'll Feel The Pain' and 'Never Love A Robin' did okay. I worked as guitarist with Inez and Charlie Foxx for awhile but when Dynamo failed, Brenda left the business, and I stayed around New York working the clubs and looking for something to benefit my career."

The beneficial break came with the formation of Ecstasy, Passion and Pain. The group's 1975 line-up is Billy Gardner (organ), Joseph Williams Jr. (bass), Althea "Cookie" Smith (drums), Alan Tizer (percussion) and Barbara Roy (lead vocals and guitar).

Veteran New York hitmakers, the Manhattans

Ecstasy Passion and Pain led by Barbara Gaskins

The discs that Bobby Martin produced on the group tended to be lacking in originality on fast numbers like "Ask Me". On slow torturous ballads such as "Don't Burn Your Bridges Behind You", however, Barbara was allowed to wail soulfully with a mature woman's voice over the delicate Don Renaldo string arrangements.

Another Bobby Martin production was Baby Washington and Don Gardner. "Both of them were pretty cold", says Bobby. "Baby had had some hits years ago." Jeanette started back in the fifties with the New York girl group the Hearts before hitting big as a solo with Sue with such numbers as "That's How Heartaches Are Made " in 1963 and "Only Those In Love" in 1965. "Don Gardner hadn't made a record for quite a while. But I did some productions with them released on Master Five Records and 'Forever' showed in the soul charts. Then Baby did some things by herself and 'I've Got To Break Away' did okay."

For a while one of Philly's subsidiary services seemed to be the revival of flagging careers. Thom Bell created a small new start for one of the all-time heroes of yesteryear. Little Anthony and the Imperials were the legendary group who in the sixties had been one of the few New York doowop teams to move successfully with the times into the "beat concerto" era. Thom remarks: "I kinda liked the group and they were cool so I did a few tracks with them." ("La La In The End" was a small hit in 1974). "But I stopped producing for them and their album came out with my things on one side and their old producer, Teddy Randazzo, on the other. Eventually my brother Tony took over producing them. I stopped producing the Stylistics on Avco as well. It was just one of those things."

Considering the brilliance of Bell's work with the Stylistics and the classic proportions of the exquisite hit, "You Make Me Feel Brand New", which Thom left with the group and Avco as a parting shot, the

Stylistics didn't miss the songs and productions of the maestro . . . at least as far as hits were concerned. Avco's presidents Hugo and Luigi along with Van McCoy, a veteran producer/arranger of hundreds of New York and occasionally Philly sessions, took over arrangements, Hugo and Luigi productions and George David Weiss songwriting. Yet their work on *Let's Put It All Together* and the *Heavy* albums only reaffirmed the subtelty of Thom Bell's production and compositional technique. Away from the warmth and brimming creativity of Sigma Sound, Russell Tompkins and co degenerated into performers of vapid, teeth-grating slush. Where before their ethereal harmonies were counteracted by the subtle rhythmic nuances of MFSB, now they floundered in seas of strings and muted trumpets. But the public seemed to go for their tasteless sentimentality and ditties like "Star On A TV Show" and "Thank You Baby" were, amazingly, big hits.

More interesting musically than the degeneration of the Stylistics was the continued excellence of Blue Magic. Their mellowed harmonies on the delightful *Magic Of The Blue* album, which provided the "Three Ring Circus" hit single, was the sweetest sound in Philly soul. "Atlantic Records were lucky to pick up on that group", observes Sigma Sound's Joe Tarsia. "Blue Magic's sound is distinct from all the other harmony groups. But to get anywhere in music you gotta have some luck, like when Atlantic picked up on the Spinners. Now they're a great, great group, but they've always been that. They had done nothing to speak of after years with Motown, but Atlantic put them with Thom Bell and there they were, a super group."

Phillippe Wynne of the Detroit super group remembers how the Spinners were able to bring a fallen star back to light again. "At the end of '73 we went on tour with Dionne Warwicke. We loved her music and she dug us. Finally we talked over the idea of recording together. There was a big hassle over contracts — she was with Warners and we were with Atlantic — but eventually some arrangement was worked out."

The sensuous, infectious "Then Came You" went gold for Dionne and the Spinners, but sadly it was a once-only concept. No album, no Dionne/Spinners follow-up 45. "Still, it was a nice sound", chuckles Phillippe, and he is right. Another large record corporation who got some nice sounds and some fair sellers out of Sigma Sound were ABC Records.

"Dave Crawford told us he wanted to bring down a couple of his acts", remembers Joe Tarsia. "We were pretty knocked out when he told us they were the Mighty Clouds of Joy and B. B. King. Sigma hadn't done much recording in the way of gospel and blues."

That, of course, was just the point. The albums that the veteran Miami gospel group and the Memphis bluesman cut with MFSB were particularly clever attempts to put the acts firmly in the soul music mainstream. Producer Crawford deftly worked in MFSB's rhythms behind the Mighty Clouds of Joy's tortured exhorting and songs like "Time" and "Mighty Cloud of Joy" burned with high energy. What they lacked in gospel authenticity they made up for in sheer professionalism. And the same could be said for Blues Boy. Encased in a cushion of electric pianos and chattering funky rhythm, B.B. still gave out with bluesy licks even when singing the distinctly non-blues Crawford presented him with. "Yeah, we dug those sessions", laughs Earl Young. "They may not have been what you call ethnic music, but everybody had a ball."

Such comments are not forthcoming about another Sigma Sound session of 1975 — even though the disc which resulted sold close to two million copies. The saga of William DeVaughn's "Be Thankful For What You Got" doesn't raise too many smiles around Sigma Sound. Producer/composer Alan Felder explains: "There's this company in Philly called Omega Sound. They're a pretty strange set up 'cause they look for talent but the artists they find have to pay them. What happens is they put adverts in the trade papers for people to send demos in. And when they get one that's some good they say okay, you come up with a thousand or fifteen hundred dollars and we'll cut a record on you. Now if the artist is desperate enough, he'll try and raise the bread and when he pays they'll go cut a record and then Omega will go try and sell the master somewhere."

So it came to pass that a guitar playing Jehovah's Witness from Washington, D.C. called William DeVaughn saw Omega's ad in *Billboard* and sent off a tape. William wrote songs and sang in a high tenor uncannily similar to Curtis Mayfield. He remembers: "They said they'd record me if I paid for a session. And that'd cost me fourteen hundred dollars. I went home and managed to raise 900 dollars. We were able to scrape by on that and I went down to the Sigma Studios." Alan Felder took up the story. "I was doing work for Omega at the time, I was the only black cat in the company. I produced the record, though John Davis was in on it too. Now they had no idea how they wanted 'Be Thankful For What You Got' to sound. They had nothing really worked out. Well, Larry Washington was tuning his conga and he says, 'how d'ya want it man?' I said 'well, the groove is here . . .' Larry heard it a bit differently, he beat it out for me and I said 'that's it, that's right'. So we did the session real quick, with the guys feeling it as they went along. It wasn't mixed properly. The whole thing was done quick and cheap. The next thing I know they've got it out [on the Chelsea-distributed Roxbury label] and the label credit says it's produced by John Davis and Frank Fioravanti."

"Be Thankful For What You Got" hitmaker, William DeVaughn

Whatever the wheeling and dealing surrounding the record, William DeVaughn's "Be Thankful For What You Got" — and to a lesser extent his follow-ups, "Blood Is Much Thicker Than Water" and "Give The Little Man A Great Big Hand" — are brilliant examples of how the superbly fluid rhythm of the MFSB band can *make* a record. "Be Thankful" 's hypnotic undulating rhythm was one of 1974's great soul moments.

But of course the Gamble/Huff/Bell family gave the listening public the biggest supply of those. "It's all been very satisfying the way the whole Philly sound' has been accepted as an important movement in music", says Kenny. "Like the international success is a great thrill to us all. When we see that the Three Degrees are number one in the British charts [as they were with the haunting "When Will I See You Again" ballad]. And the albums we recorded in Europe, Billy Paul and the O'Jays [which included their crushing, soul-baring versions of "Sunshine" and "Wild Flower"] not only sold well but were proof that the music from the City of Brotherly Love has the sound everyone wants to hear . . . But, you know, the one thing that gives me the most pleasure is the way Thom and Bobby and Leon and myself have made Philly a big music city again. LIke, popular music is about making money. That's part of the thing. But if that's all there is to it I don't want any part of it, nor does Thom Bell, or Joe Tarsia or any of these guys. It's got to be more than that . . . soul music is the lifeblood of the ghetto, it's the most beautiful thing I know. And it's my belief which has helped me put Philly's soul artists where everyone can hear them. The old concepts that used to be in Philly about the kids being mugs, give them some junk and get their bucks has gone. I'm *proud* of what I've done."

Kenny Gamble speaks from his opulent office situated in a large building at 390 S. Broad Street, the building that Philadelphia International bought from the company who wouldn't give Kenny Gamble and the Romeos an audition. 390 S. Broad used to house the studios of Cameo Records.

EIGHT:
TOWARDS TOMORROW'S SOUND

Bobby Eli quietly chuckled as he read the letter which had just been delivered to him at Philadelphia International. It was typed on impressive stationery headed "Educational Communities Inc." "We are pleased to inform you that because of your leadership and achievements you've been recommended to have your biography published in the first edition of *Who's Who of Black Americans* — 1974—75. Please complete and return our biographical data form."

Amused, but not surprised, Eli crumpled the sheet into a ball. The composer of such million-selling songs as "Just Don't Want To Be Lonely" and "Sideshow", guitarist on literally hundreds of Philadelphia soul records and a key member of the legendary MFSB houseband, Bobby Eli is white. "I was born and raised in an area of Philly which was mostly a Jewish neighbourhood but it changed into a black neighbourhood. All my buddies were black, all my experiences were black and when I started getting into music, that was black too. I grew up with Len Barry — same thing happened to him too. And there's a whole pile of other white guys from around here who just kinda naturally were led into a R&B musical thing."

Eli isn't exaggerating. "Blue-eyed soul" singers have proliferated in Philadelphia. There is Billy Harner, for example, whose rich resonant voice has been heard regularly on the East Coast club circuit. While his stream of discs on V-Tone, Parkway, Meroc, Kenta, Kama Sutra, Heritage and Bell have often skilfully utilized the fast'n'furious tempos of Uptown soul, they haven't given him the big hit necessary to

quit hairdressing. Other acts include the Magnificent Men from nearby Harrisburg, who were successful in the sixties with "Peace Of Mind" on Capitol; Ben Aiken, otherwise known as Big Ben, who recorded stunning falsetto wailers for Philly Groove; the Sons of Robin Stone, whose lead singer Jimmy Phillips sang in a convincing soul style on their 1974 Atco release, "Love Is Just Around The Corner"/"Got To Get You Back"; and recently a reactivated Soul Survivors back with the Gamble/Huff organization. All unquestionably have been performers of soul music regardless of skin colour. None of them, though, has achieved success to the same luxurious-life-style degree experienced by the key Caucasians of the Gamble/Huff/Bell family: lyricist Linda Creed, vibes man Vince Montana, string arranger Don Renaldo and guitarist Bobby Eli.

"It's kinda a paradox being white and *singing* soul", Eli continues. "If that's where your natural leaning is, you've probably got more chance getting successful if you work behind the scenes, producing, arranging, composing. That's why the MFSB band is something special. Now that band's got more ethnic groups in it than the United Nations. Yet they've made it through all that 'say, ain't some of those guys white?' shit. They get played on the black radio stations . . . consistently. And that's justice. MFSB put Philadelphia on top in the first place."

How a rag-bag assortment of leather-capped soul-brothers and near-sighted Jews, renegade jazzmen and moonlighting symphonians laid the very foundations of the Philly sound explosion is complex enough to vex a computer. As MFSB's chief arranger Bobby Martin explains: "In a sense you could say there's been an MFSB band since '65 or so, or even before that. There were the session musicians who used to record over at Frank Virtue's and at the same time there was Kenny Gamble's old group, the Romeos. Those guys were like the nucleus of MFSB today . . . they're the rhythm section musicians. Then there are guys like Vince Montana, Lenny Pakula, Ron Kersey, Don Renaldo who've been around the session scene for years. By the time Kenny and Leon got everything established in '68 they'd all kinda fused into a pool of musicians who they, and Thom Bell, would call on. But they are *session* men, so on no two records will you get *exactly* the same musicians. If one violinist or one horn player can't make a session, there's always a replacement. Some people have said the Cliff Nobles' 'The Horse' thing was the first MFSB instru-

mental or even further back." (Swan's the Locomotions or the Men From Uncle . . . who gave out with "The Spy"!) "But I don't think you can really start calling them MFSB records 'til 'Family Affair'."

Not that Gamble and Huff did call them that at first. At the end of 1971, when Leon Huff took a bunch of his regulars to Sigma to pound out a widkedly funky electric piano arrangement of Sly Stone's "Family Affair", G & H called the group Family. The disc was released on the duo's North Bay Records. Explains Kenny: "North Bay was a label we tried for developing new acts before putting them with the full label." Some North Bay acts, such as Talk of the Town and the Mello Moods made it to the "full label". Others, such as Executive Suite and Little Dooley (as Dooley Silverspoon), found a wisp of fame elsewhere. But before North Bay was discontinued in late 1972, Gamble and Huff had come to realize Family's full potential. Not that "Family Affair" hit — "it

Left to right: Norman Harris, Ronnie Baker, Bobby Eli and Earl Young

Crashed out . . . Leon Huff

Arranger extraordinaire, Bobby Martin

bubbled for ages, man, without really making the charts". Nor did its aggressively funky follow-up, "Do The Robot". Bobby Martin, however, was impressed with the concept of an instrumental combo reflecting the whole gamut of Philadelphia music. "We all got together and planned an album. It wouldn't be a hard R&B album, or a jazz album, or an easy-listening album. It'd take in everything, every kind of music. When we finished it, we called the band MFSB and it came out on Philadelphia International in mid-'73."

The press release said MFSB stood for Mother, Father, Sister, Brother — "well, maybe it stood for Mother Fuckin' Son-Of-A-Bitch". With no live performances to promote the album and a controversial "anti-dope" sleeve design, it took its time to catch on. But slowly the sales built for an album which mixed churning Philly dance rhythms with sweeping string mood pieces, jazz, soul and pop in a bewildering brew of orchestral virtuosity. For the huge MFSB orchestra, in addition to featuring the pounding percussive rhythms of Harris, Baker, Young, Eli *et al*, also gave full vent to a massive string section headed by violinist Don Renaldo, seemingly manned by Philadelphia's answer to the Milan Symphonia. For by the seventies musicians such as Albert Barone, Charles Apollonia, Angelo Petrella, Diana and Davis Barnett, Romeo Distefano, Rudy Maliazia, Christine Reeves and Joe Donofrio were carrying their violin cases into Sigma Sound to overdub their parts. A horn section headed by Leno "Zack" Zachery also featured some pretty diverse names: Joe DeAngelis, Danny Eillions, Scott Temple, Milton Phibbs, Frederich Jainer, Fred Linge, Ricci Genovese, Edward Casceralle, Rocco Bene and Robert Hartzell.

Don Renaldo comments: "A lot of the musicians play in the Philadelphia Orchestra. But somehow they've all got the *feeling* for this music. You ask any one of them — they *like* what they do at Sigma. I never always got that feeling when I was doing work for Bernie Lowe's Orchestra." (Lowe's easy-listening banalities with Cameo Records stretched right back to 1958 when they hit with "Sing Sing Sing".) "But MFSB is a *special* feeling."

The special feeling really came alive when the band's second album was released. As Bobby Martin points out, "It was the *Soul Train* TV programme which made things really happen. Don Cornelius, the programme's producer, came down and saw us and asked us to work out a theme tune for his show. We did the tune and Kenny thought up the name 'T.S.O.P.'. We used the Three Degrees as voices at the end. Then as the show went out the demand grew for the release

Mother, Father, Sister, Brother — MFSB

of the theme. At first we were a little reluctant to put it out but we did and of course it was a stone smash."

So too was the album *Love Is The Message*, released in Britain as *TSOP: The Sound Of Philadelphia*. Gold discs aren't often given to session men. And there were snags, as Norman Harris suggests. "Jamie took a record the MFSB band did with Fantastic Johnny C called "Don't Depend On Me" and they put it out without the vocals as by the Philly Sound. And American Records did something like that." They dubbed on sax on top of a MFSB track which turned up in 1974 as "100 South Of Broadway". "They couldn't use the name MFSB, that's something. Some cats just try and exploit the Philly thing. Like it's a cheap way to get a hit . . . you don't pay royalties to session men."

For the most part, though, the MFSB session men are intrigued and complimented by the kind of

anonymous stardom the Philly sound has brought them. As drummer Karl Chambers says, "It's like a kinda bonus. You do a session, be it an instrumental or a vocal thing; if you do it well you feel good. And you'll get some money for it which is nice. But *recognition* is important. All musicians need that sometimes."

In fact Karl and his brother Roland want more recognition than that available to them through the forty-musician MFSB line-ups. Karl is something rare in the ghetto, a true eclectic, thirsting for music outside of "a straight-ahead R&B thing". After the Romeos had disbanded he came to England and joined the pop group Toomorrow — artificially contrived by media manipulator Don Kirshner of the Monkees and the Archies fame. He completed a feature film with the quartet but returned disgusted to America before Kirshner had time to reap the rewards of his massive Toomorrow launch. While pop balladeer Olivia Newton John managed to emerge from the campaign's ashes, by that time Karl was back in Philly doing sessions with brother Roland. In his immediate post-Romeos days Roland had become the musical director for Marvin Gaye and Tammi Terrell, then rejoined Gamble, Huff. In 1973 Karl and Roland formed the band Yellow Sunshine with bassist Idrees Young and percussionist Lester Young. Within a few months keyboardman Dexter Wansel and electric saxist Ron Harding had been added. "We've cut one album with Philadelphia International" explains Roland. "It's what we call organic music. It's pure energy music. We derive our sound from energies under the sun. Music for the people."

Sadly, not too many people so far. The exciting eclecticism and dazzling musicianship shown on such numbers as "Apollo 70", "Yellow Sunshine" and "The Gretch" have yet to be heard by a mass audience. Though the fusion of white "progressive rock" elements has brought fantastic success to a wide range of black artists from Jimi Hendrix through to Sly Stone, Funkadelic and the Ohio Players, *Yellow Sunshine* was one of Philadelphia International's albums that didn't happen.

"The problem is", says Reverend Life, "once the Philly sound was established, that was it for acts moving in a different direction. I love the sweet soul things, but my head is somewhere else." Life isn't a member of Yellow Sunshine, but his group, Spiritual Concept, have the same problems. "Spiritual Concept's music is like a search, a constant search for a higher musical plane. I really think that we were pioneers for music in this area. We did an album with Philadelphia International but they delayed putting it out for a year. So it lost some of its impact. The group we have now is into a very theatrical thing and everyone who sees us gets excited by our concerts. But we don't get many gigs. In fact I've had most success so far as a songwriter. Conway — he's in the group — and I have written for other acts, the Ebonys, New York City . . . I'm still anxious to see Spiritual Concept out there. The problem is Philadelphia isn't a good place to break any dramatic new ground. The Philly sound developed very slowly. The city's very reactionary. The whole political regime is ultra-conservative here and that seems to reflect right through to the radio stations. Now like the black stations, they don't play anything which they consider 'way out'. The situation's starting to change on AM but on FM those jocks never show any initiative. It's the same with their attitude towards breaking hits. Now Georgie Woods or Jimmy Bishop have *never*

gone out of their way to break new records. They just go with the big hits."

Life's observations on the state of Philly's radio are borne out by even a cursory listen to station WDAL. Their playlist is depressingly stereotyped with hardly any efforts made to "make a hit", not even a Philadelphia one. "Man you could listen to them Philly deejays all day and hardly realize there were so many good Philly records which don't get any airplay". observes one record company employee. Certainly, the new small label, Andee, never gets spun in Philly. Formed by Frank Virtue and Bernie Bennick (now living in Miami), the company features such acts as Prince Johnny Robinson, an excellent soulman with vocal attack and fire not normally associated with Philly, and the Virtues, startlingly resurrected not in Ventures fifties style but wah-wah-funk seventies style. Other new independents such as Babylon, who have the sweetly mellow but highly derivative Executive Suite and Chamber of Kommerce, and Sound Gems, who have a particularly good harmony group Ebb Tide, seem to have an up-hill struggle for airplay on their hands too. Even Philadelphia International often have to go outside the city to "break" discs by their newer artists.

A second factor which makes Philly's radioland a depressing vista is the omnipresent dark cloud of "payola" which brings forth shrugs, frowns or knowing smiles but nothing else as fabulously rich disc jockeys cruise around the city in luxury cadillacs. Another problem is the general lack of distinctive presentation by the deejays. Georgie Woods was once an innovator in R&B radio "rap", but now he drawls "this is Georgie Woods, the guy with the goods" with little enthusiasm. Bland Jimmy Bishop is no better. One disc jockey who had a mountain of fire is now sadly off the air. Sonny Hopson is a human dynamo. He'll tell you how in the late sixties he

WDAS radio building

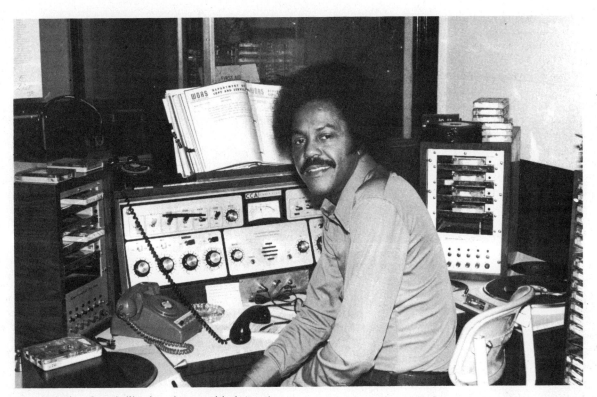

Key disc jockey Georgie Woods — the guy with the goods

gave WDAS a ratings scare when his flying torrent of words and exhortations made WHAT a serious threat to WDAS' unchallenged ascendancy. He'll tell you how he discovered jazz organist Charles Earland, which he unquestionably did; how he put up the money for the release of Fantastic Johnny C's "Boogaloo Down Broadway" on Blackjack Records and persuaded Jamie/Guyden to pick up the master, which he probably did; and how he discovered a good third of Gamble and Huff's acts, which he most certainly didn't. His latest record ventures are a jazz label, Hikeka, with album releases by Charles Earland and George Freeman, and Bamboo Records, who debuted with a progressive black rock single by Edwin Birdsong. Hopson promotes the labels with such a high flow of adrenalin it's difficult to believe one of his record ventures won't be as successful as his discotheque, a large, luxurious fun palace, crammed every night with money-paying party-ers.

Discotheques have both helped and hindered the Philly sound. The return of the discotheque took the American music industry by surprise. They had died so completely when the twist fell from favour that nobody seriously thought the day would again dawn when a club in a cellar or loft pumping out highly

amplified music on record would attract a mass audience. But, starting in the late sixties in New York City, the blacks — and to a lesser extent another minority group, the gays — had demanded a kind of club where they could drink, socialize and dance long into the night without the exhorbitant expenditure of much of America's live entertainment. So the discotheques, re-dubbed discos, re-emerged. With their rise, the industry discovered that discos were a fantastic additional way of exposing their music to a new audience. "We're heading the discotheque boom because the Philly sound is the best kind of dance music there is" was what Kenny Gamble was quoted as saying in a trade paper at the beginning of 1973. And certainly it appeared that discs such as "Backstabbers" and "For The Love Of Money" owed a large part of their startling success to their immense popularity in America's countless discos.

What's more, the New York disco boom brought about a new phenomenon: discs recorded specifically for discotheque play. At first labels were content merely to re-mix, shorten or lengthen tracks for maximum discotheque potential. By 1974, however, a new breed of producers, including New York's Bongiovi, Monardo and Ellis, had emerged. The soul records they released were orientated completely to the disco market and their production techniques, rhythm patterns and whole musical approach appeared a slavish copy of Sigma's proud Philly sound. And ironically, the singer with whom Bongiovi, Monardo and Ellis have had greatest success, Gloria Gaynor, was recorded at Sigma in 1974 with producer Norman Harris, before the trio discovered that MFSB's dance rhythms could be duplicated in a New York studio. The Bongiovi/Monardo/Ellis imitation of the Philly sound isn't the only one, just as the New York disco boom wasn't the only factor to herald a wave of studios from L.A. to Detroit to New York trying to steal Philly's glory.

"You're bound to get imitations. Once upon a time Philadelphia copied Detroit. What goes around comes around I guess." Kenny Gamble is right, of course, in noting that the endless stream of imitation "Thom Bell beats", falsetto-voiced symphonies and MFSB soundalikes isn't the real danger that faces the Gamble/Huff/Bell family and the whole Philly sound now that acclaim and riches have been achieved. The danger lies within. There is only one thing that could bring the Philly sound crashing into the abyss of yesterday's fad: inability to change.

A simplified long-term plan for success in the soul world might read this way. Evolve something of unique originality and ensure that all recordings leaving source (be it a label, a studio or a city) have the stylistic "brand" of that originality. When acceptance, popularity and profits have reached their height, gradually drop most of the stylistic characteristics that have become your trademark before criticisms about "stereotyped sound" and "conveyor-belt music" become damaging to sales. Replace the original sound with something far more in the mainstream to ensure that "an original sound" doesn't become a stylistic millstone. Just such a transition has, in fact, been carried out successfully by Motown Records who have moved from the hit-factory "Detroit sound" to a much broader stylistic base while still retaining most of their original popularity. If an original black music development fails to recognize the need for gradual change (as with the Muscle Shoals sound) it will in time cease to be a major black music force.

It remains to be seen whether Philadelphia's key creators recognize this fact. At the time of writing — mid-1975 — they are in a state of limbo. Often, instead of "gradual change", they have opted for the old music industry stand-by, diversification. And, of course, in the long term, Philadelphia International's signing of non-soul acts, be they jazz — such as the

big band of Thad Jones/Mel Lewis and funky bass player Monk Montgomery — or gospel — the Dandridge Choral Ensemble — is as irrelevant to what happens to the Philly Sound as is rock star David Bowie's recording of an album at Sigma Sound. The Philly Sound will eventually have to change, or pay the penalty.

In 1975, of course, Gamble, Huff and Bell's star remains truly ascendant. The year has already brought forth an abundance of fine Philly music, particularly on album. The Spinners' *New And Improved* is hardly that but it maintains their rich vibrancy with plenty of dazzling Thom Bell orchestrations. The Intruders' continued with *Energy of Love* which includes their nonchalantly rambling "Rainy Days And Mondays". Harold Melvin and the Blue Notes' *To Be True* featured a new falsetto (Jerry Cummings replacing Lloyd Parkes) and the first exposure of a fine new singer, Sharon Paige, to give added edge to Teddy Pendergrass' exhorting emotionalism. The O'Jays' *Survival* offers a considered balance between electronic funk on "Rich Get Richer" and fine pathos on "What Am I Waiting For". *The Trammps* album is truly blistering and contains some of the sassiest dance struts on record, including a searing instrumental re-recording of "Zing". And other Philly acts have recently made their album debuts. Major Harris left the Delfonics and has emerged as a potential big star for Atlantic. The Futures (James King, Kenny Crew, Harry McGilkerry, Frank Washington and Jon King), after years of scuffling around small clubs and various arguments over recording contracts, have emerged with a likable Buddah album, recorded in Detroit. Then too the Gamble/Huff/Bell family have established a new label, TSOP, which features an assortment of excellent acts. Pat and the Blenders have a rich, vigorous blend of harmony and grit. The Mello Moods are a fine girl group, though the fact that their management agency cannot even spell their name correctly on their publicity photographs doesn't bode well for the future. Franky and the Spindles, who once hit with producer George Kerr on the lovely "Count To Ten", offer a fine blend of harmony. People's Choice and the Soul Survivors, with "Love Shop" and "City of Brotherly Love" respectively have already made inroads into the charts and shown that Gamble/Huff are still capable of bringing acts in from the cold.

But not even *their* touch is infallible, of course. A Detroit-born former Motown vocalist, Carolyn Crawford, who possesses a swoopingly soulful vocal style, has been left to languish in exactly the same manner as she did with the Motor City corporation. And veteran producer Billy Jackson is happy to tell

Franky and the Spindles

the tale of the slip-up with the Tymes. "I scraped together some pennies of my own and did a session with the Tymes at Sigma Sound at the end of '73. Then I took the tapes of our songs around to Gamble and Huff to try and get them interested. They included this song called 'Trustmaker' which I particularly dug. But they didn't think it would happen. They said the Tymes were too good, sang too well . . . but I think they really meant they were too old. So I took the tapes and the pilot vocal to RCA and they flipped over it and we finished the tapes. The disco deejays heard 'Trustmaker' and told RCA to rush it out 'cause it could be a monster. And of course it was a smash, a gold smash.''

Similar to the way RCA pipped Gamble and Huff on "Trustmaker", "M/S Grace" and the other Tymes hits, nobody in Philly realized the potential of the old Newtown Records' group, the Bluebelles. With a new manager, Britain's Vicki Wickham, a new name, Labelle, and a totally new image of futuristic space-age glam rock, "socially significant" material and bump-and-grind sexuality, they have been successful without any help from Sigma Sound.

Such lapses are, however, exceedingly rare. The whole of Philadelphia today seems attuned to breaking as many *new* soul acts as the partying disco-ites, the complacent disc jockeys and the confused record buyer will allow them. Such acts include the Continental Four from Harrisburg, who, after a series of particularly good discs produced by Bobby Martin on independent Jay Walking, including the 1971 hit "Day By Day", are back with an excellent disc on

Philly Groove's Finishing Touch

Talk of the Town, featuring hit writers Gene McFadden and John Whitehead

The Futures

Ex-Motown singer Carolyn Crawford

A Philly "great unknown", Prince Johnny Robinson

The Mello Moods

Veteran Philly team, the Tymes

Philly's blue-eyed soul unit, the Soul Survivors

Philly freaks, Spiritual Concept

Thom Bell's protégées Derek and Cyndi

The up-and-coming Pat and the Blenders

Yellow Sunshine, featuring Karl and Roland Chambers

Master Five Records; Derek and Cyndi, whose strangely charming, though decidedly bland music might find a mass audience with Gamble/Huff/Bell's Thunder label if the world really wants another Peaches and Herb; Gerri Grainger, a fine Nancy-Wilson-style vocalist whose performance on Bunny Sigler's "Would You Believe" has an up-to-date soul sound; the TNJ's, whose name stands for Trenton, New Jersey and who added quite brilliant harmonies to Bunny Sigler's *Keep Smiling* album and made it one of the highlights of 1974; Finishing Touch, who offer the soulful lead of Charles Mack — as charismatic as Eddy Levert; Force of Nature, a raunchy black rock band whose fluid jazz—rock could broaden Thom Bell's approach; Love Committee, previously the Ethics, recently revitalized by producer Weldon McDougal on a truly memorable version of Eddie Kendricks' "Darling Come Back Home" on TSOP. And the Coalitions' beautiful "Instead . . . How Are You?" on Phil L.A. of Soul deserved to smash.

Any one of these artists could be the next Philly superstar. Any one of them could be the next to enter the world of success into which the O'Jays and the Blue Notes and the Spinners have now passed. For

Bunny Sigler's protégées, the TNJ's from Trenton, New Jersey

Jazz funk bassist, Monk Montgomery

Big band jazz greats, Thad Jones and Mel Lewis

Love Committee, previously known as the Ethics

Her first time at Sigma Sound — composer/artist Bunny Sigler helps Gerri Grainger

Sigma's owner and ace engineer Joe Tarsia with maestro Kenny Gamble working on a Billy Paul mix

success is indeed a just reward for developing such uncanny levels of sophisticated music craft which still retain the link with a cultural heritage — and for irrevocably changing the listening expectations of us all. Theirs is truly the sound of Philadelphia. And it is a sound which has now pierced the consciousness of all those who look to popular music to supply us with something more than Tin Pan Alley would have us take.

Futuristic Philly: Labelle

This book has, I trust, shown among other things that the sound of Philadelphia isn't just the sound of diamond ringed superstars. It's also the sound of singers who *didn't* get the breaks. George Tindley, for example, the one-time doowopper who just won't quit and turns out a constant stream of soul records for his own tiny label. Or Carl Holmes whose Commanders made some noise back in the twist era and who is today still in there scuffling with his group, Sherlock Holmes Investigation. Or Herb Johnson whose Impacts band gave Kenny Gamble the first chance to scramble up onto a stage and sing.

Probably the best assessment of the sound of Philadelphia and what its emergence has meant to the city so far was given to me by a man called TK who came to my assistance when I was trying to track down Lee Andrews. "The sound of Philadelphia is everything Mayor Rizzo don't want to hear. That's why there ain't no statues of Kenny Gamble or Leon Huff up in front of the city hall. To a lot of the white folk, the businessmen in the city centre, what they're doing over at Sigma is unknown to them. Or if they do know, it's crazy niggers makin' that rock'n'roll shit. They might have a sneaking admiration for the money the singers or the record companies make, but they sure ain't gonna let the city elders bestow no recognition on them to honour their music. But Kenny, Leon, Tommy — all the artists — they've got their tribute. They go drive down Chestnut Street — they can see what they've done. Now there's one helluva lot wrong with this city, like all the slums and unemployment and the gang wars. But the Philly sound guys have given everyone something. They've given the white businessmen money. They've given the white kids the best goddam kind of rock'n'roll they've ever had. And most important, they've given something to all those raggedy black kids who are out there on the streets. That's something Rizzo's never done. Kenny, Leon and Tommy have given those kids pride . . . and hope."

Philly's stars of tomorrow?

Index